"Nancy Guthrie has made the Old Testament come alive again. She connects the gospel dots from the Old Testament to the New, showing us the shadow and then the reality of Jesus Christ, who was the Lamb slain from the foundation of the world. More than once I saw Jesus in a new and remarkably beautiful way. This study has grown my love for our Savior."

> **Jessica Thompson,** coauthor, *Give Them Grace: Dazzling Your Kids with the Love of Jesus*

"User-friendly, biblically reliable, theologically astute, enthusiastically sensible, encouragingly realistic, and deeply Christ-centered—all without losing sight of the fact that the Bible student is to be a disciplined 'workman (or woman) who does not need to be ashamed.' Once again we are deeply indebted to Nancy Guthrie for giving the church an outstanding Bible study resource to help us all grow in the grace, knowledge, and wisdom of God."

> **Sinclair B. Ferguson,** Senior Pastor, First Presbyterian Church, Columbia, South Carolina

"There are few people better able to make the Old Testament come alive than Nancy Guthrie. In this accessible, balanced, and Christ-centered work, she has done it again! There is perhaps no greater theme in all Scripture than that of Jesus as the Lamb of God who takes away our sin, and it is impossible to understand what that description means without seeing it through Old Testament eyes. Nancy helps us do this with her typical clarity and passionate sensitivity to the story line of the Bible. You will find your thinking stretched, your soul fed, and your heart thrilled by her work."

> **Liam Goligher,** Senior Minister, Tenth Presbyterian Church, Philadelphia, Pennsylvania; author *The Jesus Gospel* and *Joseph: The Hidden Hand of God*

"As the title says, this book—and the entire series—is about Jesus. Instead of simply telling the stories of the Old Testament and teaching us how to be a better, more successful person, *The Lamb of God* points us over and over to the one who did it all for us. How refreshing and inspiring to bask in my Savior's love for me—to be loved and accepted because of what Christ has done and not because of what I have done. Nancy's exhaustive research, her facility in writing, and her thought-provoking questions make these studies both challenging and enjoyable. I cannot wait to lead the women in my group through each of her studies!"

> **Maureen Kyle,** Redeemer Presbyterian Church, New York City

"Nancy Guthrie masterfully draws out from the shadows the rich, Christ-centered content and themes inherent in Exodus to Deuteronomy. This book provides a needed stepping stone for those seeking a gradual introduction into biblical theology. It is a rare thing to see an author combine such rich redemptive history, natural readability, and vital applicability, but *The Lamb of God* achieves just that."

Jared Oliphint, Regional Coordinator, Westminster Theological Seminary; contributor, Reformed Forum

"In a warm, personal style, Nancy Guthrie opens up Old Testament books to reveal truths of salvation woven into every page. I am always looking for wonderful Bible studies to offer the ladies in our church, and I can't wait to recommend this book!"

Liz Emerson, pastor's wife; mother; grandmother

"Nancy Guthrie has provided yet another solid, practical, and thoroughly biblical study guide navigating the rich literature of the Pentateuch. We've used earlier volumes in this series at Parkside and have been encouraged to see people begin to connect the rich prophecies and narratives of the Old Testament to their great fulfillment in Jesus Christ. The layout of the book, the well-written studies, and the substantial questions make for a robust study guide that will challenge your people to truly see Jesus!"

Jonathan Holmes, Counseling Pastor, Parkside Church, Chagrin Falls, Ohio

"As a children's ministry director who teaches a young-women's Bible study, I love the fact that Nancy teaches in adult language and application what we seek to teach our children—that even in the Old Testament stories we see how Jesus has been in the process of redeeming us. Nancy is a master storyteller and teacher who consistently helps us see the redemptive truth of Scripture and apply that truth where we live in the real moments of everyday life."

Sherry Kendrick, Children's Ministry Director, Covenant Church of Naples, Naples, Florida

~Praise for the Series~

"The Bible is a book about Jesus. The disciples walking to Emmaus after the resurrection discovered this as Christ himself walked along with them and explained how the Old Testament pointed to the Savior. I recommend the entire series to you."

> **Alistair Begg**, Senior Pastor, Parkside Church, Chagrin Falls, Ohio

"I am thankful to God to be able to offer Nancy Guthrie's series Seeing Jesus in the Old Testament to the women of our church. For too long, studies have led us only to see what we are to *do*. Now we can see through the pages of this series what *Jesus* has done! With Nancy's help, the story of redemption jumps off the pages of the Old Testament, and the truths of the gospel are solidified in women's hearts and lives."

> **Jo Coltrain,** Director of Women's Ministry, First Evangelical Free Church, Wichita, Kansas

"It's not hyperbole to say, 'It's about time.' While there are good books out there telling pastors how to preach Christ from all the Scriptures, there have been very few Bible studies for laypeople—especially for women—along these lines. Nancy Guthrie does an amazing job of helping us to fit the pieces of the biblical puzzle together, with Christ at the center."

> **Michael S. Horton**, J. Gresham Machen Professor of Systematic Theology and Apologetics, Westminster Seminary California

"Nancy takes us by the hand and the heart on an exegetical excursion to see Christ in the Old Testament. The beauty of Guthrie's writing is that you are certain she has met him there first."

> **Jean F. Larroux**, Senior Pastor, Southwood Presbyterian Church, Huntsville, Alabama

"There are many great Christian books, but not many great Bible studies. Nancy is a master of getting the Word of God into the mouths, hearts, and lives of her students. I cannot wait to share this study with my people."

> **-Donna Dobbs**, Christian Education Director, First Presbyterian Church, Jackson, Mississippi

**Other books in the
Seeing Jesus in the Old Testament series:**

The Promised One: Seeing Jesus in Genesis

The Son of David: Seeing Jesus in the Historial Books

The Wisdom of God: Seeing Jesus in the Psalms and Wisdom Books

The Word of the Lord: Seeing Jesus in the Prophets

The Lamb of God

Seeing Jesus in Exodus, Leviticus, Numbers, and Deuteronomy

(A 10-Week Bible Study)

nancy guthrie

WHEATON, ILLINOIS

The Lamb of God: Seeing Jesus in Exodus, Leviticus, Numbers, and Deuteronomy

Copyright © 2012 by Nancy Guthrie

Published by Crossway
            1300 Crescent Street
            Wheaton, Illinois 60187

First printing 2012

Printed in the United States of America

Unless otherwise indicated, Scripture quotations are from the ESV® Bible (The Holy Bible, English Standard Version®), copyright © 2001 by Crossway. Used by permission. All rights reserved.

Scripture quotations marked HCSB have been taken from *The Holman Christian Standard Bible*®. Copyright © 1999, 2000, 2002, 2003 by Holman Bible Publishers. Used by permission.

Scripture references marked NLT are from *The Holy Bible, New Living Translation,* copyright © 1996, 2004. Used by persmission of Tyndale House Publishers, Inc., Wheaton, IL, 60189. All rights reserved.

All emphases in Scripture quotations have been added by the author.

Trade paperback ISBN: 978-1-4335-3298-6
PDF ISBN: 978-1-4335-3299-3
Mobipocket ISBN: 978-1-4335-3300-6
ePub ISBN: 978-1-4335-3301-3

Library of Congress Cataloging-in-Publication Data

Guthrie, Nancy.
    The Lamb of God : seeing Jesus in Exodus, Leviticus,
Numbers & Deuteronomy / Nancy Guthrie.
        p. cm.—(Seeing Jesus in the Old Testament ; 2)
    Includes bibliographical references.
    ISBN 978-1-4335-3298-6 (tp)
    1. Bible. O.T. Pentateuch—Textbooks. 2. Bible. O.T.
Pentateuch—Criticism, interpretation, etc. 3. Jesus
Christ—Biblical teaching. I. Title.
BS1225.55.G87   2012
222'.10071—dc23   2012003065

Crossway is a publishing ministry of Good News Publishers.

VP		25	24	23	22	21	20	19	18	
18	17	16	15	14	13	12	11	10	9	8

With gratitude to
Pastor David Owen Filson
for your sound teaching, enthusiastic encouragement,
and gracious generosity in letting me borrow
from your abundant bookshelves.
I promise to obey Exodus 20:15.

Contents

May 1

May 8

Before We Get Started

A Note from Nancy

A number of years ago I got to travel to the beautiful country of New Zealand. I came back with images in my mind of the magnificent yachts in the harbor preparing for the America's Cup race, the dancing of the indigenous Maori people, and the green hillsides spotted with grazing sheep. New Zealand has thirteen times more sheep than people, so there were plenty to see!

As we begin a book about the Lamb of God, I would really like to encourage you to picture fuzzy little lambs frolicking in a field and nuzzling their mothers. But I can't, because there are no living lambs in the books of Moses that we are about to study. The lambs we read about in Exodus, Leviticus, Numbers, and Deuteronomy do not lead us to peaceful thoughts of pastoral scenes but instead impress upon us what sin costs—the life of the lamb. All of the lambs in these books, as well as in the rest of the Old Testament, are there to point us toward one very special lamb, "the Lamb of God who takes away the sin of the world" (John 1:29). He too was slain. And, interestingly, when we come to the very end of the Bible, the focus is still on the Lamb, sitting on the throne of the universe. He lives, but not as one untouched by death. Into eternity the Lamb of God bears the marks of having been slain (Rev. 5:6).

I don't think it would be an overstatement to say that if we do not understand the story of the Lamb, we cannot fully grasp the story of the Bible. Moses has much to teach us about the Lamb of God, so I hope you will engage with all three essential parts to this study over the weeks to come. The first is the personal time you will spend reading your Bible, seeking to strengthen your grip on its truths as you work your way through the questions provided in the Personal Bible Study section of each week's lesson. This will be the easiest part to skip, but nothing is more important than reading and studying God's Word, expecting that he will meet you as you do. Because we will cover large chunks of Scripture that I will not have time to read through and explain in the Teaching Chapters or videos, the foundational understanding you will gain through your time doing the Personal Bible Study will be essential.

As you work on the Personal Bible Study, try not to become frustrated if you can't come up with an answer to every question or if you're not sure what the question is getting at. The goal of the questions is to get you into the passage and thinking it through in a fresh way, not necessarily to record all of the "right" answers. Certainly some answers to your lingering questions will become clearer as you read the chapter or watch the video and as you discuss the passage with your group.

The second part of each lesson is the Teaching Chapter, in which I seek to explain and apply the passage we are studying. If your group is using the accompanying video series, the Teaching Chapter in the book is the same content I present on the videos. If you are using the videos, you can go ahead and read the chapter as a preview, if you'd like, or simply sit back and watch the video. Or you may prefer to come back and read the chapter *after* watching the video to seal in what you've heard. It's up to you. You can also download an audio or video version of the Teaching Chapters at http://www.crossway.com.

At the end of each Teaching Chapter is a short piece called "Looking Forward," which will turn your attention to how what we've just studied in Moses's writings gives us insight into what is still to come when Christ returns. In these first few books of the Bible we find not only the history of what God has done in the past to redeem his people but also insight into what he is doing now and is yet to do in the future when the Lamb of God returns to take his throne.

The third part of each week's lesson is the time you spend with your group sharing your lives together and discussing what you've learned and what you're still trying to understand and apply. A discussion guide is included at the end of each week's lesson. You may want to follow it exactly, working through each question as written. Or you may just want to use the guide as an idea starter for your discussion, choosing the questions that suit your group and discussing key insights you gained through the Personal Bible Study and Teaching Chapter.

Each aspect is important—laying the foundation, building on it, and sealing it in. We all have different learning styles, so one aspect of the study will likely have more impact on you than another, but all three together will help you to truly "own" the truths in this study so that they can become a part of you as you seek to know your covenant God in deeper ways.

I've put the sections of this study together in a way that offers flexibility for how you can use it and in how you can schedule your time working through it. If you are going to use it for a ten-week group study, you will want to read the Teaching Chapter in Week 1, "He Wrote about Me," before the first meeting. (There is no Personal Bible Study section for the first week.) From then on, participants will need to come to the group time having completed the Personal Bible Study section of the next week's lesson, as well as having read the Teaching Chapter. You may want to put a star beside questions in the Personal Bible Study and underline key passages in the chapter that you want to be sure to bring up in the discussion. During your time together each week you will use the Discussion Guide to talk through the big ideas of the week's lesson.

There is a great deal of material here, and you may want to take your time with it, letting its foundational truths sink in. To work your way through the study over twenty weeks, break each week into two parts, spending one week on the Personal Bible Study section—either doing it on your own and discussing your answers when you meet, or actually working through the questions together as a group. Over the following week, group members can read the chapter on their own and then come together to discuss the big ideas of the lesson.

If you are leading a group study, we would like to provide you with a leader's guide that has been developed specifically for this study. To download the free leader's guide and to look over questions and

answers submitted by fellow leaders about the study, go to http://www.
SeeingJesusintheOldTestament.com.

Perhaps no book has been read and studied as long and by as many
people in as many parts of the world as the Pentateuch, the books of
Moses. But how many people who have read and studied it have never
seen the one true Lamb of God? That will be our goal—to read and
understand what Jesus meant when he said, "If you believed Moses,
you would believe me; for he wrote of me" (John 5:46). And it is there
that we begin.

Nancy Guthrie

A Prophet like Me

Teaching Chapter

He Wrote about Me

I worked at a publishing company for a long time before my name ever appeared in a book. In their acknowledgments, authors often thanked people such as the acquisitions editor who contracted the book and the editors who worked on the manuscript—people they worked with prior to the book's publication. As the publicist, I usually didn't become active in the process until after the book was shipped off to the printer, so my name never seemed to make it into the published books. But, finally, after working there for about six years, an author put my name in his book. Max Lucado, one of the most gracious and authentic authors I've ever worked with, mentioned me in the acknowledgments in the front of his book *The Applause of Heaven*. I had a new claim to fame—proof that I not only knew Max Lucado, but, more importantly, he knew me. (Thanks, Max. I hope you'll like it that now I've put your name in my book.)

When someone people know and respect writes about a person, it makes us more willing to read or listen to what that person has to say. This is why we like to read through the endorsements on the covers of book jackets looking for names we recognize in the list of endorsers. When someone we respect has taken the time to read what a writer has written and offers an endorsement that commends it as worthwhile, we're usually more inclined to read the book.

Imagine if you could say that someone who lived hundreds of years before you, someone who wrote a book that everyone you know has read and reread and sought to live by, wrote about you. Imagine that you could say that the book he wrote not only mentioned you but was actually all about you—that you were the central character in all of his writings, the person whose identity had been kept hidden from all who had read his book throughout the centuries. That would be an astounding claim.

That's exactly the claim Jesus made. In an interchange with the religious leaders of his day who were questioning his right to assume authority that had always been reserved for God alone, Jesus claimed that the book written by the one author whom his questioners respected more than any other was actually all about him. Jesus said:

> You search the Scriptures because you think that in them you have eternal life; and it is they that bear witness about me, yet you refuse to come to me that you may have life. . . . For if you believed Moses, you would believe me; for he wrote of me. (John 5:39–40, 46)

We can almost see them shaking their heads with quizzical looks on their faces, thinking, *What do you mean, that Moses wrote about you? Where exactly did Moses write about you?* These were A+ students of the book of Moses: Genesis, Exodus, Leviticus, Numbers, and Deuteronomy. Most of them could quote long passages from Moses's writings and did so on a daily basis. And here was Jesus telling them that what they had been reading and studying their whole lives was all about him, suggesting that there was a deep fault line, a huge blind spot, in their understanding.

This general lack of understanding about how to read the Old Testament was why, in the forty days between his resurrection and his ascension, Jesus sat down with his disciples—men who had grown up reading the Old Testament Scriptures—and taught them how to truly understand them, how to read them in light of their fulfillment. Luke tells us that, "beginning with Moses and all the Prophets, he interpreted to them in all the Scriptures the things concerning himself" (Luke 24:27). Jesus opened his disciples' eyes to see all the ways Moses and all of the other Old Testament writers wrote about him.

And this is what we want him to open our eyes to see. We don't want to be like the religious people of Jesus's day who regularly went to Bible study yet were so stuck in their long-held assumptions about the Bible, so bogged down by the long to-do list they derived from the Bible, that they completely missed what it was all about—namely *who* it was all about.

If you've done the previous study in this series, *The Promised One: Seeing Jesus in Genesis*, then you could probably list many of the ways Moses wrote about Christ in the first book of the Bible. When Moses wrote in Genesis 3:15 about the offspring of the woman who would crush the head of the Serpent, he was writing about Jesus. In his account of the ark in which Noah and his family found safety in the storm of God's judgment, he was writing about the nature of salvation found by those who hide themselves in Christ. When he wrote about God's call and promise to Abraham that in him "all the families of the earth shall be blessed" (Gen. 12:3), he was writing about the blessing available to people of every tribe and tongue through Abraham's future descendant, Jesus. When Moses took thirteen chapters to tell the story of Joseph, the beloved son of his father who was rejected by his brothers and became the one person all people in the world had to come to for salvation, he was writing in shadow form about the greater Joseph, Jesus.

We will see in this study, as we make our way through the rest of the writings of Moses, that he has much more to tell us about the Christ who would come fifteen hundred years after he wrote about him in his book.

◦ In Moses's account of his own life, as one who was born under the threat of death, left the royal palace to identify with his suffering brothers, and led his people out of slavery, we will see the shadow of Jesus, who left the halls of heaven to be born under Herod's murderous edict and lead his people out of their captivity to sin.

◦ In the unblemished lambs who died that first Passover night so that the firstborn son could live, we will see Jesus, God's firstborn, "the Lamb who was slain" so that we can live (Rev. 5:12).

◦ As we witness Moses leading his people through the waters of the Red Sea unscathed, we will see Jesus, who leads us through the waters of death into everlasting life.

∼ In the pillar of cloud and fire that guided God's people, the manna that fed them, and the rock that gushed with water for them to drink, we will see the light of the world, the bread of life, the living water—Jesus himself.

∼ As we listen to the law given by God on the mountain, we will hear its echo in the words of Jesus, who climbed up a mountain and spoke with authority about what it means to obey God from the heart.

∼ We will go over Moses's record of the design for the tabernacle in which God descended to dwell among his people, details that have no meaning apart from Jesus, who descended to dwell among his people.

∼ We will witness the establishment of the priesthood, those who were to be holy to the Lord and offer sacrifices for sin. In the priest's clothing and ceremonies and sacrifices we'll see that Moses was preparing his people to grasp the Great High Priest, the Holy One of God, who offered himself as a once-for-all sacrifice.

∼ We'll follow Israel's forty years in the wilderness where they repeatedly disobeyed and rebelled, seeing the contrast between them and Jesus, the true Israel, who went out into the wilderness for forty days meeting every temptation with perfect obedience.

We'll begin today by giving attention to something Moses wrote near the end of his last book, Deuteronomy, a prophetic promise and instruction for God's people as they prepared to cross over the Jordan and enter into the Promised Land. Here is what he said:

> The LORD your God will raise up for you a prophet like me from among you, from your brothers—it is to him you shall listen. . . . And the LORD said to me. . . . "I will put my words in his mouth, and he shall speak to them all that I command him." (Deut. 18:15–18)

This is interesting. Moses was a prophet—not so much in the sense that he foretold the future but in that he spoke for God to the people. God installed Moses as his first official prophet to Israel when the Israelites arrived at Mount Sinai because the Israelites were too terrified to hear God speak directly to them. They asked Moses to go up the mountain in their place and hear what God had to say and then relay it to them so they wouldn't have to hear God's thunderous voice. So Moses listened to God for the people and spoke to the people for God.

Evidently, the same Spirit who imparted God's word to Moses for the people also imparted understanding to Moses about himself—an understanding that God had woven into the fabric of his life a pattern that would also be seen in the Messiah's life. God sovereignly orchestrated Moses's life in such a way that it would one day become clear that his ministry had been a miniature version of the ministry of the coming prophet. Numerous aspects of Moses's life provided God's people with pictures of the Promised One, the Messiah whom God promised to send. If God's people would remember who Moses was and what he had accomplished and experienced, it would help them to recognize the Messiah when he came. He would be the one they would need to listen to even more intently than they listened to Moses.

So as we begin our study of these four books of the Pentateuch written by Moses, let's take a mini tour of Moses's life in order that we might see more clearly and listen more intently to the greater prophet God raised up from among God's people, who was like Moses.

Deliverer of an Enslaved People

When we read the story of the Israelites in Exodus through Deuteronomy, we cannot miss the fact that Moses was truly a great deliverer. He stood up to the greatest power in the world in his day and demanded that Pharaoh release his two-million-strong slave labor force. Moses delivered his people out of slavery in Egypt and through the Red Sea by the power of God and led them for forty years in the wilderness. But while he delivered them *out* of slavery, he could not deliver them *into* the Promised Land. He could only take them to its border. Moses could not go in. Oh, how this must have been an agony for Moses, who had invested his life and all of his hopes and dreams in delivering God's people into the land God had promised to them.

Moses forfeited that privilege by dishonoring God near the end of the journey in the wilderness. We read about the incident in Numbers 20, an event that took place as the people of Israel stood poised to enter into the Promised Land. They had run out of water and had nothing to drink. Instead of going to God and asking him to provide, the people began to complain. But they did more than that. As they voiced their complaint about the lack of water, it was as if forty years of frustration rose to the surface so that all kinds of unresolved grievances against Moses and God came tumbling out.

> And the people quarreled with Moses and said, "Would that we had perished when our brothers perished before the LORD! Why have you brought the assembly of the LORD into this wilderness, that we should die here, both we and our cattle? And why have you made us come up out of Egypt to bring us to this evil place? It is no place for grain or figs or vines or pomegranates, and there is no water to drink." (Num. 20:3–5)

Here they were, just about to enter the Promised Land, saying that they wished they had died with those who had rebelled against God and perished in the desert. They were frustrated because the wilderness had no grain or vines or fig trees or pomegranates—the very fruit the scouts had brought back with them from Canaan (Num. 13:23). In other words, "the people were blaming Moses and Aaron because the wilderness was not like the Promised Land that they had refused to enter!"[1]

We might expect that God would have had enough by this point and that he would simply sink these grumbling Israelites into a pit in the desert never to be heard from again. But instead, he gave instructions to Moses and Aaron to provide water for them to drink:

> Take the staff, and assemble the congregation, you and Aaron your brother, and tell the rock before their eyes to yield its water. So you shall bring water out of the rock for them and give drink to the congregation and their cattle. (Num. 20:8)

Moses and Aaron were to take the staff—the same staff that had summoned Egypt's plagues and divided the Red Sea. Perhaps when the people saw the staff they would remember God's past deliverances and provisions and put their trust in him. Moses and Aaron were to speak to the rock. Perhaps the stark contrast between the rock's responsiveness and their own hard-hearted unresponsiveness would shame them into repentance and faith.[2] Moses and Aaron followed the first two steps correctly. They took the staff and assembled the people. But they did not "tell the rock" to yield its water. Instead Moses spoke to the people:

> "Hear now, you rebels: shall we bring water for you out of this rock?" And Moses lifted up his hand and struck the rock with his staff twice. (Num. 20:10–11)

Moses was supposed to speak to the rock; God had not told him to speak to the people. But Moses rebuked them, setting himself up as their judge, and himself and Aaron as their deliverers, by suggesting that they were the ones who would bring water out of the rock. And what was God's response?

> And the LORD said to Moses and Aaron, "Because you did not believe in me, to uphold me as holy in the eyes of the people of Israel, therefore you shall not bring this assembly into the land that I have given them." (Num. 20:12)

Whoa, we want to say, *that seems incredibly harsh. After all that Moses has been through in the desert, after all of his faithful obedience and the difficulties of leadership, God is going to deny him the privilege of leading his people into the Promised Land?* This hits us initially as an overreaction, a great unfairness to Moses. Yet we know God is just. So what is it that we may not be seeing on the surface of things?

Once before, long ago, Moses had set himself up as judge and deliverer of his people, when he saw an Egyptian beating an Israelite. Moses killed the Egyptian without being instructed to do so by the Lord. Now, here he was, years later, once again trying to deliver God's people in his own way through his own strength. Because the rock represented God himself[3]—the source of water and refreshment to his people—when Moses struck the rock two times in anger, it was "nothing less than a direct assault on God."[4] The sad irony was that in judging the people and seeking to deliver them in their own way, Moses and Aaron became exactly what they accused the people of being: rebels against the Lord. Therefore, their consequences were the same as those experienced by the entire generation that rebelled against God: they would not enter the land God had promised.

Clearly Moses was a great deliverer. But what was needed was a greater deliverer—one who would not rebel against God but submit to him, one who would deliver God's people, not just out of their slavery but safely into the land God has promised, one who was not just a servant, but a Son—who, when he sets people free, they are free indeed (John 8:36).

Mediator for a Sinful People

In addition to being a great deliverer, Moses was a great mediator. For over forty years he listened to the complaining of the people and pleaded their case before a God who felt and heard their complaints as a personal rejection. Moses entered into the cloud of God's presence on the mountain and brought down God's law to the people, gently explaining all of its provisions and applications. More than once Moses went to God with petitions for needed provision, and God heard and provided. And more than once God told Moses to take up his rod of judgment and mediate judgment on those who rebelled against him.

Perhaps Moses's finest moment as a mediator was on that day when he came down from Mount Sinai with two tablets on which God himself had written his law. Joshua, who was with him, thought he heard singing. And when they got down the mountain, they saw the golden calf and the people dancing around it. It was clear that though the people were no longer in Egypt, Egypt's idolatry was still very much in the people.

> The next day Moses said to the people, "You have sinned a great sin. And now I will go up to the Lord; perhaps I can make atonement for your sin." (Ex. 32:30)

Perhaps Moses thought it through overnight and "remembered the sacrifices of the Hebrew patriarchs and the newly instituted sacrifice of the Passover. Certainly God had shown by such sacrifices that he was prepared to accept an innocent substitute in place of the just death of the sinner. His wrath could sometimes fall on the substitute."[5]

> So Moses returned to the LORD and said, "Alas, this people has sinned a
> great sin. They have made for themselves gods of gold. But now, if you
> will forgive their sin—but if not, please blot me out of your book that you
> have written." (Ex. 32:31–32)

Moses was asking God to forgive the Israelites, but he knew he had
no solid basis on which to ask for that pardon, so he suggested an alter-
native. As a faithful mediator, Moses presented himself as a sacrifice of
atonement, offering himself to God as a substitute, that he might take
upon himself the punishment Israel deserved because of her great sin.
Moses was willing to be damned so that Israel could be saved. But God
was not willing to accept the life of Moses to atone for Israel's sin. Exodus
32 doesn't tell us why God didn't accept the sacrifice of Moses as Israel's
mediator, but we know why from the rest of Scripture. Moses could not
die for his people's sin because he himself was a sinner. As great as Moses
was as a mediator, a better mediator was needed—a sinless substitute
who would not only be willing to lay down his life for his friends (John
15:13) but would also be worthy to atone for the sins of God's people.

Prophet to a Stiff-Necked People

So Moses was a great deliverer and mediator, and he was also a prophet
among prophets. In the years after Moses had said that God would raise
up "a prophet like me," God raised up many prophets who spoke for
God to his people. As God moved his eternal purposes forward, history
was punctuated with new words from God that were spoken through
his many prophets. But the people of Israel revered Moses the most
because he surpassed all of the other prophets God sent over the years.
God himself described Moses's distinction this way:

> Hear my words: If there is a prophet among you, I the LORD make myself
> known to him in a vision; I speak with him in a dream. Not so with my
> servant Moses. He is faithful in all my house. With him I speak mouth to
> mouth, clearly, and not in riddles, and he beholds the form of the LORD.
> (Num. 12:6–8)

At the very end of Deuteronomy we read an addendum to Moses's writings, likely added after his death, which also emphasizes Moses's distinction:

> And there has not arisen a prophet since in Israel like Moses, whom the LORD knew face to face, none like him for all the signs and the wonders that the LORD sent him to do in the land of Egypt, to Pharaoh and to all his servants and to all his land, and for all the mighty power and all the great deeds of terror that Moses did in the sight of all Israel. (Deut. 34:10–12)

Other prophets performed miracles, such as Elijah, who brought down fire, and Elisha, who brought a dead boy back to life. But no prophet's miracles compared with Moses's miracles of plagues striking and Red Sea parting and manna falling and water gushing from a rock. God spoke to other prophets through visions and dreams, but Moses met personally with God in the tent of meeting.

> Now Moses used to take the tent and pitch it outside the camp, far off from the camp, and he called it the tent of meeting. . . . When Moses entered the tent, the pillar of cloud would descend and stand at the entrance of the tent, and the LORD would speak with Moses. . . . Thus the LORD used to speak to Moses face to face, as a man speaks to his friend. (Ex. 33:7, 9, 11)

When we read that they spoke "face to face," it doesn't mean that God had a human face or that Moses could fully see God. Just a few verses later we read that God said, "Man shall not see me and live" (v. 20). "Face to face" is a figure of speech that reveals the personal nature of Moses's communication with God, which was unlike any man had ever experienced since Adam and Eve had walked with God in the garden of Eden.

But this incredible communication was not enough for Moses. He wanted to see and experience everything of God that there was to see and experience. So he pleaded with God, "Please show me your glory" (Ex. 33:18). Though he had seen God's glory blazing in the bush and burning in the pillar of fire and had been engulfed in the cloud when he went up on the mountain, somehow Moses knew there was still more to see of God's glory. In kindness God responded to Moses's request, saying:

> "I will make all my goodness pass before you and will proclaim before you my name 'The LORD.' And I will be gracious to whom I will be gracious, and will show mercy on whom I will show mercy. But," he said, "you cannot see my face, for man shall not see me and live." And the LORD said, "Behold, there is a place by me where you shall stand on the rock, and while my glory passes by I will put you in a cleft of the rock, and I will cover you with my hand until I have passed by. Then I will take away my hand, and you shall see my back, but my face shall not be seen." (Ex. 33:19–23)

God's answer to Moses's request was a yes and a no. His goodness would pass by for a moment, but Moses would not be able to gaze upon the fullness of God's glory. "If Moses were to see a complete revelation of God in his eternal being, it would be so overwhelming that it would destroy him."[6] When Moses emerged from the presence of God, his face glowed with the glory of God. The skin of his face was shining so that the people were afraid of him, and he had to put a veil over his face. But with time the glory faded. It was imparted glory, a glory that he only reflected for a time. What was needed was a prophet who was no mere reflector of God's glory, but one who radiated God's glory from his own being, one who was in himself the "radiance of the glory of God" (Heb. 1:3).

A Prophet like Me

When God promised to raise up a prophet like Moses, he was promising to send one who communed with God face-to-face as Moses had done, which is what makes the first words of John's Gospel so significant: "In the beginning was the Word, and the Word was with God" (John 1:1). Here was more than a word from God but the very Word who was God, the Word who had related to God face-to-face since before the beginning of time. Here was a prophet who had not only seen God's form but was "in the form of God," yet "did not count equality with God a thing to be grasped, but emptied himself, by taking the form of a servant, being born in the likeness of men" (Phil. 2:6–7).

The glory of God was emptied into a human body so that it was veiled by flesh day to day. But there was one point in his ministry when Jesus gave his inner circle a glimpse of this intrinsic, luminescent glory. It was a few days after Peter had boldly proclaimed Jesus to be "the Christ, the Son of the living God" but then foolishly rebuked Jesus for saying he would be going to Jerusalem and would suffer many things and be killed and on the third day rise again (Matthew 16). Jesus knew the disciples needed to have their confidence grounded so firmly in Christ that they would be able to take up their own cross and follow him. What they needed was a glimpse of his glory.

> And after six days Jesus took with him Peter and James, and John his brother, and led them up a high mountain by themselves. And he was transfigured before them, and his face shone like the sun, and his clothes became white as light. (Matt. 17:1–2)

For a brief moment, the veil of humanity was peeled back and Jesus's true essence was allowed to shine through. The glory that was always his became visible. Luke tells us:

> Behold, two men were talking with him, Moses and Elijah, who appeared in glory and spoke of his departure, which he was about to accomplish at Jerusalem. (Luke 9:30–31)

Moses and Elijah, two Old Testament prophets, were there on the mountain talking with the glorified Jesus. Both of these prophets had previously stood on a mountain and experienced God's glory. Moses caught a glimpse of it from inside the cleft of a rock, Elijah from the entrance of a cave. But they were not there to talk with Jesus about their previous experiences. Luke tells us they were talking with Jesus about "his departure" or literally "his exodus."

Imagine it: Moses, who had led the great exodus of God's people from Egypt was talking to Jesus about the far greater exodus he was about to accomplish through his death. Moses must have realized that the exodus he had led was really only a preview of the main event to come. The death of Jesus would offer exodus not just to one oppressed people group at one point in history but to people from every nation of the earth for all time. This would be not merely a political or economic liberation but a pervasive liberation from the power of sin and death.

It makes perfect sense that Moses would want to talk to Jesus about his exodus. If Jesus did not die, the exodus Moses had led would have no lasting meaning. The Passover he instituted and the entire sacrificial system he set up would have been pointless. If Jesus did not die, there would be no way for Moses or anyone else to enter into the true Promised Land that Canaan always pointed to. Everything Moses lived for and wrote about depended on the coming of this prophet like him, the sacrifice of this perfect Lamb, his passing through the waters of death and emerging alive to lead his people through the wilderness of life in this world into the land God has promised and prepared. No other topic of conversation was worthy of this mountaintop meeting. As they spoke, another voice entered into the conversation:

> *Imagine it: Moses, who had led the great exodus of God's people from Egypt was talking to Jesus about the far greater exodus he was about to accomplish through his death.*

> A cloud came and overshadowed them, and they were afraid as they entered the cloud. And a voice came out of the cloud, saying, "This is my Son, my Chosen One; listen to him!" (Luke 9:34–35)

Since we've just read God's promise in Deuteronomy about the prophet he would raise up, we realize that here on the mountain God was quoting himself. He had instructed his people through Moses that they should listen to the prophet he would raise up. Surely Peter, James, and John, having grown up hearing the promise of the prophet to come, would have made this connection when they heard the words about Jesus, "Listen to him."

But more important than making the connection was following the instruction. It is more important for us too. Throughout this study, if we find the connections between Christ and the book of Moses interesting but do not truly listen—do not truly take to heart their implications—we will miss what God intends for us. These words, "listen to him," bring us to a crossroads at the center of our souls, forcing us to answer the questions: Will I listen to Jesus? Will I listen to what he has to say about what brings true freedom? Will I take him up on his offer of himself as true bread and living water that will satisfy my soul forever? Will I allow what he says about himself to shape my view of God and what pleases him, even if it contradicts my long-held understandings? Will I respond to his invitation to come to him and take his yoke upon me and find rest for my soul?

Jesus said, "My sheep hear my voice" (John 10:27). Are you willing over the weeks to come to carve out time to open up your Bible and engage it, listening for the voice of your Shepherd, who is also the Lamb? God has raised up his prophet, and we must listen to him. Don't turn down the volume on him. Don't dismiss him as irrelevant. Give his words more weight than those of even your own inner voice and opinions. He speaks the very words of God, words we are desperate to hear, words that reach places in our lives that nobody else knows anything about. So, over the weeks to come, as we study the book of Moses, let's tune our ears to listen and our hearts to respond. Let's say to him gladly as many faithful hearers have said before us, "Speak, Lord, for your servant is listening."

Looking Forward

His Face, like the Sun Shining in Full Strength

Moses was allowed to see only the backside of God as it passed by him on the mountain. In his sinful state, he could not look upon the face of God and live. But the day came fifteen hundred years later when Moses stood on another mountain and gazed into the face of God in the transfigured Jesus. Peter, James, and John were there too as "eyewitnesses of his majesty" (2 Pet. 1:16). They were given the privilege of seeing the veil of flesh pulled back so that they could see Jesus as he truly is, radiating the glory he has shared with his Father since before the world existed (John 17:5). This was the same glory that burned in the bush and blazed in the pillar of fire and descended into the tent of meeting, where it was reflected on Moses's face.

That day on the mountain, Peter, James, and John were given a glimpse of the glory that Jesus has had since before the creation of the world and will have into eternity future, the glory that will never dim or fade, the glory we will one day be able to feast our eyes upon without fear of being destroyed. John did his best to describe what the glorified Jesus looked like in his vision while on Patmos:

> [I saw] one like a son of man, clothed with a long robe and with a golden sash around his chest. The hairs of his head were white, like white wool, like snow. His eyes were like a flame of fire, his feet were like burnished bronze, refined in a furnace, and his voice was like the roar of many waters. In his right hand he held seven stars, from his mouth came a sharp two-edged sword, and his face was like the sun shining in full strength. (Rev. 1:13–16)

Into eternity future, the face of Jesus will shine as it shone that day on the mountain, unveiled even more completely. The Bible promises that the day will come when we will stand before him like Peter, James, and John did, and we will see his face (Rev. 22:4). We will gaze upon the radiance of our glorified Savior, and there will no longer be any need for hiding from him in the cleft of a rock or seeing only his backside. Nothing will be needed to shield us from what we were made for—gazing upon the beauty of the Lord for all eternity (Ps. 27:4).

When that day comes, something even more glorious than what happened to Moses will have happened to everyone who has trusted in Christ. The Spirit's work of transforming us from one degree of glory to another will be complete (2 Cor. 3:18). Our faces will radiate his glory for all eternity. We will live forever in the abundant blessing God promised through Moses:

> The LORD bless you and keep you;
> the LORD make his face to shine upon you and be gracious
>   to you;
> the LORD lift up his countenance upon you and give you peace.
>   (Num. 6:24–26)

Discussion Guide

A Prophet like Me

Getting the Discussion Going

1. We are preparing to spend a lot of time over the coming weeks studying the books of Exodus, Leviticus, Numbers, and Deuteronomy. Why do you think these ancient books are worth studying?

Getting to the Heart of It

2. We started our study by looking at an interesting interchange between Jesus and the religious leaders of his day regarding the writings of Moses recorded in John 5. Moses was someone those leaders had great respect for. Why? What are some things we know about Moses?

3. Our aim as we work our way through these books is to consider what Moses intended to communicate to his original audience, the children of Israel, as they prepared to enter into the Promised Land. We also want to see what the divine author intends for us to see in light of the fuller revelation of Christ. Considering the previews set forth in the introduction of how we will see Jesus in these Old Testament books (pages 19–20), what are your thoughts or reactions?

4. We saw that Moses was a great deliverer, mediator, and prophet but that a greater deliverer, mediator, and prophet was needed. How was Jesus greater than Moses in each of these roles?

5. Moses had an incredible experience of the glory of God, which transformed him. The disciples also had an incredible experience of the glory of God when Jesus was transfigured. But what, according to John 17:1–5, was the greatest display of the glory of God in the life of Jesus? And how does seeing this glory impact us?

6. Read John 17:22–24, more of Jesus's prayer before his crucifixion. What does Jesus say in his prayer about eternity past and eternity future? How does this define our hope as believers?

Getting Personal

7. Moses said that when the prophet like him came, we should listen to him. And twice during the life of Jesus, God spoke from heaven identifying Jesus as his Son and commanding us to listen (Matt. 3:17; 17:5). The truth is that it can be challenging to tune out the voice of the world to be able to truly listen to Jesus. What do you think is going to be key for you to be able to truly listen and hear what God wants to say to you through this study of the writings of Moses over the coming weeks?

Getting How It Fits into the Big Picture

8. Let's think for a moment about what it means that Moses's life gave God's people a preview of the greater deliverer, mediator, and prophet to come and that Moses was inspired by the Holy Spirit to be able to write down all that was revealed to him. What does this tell us about history and the future—about who is in charge and how it will turn out? What does it impress upon us about the Bible?

Where do I see God's glory so that
I can take up my cross + follow
him.

Slavery and a Savior

Exodus 1–4

Personal Bible Study

Exodus 1–4

1. Read Acts 7:1–20, which gives a synopsis of Israel's history up to the time where we pick up the story in Exodus 1. Notice that Acts 7:17 refers to "the time of the promise." What was the promise the people of Israel were holding onto, according to Acts 7:5–7?

v.8 *God promised that one day the whole land would belong to Abraham + his descendants.*
But 1st they would live in a foreign country for 400 yrs as slaves.

2. Read Exodus 1:1–7 and compare with Genesis 1:28; 9:1; and 35:10–11. How is God clearly at work bringing about his plans for fulfilling his promise to his people? *G 1:28 God blessed them + told them to multiply + fill the earth (creation) ^ G 9:1 God's covenant to Noah - Multiply + fill the earth after the flood G35 God blessed Jacob, called him israel - multiply .... Become a great nation*

3. For those Israelites who were holding onto the promises that God would bless them and give them the land of Canaan, how did their current circumstances as revealed in Exodus 1:8–14 seem to call that promise into question?

They were made into slaves and severely oppressed but continued to multiply.

4. Read Exodus 1:15–22 and 2:1–10. To what would you attribute the multiplication of the Israelites under oppression, the courageous defiance of the Hebrew midwives, and the survival of the baby boy placed in a basket on the Nile? *The midwives feared God and would not kill the baby boys., God gave them families & strength. They were also smart, by placing moses in basket where he would be found*

5. Read Exodus 2:1–22 and Luke's version of these events in Acts 7:20–29. What facts about Moses or insights into his character and actions does Luke provide in the following verses from Acts 7, which are not explicit in the Exodus 2 account?

v. 22: *That moses was taught all the wisdom & was mighty in word & action.*

v. 23: *moses knew he was a man of israel & assumed the israelites would recognize this but they didn't.*

v. 25: *(he was visiting his relatives) He fled as he was betrayed by israel as they knew he killed an egyptian —*

6. What was the result of Moses's taking matters into his own hands, according to his own timing? *He delayed the work w/ israel for 40 years as he fled & went to a diff land (midian)*

7. During the first forty years of Moses's life in Egypt, and even through the forty years of his life in Midian, Israel was in bondage and captivity. But what is the new development, according to Exodus 2:23? *The King of Egypt died & the slaves asked God for help.*

8. What is God's response, indicated by four verbs in Exodus 2:24–25? *God heard (cries) remembered (covenant) looked down felt concern (for their welfare)*

9. Is there any indication that the people of Israel had any awareness of God's response? What are the implications of this for us when we think that God has forgotten us or does not hear our cries or care about our suffering?

no, they did not have anyone like moses to help talk to God & receive a response

10. Read Exodus 3:1–6. Though God may be silent, he is not absent, and in Exodus 3, God breaks his four-hundred-year silence by speaking to Moses from the burning bush. What were the first words Moses heard God say from the burning bush, and what difference do you think this made to Moses? Consider that Moses likely thought his rash actions back in Egypt had disqualified him from being the deliverer for his suffering people. *moses said*

"Here I am". God said take off your sandles you are on Holy Ground, I am the God of your ancestors.

11. How did God protect Moses in Exodus 3:5, and what or whom is he protecting him from? *asked him to remove sandles—*

he didn't want moses to sin on Holy Ground

12. In Exodus 3:7–10 God makes five statements about what he has seen and heard and known. What are they?

1. (v. 7) *seen misery*

2. (v. 7) *heard cries for deliverance*

3. (v. 7) *aware of their suffering*

4. (v. 9) *cries reached me*

5. (v. 9) *seen the oppression*

13. In these same verses (Ex. 3:7–10) God also outlines five points of his plan for Moses and the Hebrews. What are they?

1. (v. 8) _I will rescue them_

2. (v. 8) _lead them out of Egypt to their own land_

3. (v. 8) _I have come_

4. (v. 10) _I am sending you (moses) to Pharoah_

5. (v. 10) _You will lead my people from Egypt._

14. Moses came from an Egyptian background in which all Egyptian gods had names, so it seemed logical to him that the God of Abraham, Isaac, and Jacob must therefore also have a name, which the Hebrews would want to know. But Moses sought to know not just God's name but also his essence and character. What is the name God revealed to Moses, and what do you think is significant about this name?

I am the one who always is —
"I am" sent me to you
The Lord — the God of your ancestors,
God of the Hebrews

15. In Exodus 3–4 Moses continues to ask God questions and express concern about his suitability for such a task. How does God address and respond to each of Moses's concerns? [1]

Moses's Questions and Concerns	Yahweh's Response
Who am I that I should go? (3:11)	3:12 _I will be with you_
What is your name, that I may tell the people who sent me? (3:13)	3:14–15 _I am_ _The Lord_

How will the people believe that you have sent me? (4:1)	4:2–4, 6–7, 9 *shepherds STAFF/snake*
I am not eloquent: I am slow of speech and of tongue. (4:10)	4:11 *who makes mouths? I will help you speak well*
Please send someone else. (4:13)	4:15–16 *Aaron, his brother, will help him.*

16. Moses was one of the many people in the Old Testament who was a type of Christ, meaning that there were aspects to who he was and what he did that pointed to who Christ would be and what he would do. Work your way through the chart below, looking up the New Testament references if needed, and write a corresponding statement that shows how Moses pointed to Christ in each of these different ways. An answer for the first one is provided as an example.

Moses	*Jesus*
Moses was born when his nation was under the dominion of a hostile power, Egypt, and a cruel leader, Pharaoh. (Ex. 1:8–14)	(Matt. 2:1; Luke 24:21) *Jesus was born when his people, the Jews, were under the dominion of a hostile power, the Romans, and a cruel leader, Herod.*
Moses was born under threat of death, because Pharaoh had given orders that every Hebrew boy be cast into the Nile. (Ex. 1:22)	Matt. 2:16 *Herod sent soldiers to kill all the boys around Bethlehem 2 & ↓*
Moses was given a name to match his destiny: "he who draws out of." (Ex. 2:10)	Matt. 1:21 *name him Jesus "the Lord saves" for he will save his people from their sins*
Moses spent his childhood in Egypt. (Ex. 2:10)	Matt. 2:13 *Angel told Joseph to flee to Egypt*

The Lord told Moses to return to Egypt saying, "All the men who were seeking your life are dead." (Ex. 4:19)	Matt. 2:19 *When Herod died the Lord appeared in a dream to tell them to ret to israel*
Though Moses was legally the "son of Pharaoh's daughter" (Heb. 11:24), he went down to the enslaved Hebrews, his brothers. (Ex. 2:11)	Heb. 2:11 *Jesus & the ones he makes Holy have the same father & he calls them his bros & sisters*
Moses left the comforts of Pharaoh's palace to become a servant of God's people. (Heb. 11:24–26)	Phil. 2:6–7 *Though he was in the form of God he emptied himself & became a servant.*
The Hebrews rejected Moses's salvation, saying, "Who made you a prince and a judge over us?" (Ex. 2:14)	Luke 19:14; John 1;11 *Parable - his citizens hated him. He came to his own but they did not receive him*
Before he embarked on his saving mission, Moses spent forty years in obscurity on the far side of the desert. (Ex. 3:1)	Matt. 4:1; Luke 3:23 *tempted by devil 40 days. Jesus began ministry @ age thirty*
God sent Moses to emancipate his people from their bondage. (Ex. 3:10)	John 3:17 *God gave his son so that those believing in him had eternal life - to save the world*
Moses's commission from God was confirmed by the power to work miracles, including power over the serpent and over leprosy. (Ex. 4:1–9)	Matt. 4:10, 11; 8:3; 11:4–5 *Be gone satan! healed leprosy Blind see, lepers cleansed dead raised deaf hear*

Teaching Chapter

What's Your Story?

We all have a story. When we meet someone new and are asked to tell something about ourselves, we offer up a version of our lives, usually where we were born and raised, the family we were raised in, and a run-down of our interests, pursuits, education, vocation, and marital status. There are many things about our stories that we have no control over: where and to whom we were born, aspects of our personalities and abilities and struggles. But there is also a sense in which we often-times seek to write into our lives some greater story line.

Many of us grew up with stories of princes and princesses. We read the story of the beautiful princess, whom we wanted to be, and the handsome prince, whom we hoped to find, and their grand romance and living happily ever after, which we hoped to experience. For many of us, this is the story we want our lives to tell. Oftentimes, however, those who chose this story line to which to conform their lives end up frustrated and disappointed because instead of being crowned with a tiara, they have been handed dishrags and colicky babies; instead of being married to perfect princes, they are married to men with college debt and smelly feet.

The Bible and the God of the Bible offer us a story meant to tell us who we are and why we are here and what our lives are about.

Others of us haven't had our expectations for our lives shaped by the Disney happily-ever-after story line but by the narrative of the

43

American dream: the immigrant who comes to America with nothing and works hard and smart and makes something of himself or herself; the professional who gets an education, puts in years at the company, and retires to spend time on the golf course and live off investment income; or the young tech-savvy college grad who bypasses the work-a-day job in an office to launch a little blog that blossoms into a must-read on the web. Still others eschew these conformist stories for their lives and embrace the more rugged, nonmaterialistic lifestyle of simplicity, seeking to make their story one of giving their lives away building wells in Africa or simply building a close-knit, healthy family.

But these are all stories about what we will do, what we can accomplish—stories we want to write for ourselves. The Bible and the God of the Bible offer us a story meant to tell us who we are and why we are here and what our lives are about. It is the story we are about to study in Exodus, Leviticus, Numbers, and Deuteronomy. This is *the* story. It is this story that the Bible offers to you, inviting you to make this story the story of your life.

Cruel Bondage

To understand who the people are in this story, we have to go back a bit, even as far back as the garden of Eden when God gave Adam and Eve a promise of grace in the midst of the curse, promising that a descendant would one day come and do battle with the Serpent and put an end to evil. Genesis traces this promise of an offspring to God's call of one man and the growth of his family into the descendants of twelve sons, seventy people in all, who find themselves in Egypt because one of these sons, Joseph, has been put in charge of supplying grain in the midst of a worldwide famine. They carry with them the promise that God will bless all peoples in the world through this family.

At the beginning of Exodus we find this family four hundred years later, and we read:

> The people of Israel were fruitful and increased greatly; they multiplied and grew exceedingly strong, so that the land was filled with them. (Ex. 1:7)

There is something there that sounds familiar, isn't there? We can't help but remember God's repeated instruction in Genesis to be fruitful and multiply and fill the earth. God had promised Abraham that his descendants would be as numerous as grains of sand on the seashore and stars in the sky, so, in this initial report of fruitfulness, multiplication, and the land's being filled, it seems that God is at work bringing about his good plan for his people. But then we keep reading, and we're not so sure anymore:

> Now there arose a new king over Egypt, who did not know Joseph. And he said to his people, "Behold, the people of Israel are too many and too mighty for us. Come, let us deal shrewdly with them, lest they multiply, and, if war breaks out, they join our enemies and fight against us and escape from the land." Therefore they set taskmasters over them to afflict them with heavy burdens. They built for Pharaoh store cities, Pithom and Raamses. (Ex. 1:8–11)

Clearly these carriers of God's promises have gone from being welcomed guests of the pharaoh to becoming an abused slave-labor force. Pharaoh, an ancient version of Pol Pot, Stalin, or Hitler, imagines a threat, and uses that imagined threat to justify his evil scheme plan A.[2] He will turn these foreigners into slaves, oppressing them with labor so that the men will be kept away from their wives and will likely die young from overwork. In this way their population will decrease and the threat will be diminished.

Back in Genesis, when God cursed the serpent he said that he would "put enmity . . . between your offspring and her offspring" (Gen. 3:15). Here in Exodus we see the offspring of the Serpent, Pharaoh, the king of Egypt who wears a serpent on his crown, at enmity against the offspring of "the woman." Had this evil offspring's effort succeeded, had all the male children of the Hebrews been slain, the channel through which the Savior was to come would have been destroyed. But we discover in verse 12 that Pharaoh's plan A has clearly backfired:

> The more they were oppressed, the more they multiplied and the more they spread abroad. And the Egyptians were in dread of the people of Israel. (Ex. 1:12)

This is no fluke; this is the sovereign work of the One who had made the promise that this family would become a numerous people.

Since plan A backfired, Pharaoh turned to plan B, instructing the midwives to kill the baby boys born to Hebrew women to keep them from growing up to be warriors. Why not the girl babies? Perhaps he assumed that the women would easily become assimilated into the Egyptian population once the men were eliminated. But plan B failed too. So finally Pharaoh stopped hiding behind his secret strategies and went to plan C, moving from forced enslavement to secret suffocation to outright slaughter:

> Then Pharaoh commanded all his people, "Every son that is born to the Hebrews you shall cast into the Nile, but you shall let every daughter live." (Ex. 1:22)

This is ethnic cleansing on an enormous scale, and we realize this is not at all a quaint, "safe for the whole family" Bible story. Imagine the fear of every pregnant mother when the midwife announced, "It's a boy!" Imagine the agony of having your child ruthlessly ripped from your arms to be unceremoniously thrown into the river. Imagine the wailing that rose up night after night in the homes of Goshen as mothers mourned their murdered sons.

This was a terrible time to be the people of God. If we're looking for a story line for our lives, certainly this wouldn't be it. But, in reality, this cruel bondage is a part of each of our lives. Have you ever seen it in your life? Until we see ourselves as living in cruel bondage, we will never see our need for a Savior.

Perhaps you see your self as perfectly free. You do what you want, and you are a slave to no one. Perhaps you're like the Pharisees who said to Jesus, "We . . . have never been enslaved to anyone" (John 8:33). Jesus said to those Pharisees,

> Truly, truly, I say to you, everyone who commits sin is a slave to sin. (John 8:34)

What does it mean to be a slave to sin? It means that you are unable to escape from sinful patterns of conduct and cycles of guilt and regret. This is the bondage we are born into and are powerless to break free from until God sends us a deliverer. Just as God sent Moses to lead the children of Israel out of their bondage to the Egyptians, God sent Jesus to deliver you from bondage to the slave master of sin—bondage to binging and purging, to materialism, perfectionism, pride, hypocrisy, hate, or whatever it is that rules you and robs you of relationship with the one who made you. If you are united to Christ, this bondage has been broken, and you are no longer subject to the tyranny, domination, and rule of sin. You may still be tempted, and you may still sin, but sin no longer has the power to control you as it once did.

Perhaps there was an event somewhere in the story line of your life when you made a decision to turn away from your sinful ways or prayed a prayer or even wept over the sin that has enslaved you, yet you find you are still serving those same old slave masters. If so, you are not living in the freedom Christ has purchased for you.

When we look at the cruel bondage the people of Israel endured, and if we look ahead to their deliverance, we realize that their freedom did not come solely by leaving Egypt but by going to the mountain to worship. God told Moses, "When you have brought the people out of Egypt, you shall serve God on this mountain." The secret to finding freedom is not trying harder but turning wholly toward God, sensing his greatness and goodness, looking away from all that enslaves you and looking up to who he is. It is being moved by the wonder of this one who lost his freedom so that you could be free, this one who was nailed to a cross so that your chains could be broken, this one who was whipped and beaten so that you could be healed. Here is the invitation he offers you:

> Come to me, all who labor and are heavy laden, and I will give you rest. Take my yoke upon you, and learn from me, for I am gentle and lowly in heart, and you will find rest for your souls. For my yoke is easy, and my burden is light. (Matt. 11:28–30)

Won't you trade in your yoke to whatever it is that you once thought would bring you so much pleasure and freedom, but has only made you its slave, for this yoke that binds you savingly to Christ?

Compassionate Brother

To this point in the story we really have no interest in this being the story of our own lives, do we? Certainly from the vantage point of those who were suffering, all must have seemed hopeless. Many of the Israelites had probably altogether forgotten about God and his promises that were made to their ancestors Abraham and Jacob. Those who remembered must have wondered if it was foolish to hang on to them. But when Exodus 2 opens, hope has been born in the form of a baby boy.

> Now a man from the house of Levi went and took as his wife a Levite woman. The woman conceived and bore a son, and when she saw that he was a fine child, she hid him three months. When she could hide him no longer, she took for him a basket made of bulrushes and daubed it with bitumen and pitch. She put the child in it and placed it among the reeds by the river bank. (Ex. 2:1–3)

When we read that this mother saw that this was a "fine child" or, as the New International Version puts it, "he was no ordinary child," we might think that this is simply a description of what every mother feels about her child. The truth is that we don't know exactly what is meant by this description. The first-century historian Josephus wrote that Moses's parents received divine revelation about God's intentions for this child—that he would be the one who would save the Israelites.[3] But however it came about, it seems clear that Moses's parents were convinced that this baby would have a significant place in God's plan to fulfill his promises to his people. And while we might assume it was simply desperate mother love that drove Moses's mother to weave a basket and put her beautiful baby into the Nile River, Scripture corrects our assumption:

> *By faith* Moses, when he was born, was hidden for three months by his parents, because they saw that the child was beautiful, and they were not afraid of the king's edict. (Heb. 11:23)

Moses's parents were not acting primarily out of parental passion or even creative desperation, but *by faith*. And we know that faith is being confident of what we can't see, based on what God has said (Heb. 11:1), so perhaps Moses's parents did receive direct communication from God telling them what to do. This possibility becomes even more probable when we consider where they put the baby and the basket:

> She put the child in it and placed it among the reeds by the river bank. (Ex. 2:3)

If they were acting purely on parental instinct rather than on faith, surely they would not have placed the basket in the very place where babies were being drowned—in the river—but would have taken him as far away from the river as possible. Yet here is this baby, in whom God's entire plan for triumphing over evil rests, and he is floating in the Nile River in a little papyrus basket.

In the story that God is writing in this world he made, nothing happens merely by coincidence. And it was no coincidence that Pharaoh's daughter picked that day and that location for a swim. God was at work, not only getting her to that place where she would find Moses but moving her heart to have compassion on this Hebrew baby. Her daddy had just given the edict to have all Hebrew baby boys killed, and it was no small thing to defy her father, the pharaoh. But she did. And when she named the baby, it would seem she knew at least a little Hebrew:

> She named him Moses, "Because," she said, "I drew him out of the water." (Ex. 2:10)

But evidently her Hebrew needed a little work, because *Moses* literally means "he who draws out of." Without realizing it, the daughter of Pharaoh gave this child a name that is less about where he came from and more about what he will do: draw his people out of Egypt through the Red Sea.[4]

So Moses grew up "instructed in all the wisdom of the Egyptians" (Acts 7:22), learning linguistics, mathematics, astronomy, architecture, music, medicine, law, and the fine art of diplomacy.[5] Ironically, the training Moses would need to lead his people out of Israel and shepherd them in the desert was provided in the household of the pharaoh himself. While Exodus doesn't tell us about what went on in Moses's life during these years, once again the writer to the Hebrews draws back the curtain, allowing us to see into what motivated Moses and what he valued and the choice he made in regard to where to place his confidence:

> By faith Moses, when he was grown up, refused to be called the son of Pharaoh's daughter, choosing rather to be mistreated with the people of God than to enjoy the fleeting pleasures of sin. He considered the reproach of Christ greater wealth than the treasures of Egypt, for he was looking to the reward. (Heb. 11:24–26)

How could it be that Moses "considered the reproach of Christ greater wealth than the treasures of Egypt"? Moses lived fifteen hundred years before Jesus was born. The truth is that although Moses might not have known Jesus, he knew about the Christ, the Messiah. He knew that the Christ, the offspring of the woman God had promised, was coming and would one day put an end to suffering and cruelty of life in this world. Moses, who had lived for several years in the Hebrew home of his believing parents before being schooled in the halls of Pharaoh's palace, held on to the promise of a Messiah he had learned about from his parents, and eventually he put everything on the line demonstrating his faith in the promised Christ:

> One day, when Moses had grown up, he went out to his people and looked on their burdens, and he saw an Egyptian beating a Hebrew, one of his people. He looked this way and that, and seeing no one, he struck down the Egyptian and hid him in the sand. When he went out the next day, behold, two Hebrews were struggling together. And he said to the man in the wrong, "Why do you strike your companion?" He answered, "Who made you a prince and a judge over us? Do you mean to kill me as you killed the Egyptian?" (Ex. 2:11–14)

Moses was moved by compassion for his brothers, but his efforts to intervene in their mistreatment were rejected and even ridiculed, and he was forced to flee Egypt and head into the wilderness. There we see Moses exercise this same compassionate intervention on behalf of a group of young women who were being abused by a group of shepherds. One of those young women, the daughter of the priest of Midian, became his wife and then the mother of his child. Moses named the child Gershom, which means "I have become an alien in a foreign land." Obviously, what was weighing heavily on Moses's heart when this baby was born was that his brothers were suffering in Egypt, and seemingly he could do nothing about it.

As we read this story of Moses's birth, deliverance, and rejection, it begins to dawn on us that this story reminds us of another story that will take place fifteen hundred years later. We remember that there will be another cruel dictator who will make a decree that all male infants should be killed. There will be another baby who will escape the death sentence while many other baby boys are killed. We remember that there will be another group of oppressed people longing for deliverance from those who rule over them, and one who will leave the royal splendor of his heavenly home to enter into their suffering. This deliverer will also be rejected by those he came to save and sentenced to death. But, unlike Moses who escaped the king's edict, this deliverer will be put to death. In fact, his death and resurrection will be exactly what is required to deliver his people from their cruel bondage to sin and death.

When we begin to make these connections between the great deliverer, Moses, and the greater deliverer, Jesus, it becomes clear that we are not the key characters in this grand story. This story is really about this great Deliverer, this compassionate brother. So, I must ask you, does this compassionate brother have a starring role in your story? Is he even a part of your story? Or have you looked him in the face and said, by your suspicion of him, your rejection of him, or simply your apathy toward him, the same thing his enslaved brothers said to Moses: "Who made you a prince and judge over me?"

At this point in the story in Exodus, if we knew nothing else of the Bible, we might well wonder if God had abandoned his original plan, his promise, and his people, because there has been little sign of God and barely a mention of him so far. But then, at the end of Exodus 2, we come to this insight into unseen realities:

God: heard remembered saw knew

> During those many days the king of Egypt died, and the people of Israel groaned because of their slavery and cried out for help. Their cry for rescue from slavery came up to God. And God heard their groaning, and God remembered his covenant with Abraham, with Isaac, and with Jacob. God saw the people of Israel—and God knew. (Ex. 2:23–25)

If we have wondered what God was doing, now we know. He was listening. He was remembering. He was watching. God was not unaware or uncaring about his people's suffering. He had not forgotten his promise. Even if his people had forgotten his covenant promise to them, God still remembered the promise he had made. And that is what matters. From beginning to end, our salvation depends not on our remembering or fulfilling our promises to him, but on God remembering and fulfilling his covenant with us.

Burning Bush

> Now Moses was keeping the flock of his father-in-law, Jethro, the priest of Midian, and he led his flock to the west side of the wilderness and came to Horeb, the mountain of God. (Ex. 3:1)

You can't get much farther away from the throne of Egypt than tending sheep on the western side of the wilderness. Remember that Moses grew up in a household in Egypt, where all shepherds were detestable (Gen. 46:34), so Moses probably could not help feeling that this was as low as he could get. But while this wilderness didn't glimmer with the treasure of Egypt, it did deliver regular doses of reality. Sinclair Ferguson said, "Forty years of humiliation and loneliness and isolation and shepherding foolish sheep has rendered Moses meek and prepared him to be the shepherd of Israel whom God will use to bring his people out of bondage."[6] In Exodus 3 we no longer see Moses as a beautiful baby or a pampered prince but as a meek shepherd.

> And the angel of the LORD appeared to him in a flame of fire out of the midst of a bush. He looked, and behold, the bush was burning, yet it was

not consumed. And Moses said, "I will turn aside to see this great sight, why the bush is not burned." (Ex. 3:2–3)

At first Moses was drawn to this "great sight" because he couldn't figure out what it was. He saw fire in a bush that did not depend on the bush for its existence. But Moses quickly discovered that the correct question was not so much, *What* is this? as it was, *Who* is this? Moses wrote that it was "the angel of the Lord" who appeared to him in the flame of fire. But it is clear that this was more than the typical angel or messenger. And we know this for a number of reasons.

First, fire is a sign of God's presence throughout the book of Exodus, as we see later in the pillar of fire that leads and protects the Israelites (13:21–22); in the fire of God's presence on Mount Sinai (19:18); and in the tabernacle (40:38). Second, Moses wrote that "*God* called to him out of the bush." Moses clearly identified the person speaking to him as God himself, writing that he hid his face from this fire because he was afraid to look at *God*. And third, Moses was told to take off his sandals because he was standing on holy ground. It is not a mere angel whose presence makes a place holy, but only God himself.

So who is this angel of the Lord? The "angel of the Lord" is clearly distinguished from all other angelic beings throughout the Old Testament in a number of ways and yet is called an "angel." Hagar met this angel in the desert, and he comforted her with predictions concerning the future. Abraham heard the angel of the Lord's voice on Mount Moriah telling him not to kill his son Isaac. Jacob spent the night wrestling with the angel of the Lord. This angel of God was in the pillar of cloud and the pillar of fire that led Israel through the wilderness.

Nowhere does Scripture spell it out absolutely, but it does seem to indicate that the angel of the Lord was none other than the pre-incarnate Son of God. Centuries before Jesus was born as a baby in Bethlehem, he occasionally manifested himself among his people as a ministering angel. It would seem that this angel of the Lord who appeared in the flame of fire is the same person who later wrapped himself in the flesh of humanity.

As we see this burning bush in our mind's eye, we realize that even

Moses is not going to be the main character in this salvation story. That is reserved for God himself. Notice the first-person-singular verbs in what Jehovah says to Moses:

> Then the LORD said, "*I* have surely seen the affliction of my people who are in Egypt and have heard their cry because of their taskmasters. *I* know their sufferings, and *I have come down* to deliver them out of the hand of the Egyptians and to bring them up out of that land to a good and broad land, a land flowing with milk and honey, to the place of the Canaanites, the Hittites, the Amorites, the Perizzites, the Hivites, and the Jebusites. And now, behold, the cry of the people of Israel has come to me, and *I have also seen the oppression* with which the Egyptians oppress them. (Ex. 3:7–9)

I have seen, I know, I have heard, I have come down, says God. Forty years earlier Moses had taken the salvation of his people into his own hands. But now we see that God alone takes the salvation of his people into his hands. This is the Lord who comes down to deliver his people. By using Moses to accomplish his deliverance, he will give us a preview of the day when he will come down to deliver—not as fire but as flesh. He will deliver his people—not out of the hand of the Egyptians but out of their slavery to sin; not by parting the waters of the Red Sea, but by rolling away the stone.

"Here I am," Moses replied when God called to him (Ex. 3:4). Then Moses took off his sandals, a sign in ancient times of willing servant-hood, as slaves usually went barefoot. But, of course, this was before Moses knew what God was calling him to do. As we continue in this account, we find that Moses becomes less eager. He has some questions, and his most significant question is about himself. God said to him:

> "Come, I will send you to Pharaoh that you may bring my people, the children of Israel, out of Egypt." But Moses said to God, "*Who am I* that I should go to Pharaoh and bring the children of Israel out of Egypt?" (Ex. 3:10–11)

Moses knew that he was inadequate to accomplish such a great deliverance. But it was becoming clear that this story was not going to be about who Moses was, but about who God is, the one who called him, and sent him, and promised to be with him.

We might expect that God would answer Moses's question, Who am I? by pointing out all of the ways he has prepared Moses for this task: his Hebrew ancestry, his Egyptian education, his shepherding experience. But this deliverance was not going to be about who Moses was, but about who God is. It will not be up to Moses to do the saving, but up to God alone.

> Then Moses said to God, "If I come to the people of Israel and say to them, 'The God of your fathers has sent me to you,' and they ask me, 'What is his name?' what shall I say to them?" God said to Moses, "I AM WHO I AM." And he said, "Say this to the people of Israel, 'I AM has sent me to you.'" (Ex. 3:13–14)

Now, this is a bit perplexing, isn't it? What kind of a name is this? By giving Moses his name, God showed that "he aims to be known not as a generic deity, but as a specific Person with a name that carries his unique character and mission."[7] This name speaks of his eternal and unchangeable nature, his self-existence and self-sufficiency. Clearly he is differentiating himself from the gods of Egypt that Moses grew up hearing about day after day in Pharaoh's household. This God is dependent on nothing and no one, but in fact everything and everyone is dependent for its existence upon him. This name forces us to reckon with the vast chasm between who God is and who we are. When God says, "I AM WHO I AM," he puts an end to our inflated view of ourselves.

He also does away with our notion that God can be whoever we want him to be. God did not say, "I am who you want me to be." God is a person, and we cannot shape him into the god we have put on order who suits our ideas of what a god should be. Instead, he ignores our personal preferences and says, "I AM WHO I AM." Does this sound like a god you could assign to be your copilot, a god you could put in your pocket like a lucky charm? When we discover I AM WHO I AM, perhaps there are things about him we don't like, things that rub us the wrong way and don't sit well with our preconceived notions or politically correct ideals. But he is real. And he must be reckoned with as he truly is.

By revealing his personal name, God demonstrated that he is personal. This revelation of his name was a promise of his personal presence. Whereas "the deities of the ancient Near East were impersonal and little more than personifications of natural forces, requiring acts of appeasement with no relationship, no communication, no reciprocal action, no moral obligation, . . . this is a God who enters into covenant relationship with people, who makes promises to them and keeps them."[8]

> God also said to Moses, "Say this to the people of Israel, 'The LORD, the God of your fathers, the God of Abraham, the God of Isaac, and the God of Jacob, has sent me to you.' This is my name forever, and thus I am to be remembered throughout all generations." (Ex. 3:15)

And this name was remembered. That's what made it so unbelievable and even offensive when Jesus, who seemed like an ordinary person, began to take this divine name upon himself. The people of Jesus's day recognized that he was claiming to be God, and it was such an offense, such seeming blasphemy, that they picked up stones to throw at him.

Again and again, when we come to the New Testament we hear the words, "I am" from the mouth of Jesus as he drew out for us all what it means for him to be God with us. "I am the living bread that came down from heaven" (John 6:51). "I am the light of the world. Whoever follows me will not walk in darkness, but will have the light of life" (John 8:12). "I am the door. If anyone enters by me, he will be saved and will go in and out and find pasture" (John 10:9). "I am the good shepherd" (John 10:11). "I am the resurrection and the life" (John 11:25). "I am the way, and the truth, and the life. No one comes to the Father except through me" (John 14:6). "I am the true vine, and my Father is the vinedresser" (John 15:1).

But perhaps the most significant time Jesus identified himself as "I am" was when a mob came to arrest him in the garden of Gethsemane. John tells us:

> Then Jesus, knowing all that would happen to him, came forward and said to them, "Whom do you seek?" They answered him, "Jesus of Nazareth." Jesus said to them, "I am he." . . . When Jesus said to them, "I am he," they drew back and fell to the ground. (John 18:4–6)

Why would this mob of angry people and brutish soldiers draw back and fall to the ground? Before them stood the same "I AM WHO I AM" that Moses hid his face from in the wilderness. They didn't fall down when he asked them what they wanted but only after he said, "I am he" or literally, "I Am."

That night Jesus, the great deliverer of whom Moses was only a type, was about to accomplish the great act of deliverance from the cruel bondage of sin that Moses's leading his people out of the cruel bondage of Egypt had been pointing to all along. This one, who served as mediator between holy God and sinful Moses in the flaming fire of the bush, was about to become mediator of a new covenant. He would not be protected from the flame as Moses was. Instead, when he became sin for us, the fire of God's wrath enveloped him.

The very real story of the suffering of God's people and the raising up of a savior sent by God, told in Exodus and celebrated throughout the rest of the Bible, is a living preview of the story of salvation accomplished through Jesus Christ. In this story, we see that our salvation is not about who we are or what we can accomplish, but about who I Am is and what he has accomplished.

> *The very real story of the suffering of God's people and the raising up of a savior sent by God is a living preview of the story of salvation accomplished through Jesus Christ.*

This is an amazing and important story. And I have to ask you: Is this the story that your own story revolves around and draws from? Have you ever seen yourself in cruel bondage, and have you experienced the deliverance that can only be accomplished by your compassionate brother Jesus Christ? The more your story is about this rescue from bondage, this savior God sent, this God who has come down and revealed himself, the less your story will be about you and your failures or achievements, your abilities or inadequacies, your circumstances, opinions, or questions. This is the story that enables you to make sense of your suffering and make much of your Savior. It is this story, and only this story, that can fill your story with meaning that will last forever.

Claim new person in Christ, so are others

Looking Forward

I Am Comes Down

The people of Israel groaned because of their suffering and cried out for help. Their cry for rescue from slavery came up to God. And so what did God do? God came down in a flame of fire and spoke to Moses out of the midst of a bush, saying, "I have surely seen the affliction of my people. . . . I know their sufferings, and I have come down to deliver them" (Ex. 3:7–8). And when Moses wanted to know the name of this God who had come down in fire, God told him, "I AM WHO I AM."

I Am came down in compassion and power to fulfill his covenant promise by delivering his people from the cruel bondage of the Egyptians. But this was really just a down-payment on the greater deliverance that was to come. Coming down in fire in the bush was just a preview of his coming down in flesh in the person of Jesus. When God came down in the person of Christ, he not only condescended to come to earth, but he descended into death to accomplish our deliverance.

> Since therefore the children share in flesh and blood, he himself likewise partook of the same things, that through death he might destroy the one who has the power of death, that is, the devil, and deliver all those who through fear of death were subject to lifelong slavery. (Heb. 2:14–15)

There is another "coming down" we still long for. The great deliverance that Christ accomplished was inaugurated on the cross and by his resurrection from the dead, but it has not yet been consummated. Just as the Israelites groaned under their suffering in Egypt and cried out to God for deliverance, we continue to cry out for deliverance. In fact, all of creation longs for God to come down again and bring his work of redemption to its glorious completion. Paul put it this way in Romans 8:

> For the creation waits with eager longing for the revealing of the sons of God. For the creation was subjected to futility, not willingly, but because of him who subjected it, in hope that the creation itself will be set free from its bondage to corruption and obtain the freedom of the glory of the children of God. For we

> know that the whole creation has been groaning together in the pains of childbirth until now. And not only the creation, but we ourselves, who have the firstfruits of the Spirit, groan inwardly as we wait eagerly for adoption as sons, the redemption of our bodies. (Rom. 8:19–23)

The same God who heard the groans of his people Israel in Egypt, the same God who came down in flesh to offer himself in weakness, will indeed come down again—this time in glorified flesh to rule and reign with glory and power.

> For the Lord himself will *descend from heaven* with a cry of command, with the voice of an archangel, and with the sound of the trumpet of God. (1 Thess. 4:16)

This will be the great deliverance that the people of Egypt were given a taste of when they were delivered physically out of Egypt. It will be the great deliverance we have been given a taste of as we experience spiritual freedom from the bondage of sin that once held us captive. On this day, evil powers that enslave will be gone for good. The very thought of it causes us to cry out for our Deliverer to come again, and quickly. He said, "Surely I am coming soon," and we say, "Come, Lord Jesus!" (Rev. 22:20).

Discussion Guide

Slavery and a Savior

Getting the Discussion Going

1. Most of us have had our mental pictures of this story of Israel's slavery in Egypt and the raising up of Moses as a deliverer shaped as much by Hollywood as the biblical account. As you've re-familiarized yourself this week with this story, what fresh images or scenes made an impression on you, stirring your imagination or emotions?

[handwritten note in margin: Moses as shepherd]

Getting to the Heart of It

2. As we study Exodus, we're recognizing that this story is really *the* story of bondage to sin and deliverance through Christ. Let's think more about sin as bondage. Is that how you see sin? In what ways is sin bondage, and how does Christ bring us out of this bondage? (You might read Titus 3:3–7 together to add to this discussion)

[handwritten note: He saved us because of his mercy]

3. If we were to translate Exodus 1:13–14 literally, it wouldn't sound very good to our ears because it uses the same Hebrew word, *avad*, seven times. But it would get a message across to us. It would sound something like this: "So they ruthlessly made the people of Israel serve with service and made their lives bitter with hard service, in mortar and brick, and in all kinds of serving in the field. In all their serving they ruthlessly made them serve as servants." Later we read that God said to Moses, "When you have brought the people out of Egypt, you shall serve God on this mountain" (3:12), and we realize that God does

not intend to end their service but to transfer it. What will the differences be between their service in Egypt and their service when they emerge from Egypt? *Do you choose to serve God or man? Serving egypt was forced. They can 'choose' to serve god.*

4. We know that God always works for the good of those who are called according to his purpose (Rom. 8:28), so we know that God intended to use even this cruel time of slavery for good in his people's lives. What are some ways you can think of that God used their suffering in Egypt for good? *He did multiply them. They had such dire straights they had to trust God to take care of them*

5. Put yourselves in the shoes of some of the people in this story. What drives you, and what is your life like? Let's quickly throw out one-word or one-sentence answers for each of these people and situations: *Sacrifice, Calm   Compassion   conflicted* Moses's parents, Pharaoh's daughter, Moses living in Pharaoh's house *jealous? hopeful?* knowing he's a Hebrew, Hebrew slaves who know Moses is Hebrew, Moses as a shepherd over the sheep of his father-in-law. *responsible, patient?, torn, scared*

6. What lasting impact do you think the experience at the burning bush had on Moses? *Personal relationship w/ God He had a sign to believe in — miracle, could tell about it*

7. Look back over your list on pages 41–42 of the Personal Bible Study where you saw many ways that Moses points to Christ in just these first four chapters of Exodus. What thoughts do seeing these connections leave you with? What do these connections tell you about this story, about the Bible, or about Moses? *Fascinating parallels Why so much time until Jesus comes?*

Getting Personal

8. We've seen in this story that real freedom is not just freedom *from* slavery to sin, but freedom *to* worship, freedom to take upon ourselves the yoke of Christ. Would several of you be willing to share briefly how you have experienced one or both of these things—freedom from bondage to a sin and/or freedom to worship God by taking on the yoke of Christ?

By taking the yoke of Christ we share our burden with him, side by side, w/ his direction.

Getting How It Fits into the Big Picture

9. Throughout this study, we will be seeking to grasp how the passage we're studying fits into the bigger story of God's plan for redemption. While the book of Genesis shows the plight of the human race, its need for salvation, and the call of Abraham to begin the process of divine rescue, what do these first four chapters of Exodus tell us about how God is going to accomplish the redemption of sinners and the nature of that redemption?

Plagues and Passover

Exodus 5–12

Exodus 5–12

1/30   *plagues*

To seek to grasp what the writer of Exodus (Moses) intends for us to grasp from this portion of Exodus, we will focus in on a number of repeated words and phrases in chapters 5 through 12.

"I am the Lord"

1. Read Exodus 6:1–13 and notice the repeated phrase, "I am the Lord." What reasons can you think of that God might emphasize and reemphasize that he is the Lord, or Jehovah?

The "I am" and the one and only
God longs for relationship

2. Along with emphasizing who he is, the Lord reveals what he will do. What seven or eight things does he indicate in verses 6–8 that he will do for his people?

Free you from slavery
redeem you w/ mighty power
bring you into Promised land

Firstborn Son

Back in Exodus 4:22–23, God told Moses:

> Then you shall say to Pharaoh, "Thus says the LORD, Israel is my firstborn
> son, and I say to you, 'Let my son go that he may serve me.' If you refuse to
> let him go, behold, I will kill your firstborn son."

By calling Israel "my firstborn son," God is saying that the Israelites
are the people who represent the future, the destiny of his family.
Everything rested on the firstborn son in this ancient culture. By "firstborn," Israel was given a status in relationship to God that was supreme
and familial. It is Israel's status as God's firstborn son that explains why
God had a quarrel with Pharaoh. While to Pharaoh the Israelites were
lowly slaves, to God they were beloved sons.

3. Throughout the Old Testament, as we trace the story of God's firstborn son, the Israelites, we realize that while God is a father who
desires a son to serve him, his son Israel always proved to be a disap-
pointment. A greater firstborn son was needed. What do Matthew 2:15
and 3:17 reveal about the greater firstborn?

2:15 "I called my son (Jesus) out of Egypt
3:17 'this is my beloved son (Jesus) and I am
fully pleased with him (after baptism)

4. If we are tempted to think God was harsh for bringing down judgment on the firstborn of Egypt, how does understanding that Jesus was
God's firstborn make a difference?

He was making them understand his
future sacrifice?
└ sin needs a sacrifice

Hardness of Heart

We tend to think of someone who is hard-hearted as cold and cruel.
But in the Scriptures, the heart speaks of the mind, will, and intentions. And the word *harden* means "to stiffen." So to harden your heart
can mean to stiffen your resolve. *Harden* can also mean to make heavy
or weighed down so that it cannot be moved. So when we read that
Pharaoh hardened his heart or that God hardened Pharaoh's heart, we
understand that Pharaoh stiffened his resolve to defy God and determined that he would not change his position in regard to the Hebrews.

stubborn

In Exodus 7–11 we read numerous times that Pharaoh hardened his own heart. But behind that choice is the sovereign will of God, who softens or hardens human hearts as he pleases. We struggle with the idea that God could harden Pharaoh's heart and yet hold him responsible for that hard-heartedness. We can't understand how it can be true that God can be in control of everything, hardening Pharaoh's heart, while Pharaoh's hard heart can still be his own fault. But just because we can't understand it does not make it any less true.

God needed to demonstrate miracles to gain faith

5. Read through Exodus 7–11, marking each occurrence of the phrase "hardened his heart" or "heart was hardened." Why do you think Pharaoh's hardness of heart is mentioned eighteen times throughout these chapters? What do you think Moses, and ultimately God, intends for us to take away from this repetition?

constant testing and teaching
need to recognize when heart is being
hardened?

"Let my people go that they may serve me."

Perhaps because we've been influenced by the Charlton Heston version of this biblical story, we often think Moses's declaration to Pharaoh was simply, "Let my people go!" But that condensed version clearly does not express what God tells Moses to say to Pharaoh at least seven times in these chapters (Ex. 7:16; 8:1, 20; 9:1, 13; 10:3, 7).

Let my people go, so that they can worship me —

6. What is it that God wants, and why is it important that we understand the two-part nature of this command?

He wants their freedom but also their
compliance. He wants Pharaoh to ack.
he is the Lord and should be worshiped.

"So that you may know that I am the Lord."

In Exodus 5:1–2 we read:

> Moses and Aaron went to Pharaoh and said, "Thus says the Lord, the God of Israel, 'Let my people go, that they may hold a feast to me in the wilderness.'" But Pharaoh said, "Who is the Lord, that I should obey his voice and let Israel go? I do not know the Lord, and moreover, I will not let Israel go."

7. Pharaoh does not know Yahweh, but eventually he will know him through his judgments. The phrase "so that you may know that I am the LORD" or something similar is repeated numerous times in Exodus 7–10. In the chart below, make a note of (1) whom the LORD intends to have know him, (2) what he intends for them to know about him, and (3) how they will know.

	Who will know	What they will know	How they will know
7:5	Egyptians	"that I am the LORD"	When Moses stretches out his hand against Egypt and brings out the people of Israel
7:17	Pharoah + egyptians + israelites	I Am the Lord	No water will be avail in Nile or even in jugs. All blood
8:10	Pharoah	No one is as powerful as the Lord our god	Frogs destroyed
8:22	Egyptians Pharoah israelites	Flies infest egypt but not israelites	I am Lord & I have power in heart of Land, can differentiate
9:14	pharoah officials	No other God like me in the earth	new plague (hAil) worst in history.
9:16	I	.	I could have wiped you all from face of the earth
9:29		The earth belongs to the Lord	make thunder + hail stop on command
10:2	children of israel	prove I am lord	stories of the miracles

When we read Exodus 7–12, we must realize that we are not only reading the history of Israel in Egypt but also discovering a pattern that we will see throughout the rest of Scripture: that God brings salvation through judgment.

We also see that through the sacrifice of the Passover lamb, God is preparing his people to recognize Jesus as the fulfillment of all that this sacrificed lamb pointed to. In fact, while there are many symbols and shadows throughout the Old Testament that point to the person and work of Christ, perhaps no other is as clear and profound as this picture in Exodus 12.

8. Read Exodus 12 and then work your way through the New Testament passages indicated, writing a corresponding statement that indicates how Christ is a fulfillment of each aspect of Passover.

The Passover lamb of Exodus	*Christ, our Passover lamb*
The Lord gave instructions for selecting a Passover lamb. (Exodus 12)	1 Cor. 5:7 Christ, our passover lamb has been sacrificed for us.
The Passover lamb was sacrificed for the sin of one household. (v. 3)	John 1:29 John the Baptist said — There is the lamb of God who takes away the sin of the world.
The Passover sacrifice had to be a lamb free from all defects. (v. 5)	1 Pet. 1:18–19; 2:22 God sacrificed — sinless, spotless lamb of God; he never sinned and never deceived anyone
The paschal lamb died on the fourteenth day in the month of Nisan. (v. 6)	John 13:1; 18:28 Passover; knew he was leaving this world; during passover feast.
The paschal lamb was killed at twilight. (v. 6)	Matt. 27:46 at noon, darkness fell across land until 3 pm.
The Israelites had to ingest the whole lamb as their nourishment. (vv. 4, 8–10)	John 6:35, 53–56 Jesus proclaimed true bread of life; no one will be hungry again. Flesh – bread Blood – drink

The Israelites would be spared from death when the destroyer passed over, not because they were guiltless but because they were under the blood. (vv. 12–13)	Rom. 3:24–25; 5:9 We are sinners God declares us not guilty as Jesus freed us by taking away our sins. saved from judgement
No bones in the paschal lamb were to be broken. (v. 46)	John 19:36 They did not break Jesus' legs to get him off the cross.
Israel was delivered out of slavery in Egypt. (v. 51)	Heb. 2:14–15 Jesus delivers those who live in fear of dying.

If You Really Want to Know Me

Getting to know someone usually comes in stages. Chatting about superficial things develops into discussions about more significant things. Occasional connections develop into regular interactions. Seeing someone somewhere evolves into inviting that person into your home. But perhaps the real knowing comes when he or she dives into knowing not only who you are today but how you became who you are today. And one of the best ways to help someone understand who we are is, perhaps, to open up a photo album and work our way through pictures of our childhood, our teenage years, and beyond. When we look through people's photo albums, we discover the activities they enjoy, the people who have been most involved in their lives, and the events they perceived as significant (at least, significant enough to forever capture on that precious roll of film back in the days of twenty-four exposures and six dollars for processing).

I remember the first time I made the trip across the country to Oregon, where David's family lives. One night they pulled out the old home-movie projector and threaded in the 8-mm film, and I got a glimpse into the growing-up years of David Guthrie, complete with commentary by parents and siblings. Like most families, the home-movie camera with its blinding lights got pulled out mostly at birthday parties and on Christmas morning. (I suppose if aliens came to earth and took our home-movies back with them, hoping to discover what life is like on earth—at least, what it was like in America in the

[handwritten margin note: Would your photos do that? How about social media]

71

era in which I grew up, before there were flip cameras and YouTube—they might think that life was pretty much one Christmas morning after another interspersed with a Little League home run, a trip to the Grand Canyon, and a graduation tassel toss here and there.) Certainly I learned a lot about David as we watched those home movies and looked through family photo albums.

If God had a photo album filled with pictures of his family history, what pictures would be in it? What pictures from his personal history would he point to and say, "If you really want to know me, you've got to see this"?

I want to suggest that there are two pictures in particular that God would lift out of the album of human history to put before you so that you could take a long, lingering look. One is a picture of national devastation. This is a wide-angle shot of Egypt in ruins, in the wake of the plagues. This is a picture of judgment. The other picture captures a row of homes in Goshen in which doorway after doorway is framed by brush strokes of blood. This is a picture of salvation—salvation through judgment.

What would make us think that these would be the pictures God would point to? Two reasons. First, when we read the chapters in Exodus where we find the story surrounding these pictures, again and again we hear God give the same reason for what is being pictured, which is: "so that you will know me." Here's just a couple of examples:

> The Egyptians shall know that I am the LORD, when I stretch out my hand against Egypt. (Ex. 7:5)

> By this you shall know that I am the LORD: behold, with the staff that is in my hand I will strike the water that is in the Nile, and it shall turn into blood. (Ex. 7:17)

And a little later:

> For this purpose I have raised you up, to show you my power, so that my name may be proclaimed in all the earth. (Ex. 9:16)

Certainly God could have taken Pharaoh out in one swift sweep of his power. But he didn't. Why? Because he intended to be known, not just in the homes and hearts of his people Israel, and not just inside the palace of Egypt or even within the borders of Egypt, but throughout all the earth. He intended the story of salvation that he was accomplishing in the lives of his people to be proclaimed throughout the whole earth and throughout all generations. There is a much grander plan and a much larger story taking shape here than simply the salvation of one ethnic group at one point in history. God intends for the whole world and every generation to know that he is the Lord who saves through judgment. These pictures will forever tell that story.

A second reason we might think that these are pictures God would point to if we want to know him is that he ordered Israel's calendar to be oriented to these events, and for these events to be commemorated year after year through a feast. In this way, as the years progressed, his people would pull out this album and look at these pictures and would orient not only their calendars but also their hearts and lives according to these pictures. In observing this feast they would not merely glance at these pictures and quickly look away but would enter with all five senses into the story the pictures told. These pictures would tell them about the past as well as prepare them for the future.

So let's look closely at these two important pictures, allowing them to be seared into our understanding, shaping our knowledge of who God is and what he is doing in the world and in our lives.

A Picture of Destruction and Death

The first picture is a scene of devastation and death. Of course, the picture of this place was not always this grim. Egypt was once a great world power, a country of culture and wealth and wonder. What brought such a dynasty down to dust? We see four things in this picture that explain what brought about this devastation and death.

First, we see a *stubborn Pharaoh,* approached by a stuttering prophet and his brother, and they have a startling proposal:

> Moses and Aaron went and said to Pharaoh, "Thus says the LORD, the God
> of Israel, 'Let my people go, that they may hold a feast to me in the wilder-

ness.'" But Pharaoh said, "Who is the LORD, that I should obey his voice and let Israel go? I do not know the LORD, and moreover, I will not let Israel go." (Ex. 5:1–2)

Are we resistant?

Pharaoh is not only ignorant about God's identity; he is resistant to God's authority. But this should have been no surprise to Moses and Aaron. God had told Moses:

> When you go back to Egypt, see that you do before Pharaoh all the miracles that I have put in your power. But I will harden his heart, so that he will not let the people go. Then you shall say to Pharaoh, "Thus says the LORD, Israel is my firstborn son, and I say to you, 'Let my son go that he may serve me.' If you refuse to let him go, behold, I will kill your firstborn son." (Ex. 4:21–23)

While Pharaoh sees the Israelites merely as his slave-labor force, to God these people are his firstborn son. And while Pharaoh is enjoying having the Israelites serve him, calling him "Master," God intends for the Israelites to worship him alone, calling him "Father." There is a clash of wills here, a battle between two powers. But there is never any question regarding who will win this battle.

Clearly Pharaoh does not know who he is dealing with. He thinks he can refuse Yahweh's interfering demand. Pharaoh's arrogant response to God's word begins, continues, and culminates with a defiant no. He will not say yes to God, which is the definition of a hard heart. Repeatedly we read that Pharaoh hardened his heart. But don't even begin to think that Pharaoh's stubbornness and stiffness will thwart God's purposes. In fact, Pharaoh's hard heart is actually a part of God's purpose to make himself known, and it will, in fact, serve to make God's glory more fully known.

Both Pharaoh's hardening of his heart and God's hardening of Pharaoh's heart are clear from the beginning when we read that God says to Moses: "I will harden Pharaoh's heart, and though I multiply my signs and wonders in the land of Egypt, Pharaoh will not listen to you" (Ex. 7:3–4), through to the end when we read that the Lord said to Moses, "'Pharaoh will not listen to you'. . . . And the LORD hardened *when have you had to harden your heart?*

Pharaoh's heart"(Ex. 11:9–10). While we wonder how this hardening can be both Pharaoh's free choice and God's sovereign plan, the narrator simply states both as true. We find it hard to understand how God can be sovereign over all things and yet rightly hold people responsible for their choices. But he is, and he does. We are accountable to God, but he is not accountable to us.

Next, we see a *series of plagues.* Pharaoh's stubborn refusal to obey God's instructions to let his people go so that they can worship him is met with a series of plagues intended to offer Pharaoh an opportunity for repentance, even as they make God more fully known. Each plague will magnify the greatness of the one true God while also exposing the weakness of the gods of Egypt. These are not random ills that come upon Egypt; rather, each is a targeted attack on one or more of Egypt's panoply of gods. The plagues assaulted them one by one. They began with this instruction to Moses from God:

> Go to Pharaoh in the morning, as he is going out to the water. Stand on the bank of the Nile to meet him, and take in your hand the staff that turned into a serpent. (Ex. 7:15)

Pharaoh will be going out to wash, but more than that, Pharaoh will be going out to worship. He will be headed out to bow down to Hapi, the God of the Nile, with every dip he takes in the water.

> And you shall say to him, "The LORD, the God of the Hebrews, sent me to you, saying, 'Let my people go, that they may serve me in the wilderness.' But so far, you have not obeyed. Thus says the LORD, 'By this you shall know that I am the LORD: behold, with the staff that is in my hand I will strike the water that is in the Nile, and it shall turn into blood. The fish in the Nile shall die, and the Nile will stink, and the Egyptians will grow weary of drinking water from the Nile.'"(Ex. 7:16–18)

The Nile, which had been full of the blood of murdered Hebrew baby boys, now became blood. This created an instant water and food shortage, a transportation shutdown, a financial disaster, and a spiritual crisis, as the object of their worship became a thing of horror. After the Nile turned to blood, frogs came from everywhere and were eventually piled in huge, stinking heaps. That plague was followed by gnats or lice, and then flies. All of these plagues were a mess and a nuisance, but it was about to get worse. Next came the plague upon the livestock, which was a huge assault on the economy of Egypt, as wealth was measured largely in terms of cattle. Then came the boils, which were an assault on the physician god that the Egyptians thought kept them healthy. Then came hail that was so heavy it could kill whoever dared to step outside in it. The hailstorm destroyed the flax and barley crops; and the next plague, the locusts, destroyed the wheat and spelt crops.

This was total devastation, an ecological, environmental, and economic disaster. And then the scene went dark. Really dark. Three days of heavy darkness, which was clearly an assault on the power of the sun god Ra, of whom Pharaoh was a representation. But the final plague would be the worst. It would find its way into Pharaoh's home and Pharaoh's heart and Pharaoh's future.

> So Moses said, "Thus says the LORD: 'About midnight I will go out in the midst of Egypt, and every firstborn in the land of Egypt shall die, from the firstborn of Pharaoh who sits on his throne, even to the firstborn of the slave girl who is behind the handmill, and all the firstborn of the cattle. There shall be a great cry throughout all the land of Egypt, such as there has never been, nor ever will be again. (Ex. 11:4–6)

Pharaoh had been exploiting the Lord's firstborn, Israel, and now justice would demand the firstborn of Egypt. Pharaoh had heard God's clear word again and again and refused it. Thinking of himself as a god, he refused to bow before the one true God. But this plague will bring him to his knees.

This awful death sentence on the firstborn came only after nine other, lesser plagues had been warned about and then brought about because of Pharaoh's refusal to obey God. God never judges without warning. But when unbelieving people refuse to listen to his warnings, he does come in judgment.

Has God warned you again and again about some ongoing, covered-up, really-not-a-big-deal-you-say sin? You have felt the rub of conviction many times but ignored it because, quite frankly, you don't want to change. You don't want to give it up. You don't even want to name it as sin. *Plenty of people have this struggle,* you say. *Besides, what right does God have to demand that I let it go?* Don't you know that when you ignore conviction again and again, a callous begins to build up on your heart so that, after time, you no longer feel the sting of conviction? That's when you know your heart has become hard.

justify

We've seen in this picture so far a stubborn Pharaoh and a series of plagues. The third thing we see is a *self-defined person.* God shows us who he is in this scene in a way that some of us might not approve of. Many people are comfortable with a kindly grandfather god who would never do anyone any harm. But they have no room for a God who would use his power to bring terror on those who refuse to obey him. Many people want to slam the photo album shut in regard to this picture of who God is. A God of vengeance who demands that blood be shed for sin seems primitive. They are embarrassed by the judgment of God and so turn judgment into an impersonal force. But it is clear from this text, and, in fact, from the entire Bible, that God is not embarrassed by this intensely personal picture of his acts of judgment. He is clear that he is the one coming to strike down the firstborn of Egypt. Listen to the personal pronouns:

> For *I will pass through* the land of Egypt that night, and *I will strike* all the firstborn in the land of Egypt, both man and beast; and on all the gods of Egypt *I will execute judgments:* I am the LORD. (Ex. 12:12)

If you want a god who would never hurt a fly, that will have to be a god you manufacture in your own imagination. That is not the God of the Bible. God will not allow you to define him on your preferred terms. The God of the Bible is dangerous. He's not capricious or impulsive about expressing his anger. In fact, it is obvious from this story that he is slow to anger. But there is always an end to God's patience. Even now we know that God "is patient toward you, not wishing that any should perish, but that all should reach repentance" (2 Pet. 3:9). But we can be sure that his patience with those who continue to reject him will come to an end, just as his patience with Pharaoh came to an end.

Finally in this first picture, we see a *scriptural pattern.* This picture shows us a preliminary, temporary judgment day that gives us a glimpse of the devastation and death of the great judgment day to come. It reveals a scriptural pattern for God's judgment on all those who refuse to obey him. But along with certain judgment we can also see in this scriptural pattern that God saves those who turn to him—not apart from, but actually *through* his acts of judgment. God saved the Israelites *through* the judgment he brought down upon Egypt. God's salvation has always been and will always be accomplished through acts of judgment.

Adam and Eve were saved through the judgment that came down in the garden by being expelled from the garden. Noah was saved through the judgment that fell on the earth in the form of rain, and Lot and his family were saved through the fire that fell on Sodom and Gomorrah. We can trace it throughout Scripture, leading all the way to the most profound act of God's judgment. Through the judgment that fell on Christ on the cross, God accomplished the greatest salvation of all time, which he makes available to all who will call upon him.

This scriptural pattern of salvation through judgment continues as we look into the future, where we see in Revelation a great day of salvation when there will be no more death. And how will we enter into that day? Through a great act of judgment that will, in fact, echo the plagues of Egypt visited on those who have refused God's word and persecuted God's people. When Jesus returns, there will be judgment. And there will be salvation through that judgment.

A Picture of Doorposts and Deliverance

So we've seen one picture, a picture of devastation and deliverance. And now the second picture, which we also must see if we want to know God. This is a picture of a doorpost, or really many doorposts, with blood painted on each one. Now, this seems strange. Why would a picture of a doorpost actually be a picture that God himself would point to if he wanted us to know him? Actually, there is no way we can know him at all if we do not take in what this doorpost pictures for us. It shows us that while God's judgment brings devastation and death, God offers a way of escape from that judgment. He provides protection in judgment for all who will put their faith in his provision of an innocent substitute. God instructed Moses and Aaron:

> Tell all the congregation of Israel that on the tenth day of this month every man shall take a lamb according to their fathers' houses, a lamb for a household. And if the household is too small for a lamb, then he and his nearest neighbor shall take according to the number of persons; according to what each can eat you shall make your count for the lamb. Your lamb shall be without blemish, a male a year old. You may take it from the sheep or from the goats, and you shall keep it until the fourteenth day of this month, when the whole assembly of the congregation of Israel shall kill their lambs at twilight. Then they shall take some of the blood and put it on the two doorposts and the lintel of the houses in which they eat it. (Ex. 12:3–7)

Wait a minute. This doesn't make sense. The greatest power in the universe is coming down to bring death on every home, and the only way to be protected is to kill a weak little lamb? Can this really be?

The only way this makes sense is to put it in context of the story of the lamb that spans the entirety of the Bible, beginning in Genesis when Abel, a keeper of sheep, brought an offering of the firstborn of his flock to God. We trace this story of the lamb to that day when Abraham was called to make an offering of his son who was spared when God provided a lamb to be sacrificed instead. In this case, God provided one lamb as a substitute for one person, Abraham's son Isaac. Here in Exodus we see that God made provision for one lamb to be sacrificed for one household. Later we'll read of God's instructions for the Day of Atonement, in which one lamb will be sacrificed for the sins of the whole nation of Israel.[1]

But all these lambs were just preparing God's people to recognize God's provision in Mary's little lamb. Finally the day came when John the Baptist "saw Jesus coming toward him, and said, 'Behold, the Lamb of God who takes away the sin of *the world*!'"(John 1:29). Jesus was God's provision of one lamb to die, not for one person or one family or one nation, but for one world. Throughout the entire Bible, we have it pictured for us again and again—that anyone who wants to be made right with God can only do so on the basis of the lamb that God has provided.

As we look closer at this second picture of doorposts and deliverance, we see that this judgment was, first, *an impartial sentence.* When God told Moses and Aaron that the destroyer was going to strike down the firstborn, this judgment would fall on both the Egyptians and the Israelites. No favoritism would be shown to the Hebrews. If they persisted in unbelief and refused to kill the lamb and spread the blood on the doorpost, they too would perish. Likewise, this way of escape was open to the Egyptians who would put their faith in the blood of the lamb, and certainly some did. We know that there were Egyptians who later left Egypt with the Israelites, having put their faith in the one true God, rejecting the gods of Egypt (Ex. 9:20). This salvation was by grace through faith expressed by brushing the blood of the lamb on the doorpost.

Second, we must see that what was required was *a perfect sacrifice.* The lamb slaughtered in the homes of the Israelites had to be "without blemish" (Ex. 12:5). Here it begins to become clearer to us what is happening. God is using the sacrifice of lambs in Egypt to prepare his people to recognize the perfect sacrifice he will one day provide in his own Son. When Jesus, who has never sinned, offers himself as a sacrifice, they will be more likely to recognize him as the Lamb God has provided, because this picture of a perfect sacrifice will have been impressed upon them year after year in the selection and slaying of the Passover lamb.

Third, we see a *precise substitution.* The Israelites were instructed:

> Every man shall take a lamb according to their fathers' houses, a lamb for a household. And if the household is too small for a lamb, then he and his nearest neighbor shall take according to the number of persons; according to what each can eat you shall make your count for the lamb. (Ex. 12:3–4)

There had to be a precise equivalency in each home to the number of people in the household. There was a substitution taking place, and a correspondence between the number and needs of the people and the lamb provided was required.

Imagine what it was like in Hebrew homes on this night as this truth of substitution began to sink in. God's instructions were that the Hebrews had to take a lamb into their home. Then, four days later, as the sun was beginning to set, Dad had to take the innocent little lamb, which everyone in the house had become so fond of, and slit its throat. Perhaps there were many little boys in Hebrew houses who had become attached to the lamb and asked, "Dad, do we really have to kill the lamb? He has done nothing to deserve this." To which the father replied, "Son, either the lamb dies, or you die."[2]

But in other homes, the scene played out quite differently. In other homes in Egypt, firstborn sons asked, "Have we killed the lamb and put its blood on the doorframe, Dad?"

And the dad perhaps said something like, "Oh, I don't believe in that stuff. It doesn't make any sense. Maybe we'll do that sometime, but not tonight."

"But, Dad, everything else Moses has warned would happen has happened just like he said. Please, Dad, let's kill the lamb and eat it and brush the blood on the doorpost right now."[3]

Because we have the benefit of hindsight, we think that certainly *we* would have taken Moses's words to heart and killed the lamb. But perhaps that is only because we have the whole Bible to put this story of the lamb into context. We have to admit, apart from the rest of the Bible's story that shows us the picture again and again of a lamb being sacrificed in our place, we would find it difficult to believe that blood brushed on a doorpost would have any saving power.

Similarly, many people today find it difficult to believe that blood shed on a cross two thousand years ago has any saving power for them. This only makes sense if we understand substitution. "[God] made him to be sin who knew no sin, so that in him we might become the righteousness of God" (2 Cor. 5:21). This is the substitution that saves us. Either the lamb dies or we die. The Lamb has died, God's very own firstborn Son, in our place, so that we need not die.

Fourth, we must see our *source of protection:*

> Then Moses called all the elders of Israel and said to them, "Go and select lambs for yourselves according to your clans, and kill the Passover lamb. Take a bunch of hyssop and dip it in the blood that is in the basin, and touch the lintel and the two doorposts with the blood that is in the basin. None of you shall go out of the door of his house until the morning. For

the LORD will pass through to strike the Egyptians, and when he sees the
blood on the lintel and on the two doorposts, the LORD will pass over the
door and will not allow the destroyer to enter your houses to strike you.
(Ex. 12:21–23)

What will be the difference between the homes where the firstborn
dies and the homes in which everyone survives the night? "When he
sees the blood . . . the LORD will pass over" (12:23). The salvation God
provides is by grace through faith. The Israelites' killing of a lamb and
sprinkling of the blood was an act of faith. The blood on the lintel and
two doorposts is proof that they are taking God at his word about the
judgment to come and the protection he will provide in the death of
the lamb. And it is the same for us. If we take God at his word, that judgment is coming, the proof is that the blood of the Lamb has become our
covering, our hiding place. Our lives are marked by that blood.

So many people have so many ideas about what it means to be a
Christian. Many people think a Christian is someone who believes
in God and tries to be good, or someone who lives by the Ten
Commandments or the Sermon on the Mount (as if anyone could!).
My friend, a Christian is a person who recognizes that he or she is a
sinner deserving nothing less than the terrifying judgment of God and
takes refuge in nothing other than the blood of the Lamb of God, Jesus
Christ. If this is you, you have no need to fear the day when we will all
stand before God. You can know that you will be protected on that day
from the judgment you deserve, not because God will go soft and over-
look your very real guilt, but because God will look at you and see that
the blood has been applied. The blood of the Lamb will be your source
of protection when judgment falls.

Finally we must see the *sacrament provided.* From the time of
Moses up to the time of Jesus and beyond, the Israelites celebrated
the Passover each spring. People from all over the country would go to
Jerusalem to sacrifice a lamb for the Passover feast. The day Jesus made
his triumphal entry into Jerusalem was the very day herds of Passover
lambs were being driven into the city to be sacrificed. Later that week
Jesus told his disciples, "You know that after two days the Passover is

coming, and the Son of Man will be delivered up to be crucified" (Matt. 26:2). Ever since John the Baptist identified Jesus as the "Lamb of God," all of Jesus's ministry had been driving toward this day, this celebration of Passover, when Christ, "our Passover lamb" (1 Cor. 5:7), would be sacrificed for us. Luke tells us:

> When the hour came, he reclined at table, and the apostles with him. And he said to them, "I have earnestly desired to eat this Passover with you before I suffer. (Luke 22:14–15)

They expected him to pick up the bread and say the familiar words of the Passover feast: "This is the bread of affliction that our ancestors ate in the land of Egypt." But instead:

> He took bread, and when he had given thanks, he broke it and gave it to them, saying, "This is my body, which is given for you. Do this in remembrance of me." And likewise the cup after they had eaten, saying, "This cup that is poured out for you is the new covenant in my blood. (Luke 22: 19–20)

In the Last Supper, Jesus endowed the Feast of the Passover with new meaning. Instead of celebrating the redemption of Israel from Egypt, it became clear that these elements now symbolize redemption from the slavery of sin provided by his death as the Lamb of God. His death was the central event toward which all of history had been moving and from which it has meaning.

There they are—two pictures that we must see if we truly want to know God. And at the cross of Christ, the picture of devastation and death and the picture of a doorpost and deliverance merged into one, a singular picture of grace and mercy. At the cross, the judgment of God came down in full force against God's own firstborn Son. The blood was spilled by our perfect substitute, providing protection for all who will come under it.

So gaze into the wonder of this picture knowing that if you want to really know God, this, indeed, is the picture you must see.

> "And this is eternal life, that they know you the only true God, and Jesus Christ whom you have sent." (John 17:3)

Looking Forward

Salvation through Judgment

Revelation 16 paints a scene of complete destruction, desolation, and death when Jesus comes to save through judgment, a picture that is reminiscent of and yet far surpasses that of Exodus.

> Then I heard a loud voice from the temple telling the seven angels, "Go and pour out on the earth the seven bowls of the wrath of God." (v. 1)

> So the first angel went and poured out his bowl on the earth, and harmful and painful sores came upon the people who bore the mark of the beast and worshiped its image. (v. 2)

> The second angel poured out his bowl into the sea, and it became like the blood of a corpse, and every living thing died that was in the sea. (v. 3)

> The third angel poured out his bowl into the rivers and the springs of water, and they became blood. (v. 4)

> The fourth angel poured out his bowl on the sun, and it was allowed to scorch people with fire. They were scorched by the fierce heat, and they cursed the name of God who had power over these plagues. They did not repent and give him glory. (vv. 8–9)

> The fifth angel poured out his bowl on the throne of the beast, and its kingdom was plunged into darkness. People gnawed their tongues in anguish and cursed the God of heaven for their pain and sores. They did not repent of their deeds. (vv. 10–11)

> The sixth angel poured out his bowl on the great river Euphrates, and its water was dried up, to prepare the way for the kings from the east. And I saw, coming out of the mouth of the dragon and out of the mouth of the beast and out of the mouth of the false

> prophet, three unclean spirits like frogs. For they are demonic spirits, performing signs, who go abroad to the kings of the whole world, to assemble them for battle on the great day of God the Almighty. (vv. 12–14)

> And great hailstones, about one hundred pounds each, fell from heaven on people; and they cursed God for the plague of the hail, because the plague was so severe. (v. 21)

Rivers of blood, painful sores, agonizing darkness, croaking frogs, crushing hail—evidently, what Egypt suffered was, in fact, only a localized preview of the judgment of God that will fall at the final judgment upon the entire earth. By the time the bowl judgments of Revelation 16 have run their course, God's wrath against sin and unbelief will be complete.

Revelation also shows us a picture of God's deliverance of his own through this judgment. Just as the people of Israel cried out to God under their harsh bondage in Egypt, so do the prayers of God's people under persecution rise before him (8:3–4). And just as God heard the Israelites in Egypt and brought them out, so does he hear the cries of believers under persecution and so will bring them out.

> These are the ones coming out of the great tribulation. They have washed their robes and made them white in the blood of the Lamb." Therefore they are before the throne of God, and serve him day and night in his temple; and he who sits on the throne will shelter them with his presence. (Rev. 7:14–15)

Here are the people of God, emerging from the great tribulation of being persecuted by those who have set themselves against God, saved through judgment, marked by the blood of the Lamb, set free to serve the one true God day and night. They have been protected from judgment by the blood of the Lamb and find their shelter in his presence.

Plagues and Passover

Getting the Discussion Going

1. Think through the first nine plagues that Egypt endured. Which one do you think would be most miserable or horrifying, and why?

Death of firstborn   or   Blood in water

Getting to the Heart of It

2. In the Personal Bible Study and then in the Teaching Chapter the emphasis is on God's intention to make himself known through the plagues and the Passover. What are some of the things about God that are made known?

3. Many people have a hard time with Old Testament stories in which they think God appears vengeful and unyielding. Do you think that is the case in his dealings with Egypt? Does this God seem different to you from the God who became flesh in Jesus Christ? Why or why not?

45 times vengeful ; God is vengeful so we don't have to be

4. While it is hard for us to understand as well as to accept, the Bible makes clear that Pharaoh hardened his heart and also that God hardened Pharaoh's heart. What are the implications in this for us in regard to how we respond when we hear God's Word?

5. Imagine that you were an Israelite who had grown up as a slave in Egypt and had little knowledge of God. What do you think your thoughts might be about Moses's instructions to slay the lamb and sprinkle the

blood? And what do you think your thoughts would have been the next morning after the destroyer came through Egypt?

6. Looking back at your chart of statements about the sacrifice of Jesus on the cross that correspond to the Passover lamb (pp. 69–70), which are particularly meaningful or significant to you?

7. Many people like the idea of a God who saves but are uncomfortable with a God who judges. Yet the reality is that God saves through judgment. What do you think the phrase "salvation through judgment" means, and where are some places you see this pattern in Scripture?

Getting Personal

8. The sign that the Israelites were putting their faith in the blood of the Lamb was physically visible on the doorposts of their houses. What sign is there in your life that the blood of Christ has been applied to you? Is it internal and invisible or external and obvious?

Getting How It Fits into the Big Picture

9. Throughout this study, we are seeking to grasp how the passage we're studying fits into the bigger story of God's plan for redemption. Apart from Christ, the Passover sacrifice and covering of blood simply wouldn't make any sense. And apart from the story of the lamb sacrificed for Passover, the death of the Lamb of God as our substitute wouldn't really make any sense. How do you see God's sovereign control of history in the details of these two events?

Salvation and Provision

Exodus 13–17

Exodus 13–17

1. Read Exodus 13:17–22. Imagine that you are one of these slaves who had barely heard of the Lord and now you are in the wilderness being led by a pillar of cloud and fire. What do you think you might understand about God from this? *just as He(God) directed them to go to the sea so they wouldn't △ their mind, this served as a constant reminder to them that God was w/ them.*

2. What has God provided as a light to give us guidance and direction? *The Bible, Jesus*

3. What did Moses take with him when he left Egypt (13:19), and why was that significant? (See Gen. 15:13–16 and Gen. 50:24–26.) *Joseph's bones, as Joseph 'knew' they would eventually leave Egypt. Fulfilled promise to Joseph*

4. Read Exodus 14:1–14. How do God's intentions in these events, Pharaoh's reactions to Israel's leaving Egypt, and Israel's reaction to Pharaoh's pursuit of them continue the pattern we saw throughout the plagues? *God continues to set a trap? for Pharaoh & knowing he will chase the israelites harden heart. And send a substantial army. God knows it will be another powerful sign for Israel + the world, and forevermore*

91

5. What, according to Exodus 14:13–15, is God's part and the Israelites' part in the victory over the Egyptians that they will experience at the Red Sea?

God's part:
Rescue them in a spectacular way

Israel's part:
Stand firm + have faith the Lord will rescue you. Bear witness

6. Read Exodus 14:15–29. Write down three or four facts from this description of the events of that crossing that are significant.

① *he allowed/had Moses lead them + use the same staff to part the sea.*
② *hardens hearts of egyptians so they follow*
③ *they will know I am Lord*
   cloud/pillar hid them. ④ *lord confused to Egyptians*

7. Last week our theme was salvation through judgment. How do you see that continuing theme in this passage?

Lord condemned egyptians + killed them
He provided safe passage to israelites

8. Read Exodus 15:1–18. A short time before this, Moses didn't know this God's name. But this song reflects a deepening knowledge of God and his saving acts. What significant aspects of God's person and power are celebrated in song in the following verses?

v. 2 *Strength + victory*

v. 6–7 *Your right hand is power/dashes the enemy to pieces*

v. 11 *who else is like you God? glorious holiness, performing wonders*

v. 13 *unfailing love*

v. 17 *Sanctuary your hands made*

v. 18 *the Lord will reign forever.*

9. Read Exodus 15:22–27. This scene is a true picture of grace. While the people ungratefully grumble against Moses, God responds by providing their needs and also revealing more about himself. What is it?

He cares for their immediate needs by cleansing the water.
Lord told them that he will save/protect them if they obey his commands + laws

10. Read or skim Exodus 16. What is God's part and the Israelites' part in the provision of manna in the wilderness?

God's part: *Provide meat in eve + bread in morning*

40 years

Israel's part: *hunt + gather + follow the rules set forth.*

11. Read John 6:1–13, 22–59. What further purpose can we see in Israel's history for the provision of manna, which comes to light in this passage?

Bread met their material hunger but "True bread of God is the one who comes down from heaven + gives life to the world" Jesus = bread of life

12. Compare Exodus 16:4 with Deuteronomy 8:3. What does this reveal about God's purpose for feeding his people with manna for forty years?

D: humbled you by letting you go hungry + feeding you manna. —to teach you people need more than bread in their lives.
E: he tested them w/ rules. they could not save it — they had to trust God each day

13. Read Exodus 17:1–7. We are beginning to see a repeated pattern here. What is it?

people continually dissatisfied w/ leaders to provide hungry/thirsty "testing the Lord" They get dramatic ... we will all die "

Jesus is bread of "eternal" life

14. What is God's part and the Israelites' part in the provision of water from the rock?

They moved at Gods command.

God's part:
Provide the water & the way to get it

Moses's part:
ask God for help/advocate

Israel's part:
Grumble to moses, argue, tested the Lord

15. Read 1 Corinthians 10:1–6. Paul is training us how to read the Old Testament and see Jesus in it. He equates the people's identification with and joining themselves to Moses, as evidenced by crossing the Red Sea, with being baptized into Christ (Rom. 6:3, Gal. 3:27). What insight does he give us into the scene recorded in Exodus 17?

In Ex 17, the people were testing whether the Lord would take care of them or not.

Think about
   Israel passed thru the water and were saved from the egyptians.
      Those that trusted & crossed were saved & in the promised land of milk & honey

Teaching Chapter

Safely to the Other Side

While I was growing up, our family enjoyed going on canoe trips. We'd get together with another family or two and drive to the Current River in Central Missouri to camp out and canoe. As we got older, my sister and I would take along our air mattresses and float down the river at points along the way. I'm not sure life in this world gets much better than floating down a gentle river on an air mattress on a sunny day with your feet dangling in the cool water.

I remember one trip, when I was seven or eight. We came to a point where we were stopping for lunch or for the day. Somehow I ended up by myself out in the water where the current was strong, and I couldn't seem to get a footing to walk across the flow of the current to where my dad was standing on the shore. I kept slipping and falling, and I remember getting very panicked that the current was going to carry me away. My dad was on the shore, telling me, "You can do it!" In addition to being scared, I remember being really frustrated that he wouldn't come out and get me. Looking back, I think he wanted me to discover that I could overcome this problem on my own under his watchful eye, and that I had it within me to get through the water and safely onto shore. And I did. I emerged from the water having saved myself, thank you very much.

I suppose it's good for little girls to learn that they can struggle through something hard and overcome it. A sense of "I can handle this myself" is not a bad thing for us to have in many areas of life. But it is

a problem when we bring our sense of self-sufficiency into our relationship with God. There are some things we cannot overcome, some
problems we cannot solve on our own, simply by trying harder. Rather
than increased self-confidence, we need increased God-reliance.

Oftentimes someone who is asked if he or she is a Christian will
respond by saying: "Well, I'm trying." Anyone who says they are "trying" to be Christian simply does not understand what it means to be
a Christian. The answer betrays belief that becoming a Christian is a
process rather than an event, something we make happen through
our own efforts rather than something God accomplishes apart from
our efforts. But do we have some part in salvation? Exodus 13–17 will
help us find an answer to the all-important question, What must I do
to be saved?

Our Light

In Exodus 13 we catch up with the people of Israel after they have left
Egypt and are headed home to the land of their ancestors. Everybody
knows that when you've been away a long time (and they'd been gone
four hundred years), you want to take the shortest, most direct route
to get home. So it would make sense that they would want to take the
well-trodden way from the delta through the coastal strip to Canaan.
But that's not the way they went.

> When Pharaoh let the people go, God did not lead them by way of the
> land of the Philistines, although that was near. For God said, "Lest the
> people change their minds when they see war and return to Egypt." But
> God led the people around by the way of the wilderness toward the Red
> Sea. (Ex. 13:17–18)

God knew that these people, fresh out of slavery, were not ready
militarily or spiritually to come against the armies of those living in
the Promised Land and the numerous other challenges they would
face there. They needed to be made stronger through testing and at
the same time more dependent on God by experiencing his supply for
all of their needs. So God charted their course through the wilderness,
leading them with a miraculous light.

> And the LORD went before them by day in a pillar of cloud to lead them
> along the way, and by night in a pillar of fire to give them light, that they
> might travel by day and by night. (Ex. 13:21)

The cloud of God's presence with them gave light and provided a covering in the hot desert (Ps. 105:39). For these ex-slaves who were used
to working long, hot days under the scorching sun in Egypt, it must
have provided welcome relief. The God who had brought them out of
bondage was evidently going to care for them tenderly. But this indi-
rect route was confusing. They were well on their way to freedom when
God ordered them to turn around, go back, and camp between the desert and the sea.

It was as if God had led them into a blind alley with walls on both
sides, and they quickly discovered that they couldn't go backwards
either. When they looked back over their shoulders, they saw a growing
dust cloud drummed up by the hooves of Egyptian horses pulling six
hundred "chosen chariots" (Ex. 14:7). Pharaoh was coming out against
a trapped mass of ex-slaves with his most prestigious and imposing
force. And as the world's most fearsome army thundered toward them,
the Israelites were understandably afraid. They could see clearly the
power and purposes of Pharaoh, but they had lost sight of the power
and purposes of God.

The Israelites were caught between an unconquerable army and
an impassable sea. If it were true that God helps those who help
themselves, then this is when we might expect Moses and some
other quick-thinking heroes among the group to come up with some
kind of plan for thwarting this attack, some trick play or surprising
strategy. But the truth is that God helps those who cannot help themselves, and he does so when there is nothing they can do, no chance
for escape.

Our Salvation

"It would have been better for us to serve the Egyptians than to die in
the wilderness," the Israelites cried out to Moses (v. 12). They saw only
two options: death or slavery. They did not see God. But then instruc-

tions came from the LORD to Moses and the people waited expectantly
to hear Moses pass along the strategy.

> And Moses said to the people, "Fear not, stand firm, and see the salvation
> of the LORD, which he will work for you today. For the Egyptians whom
> you see today, you shall never see again. The LORD will fight for you, and
> you have only to be silent." (Ex. 14:13–14)

Moses did not tell the Israelites to pull themselves together so that they
could mount a strong defense. There was nothing they could do and
nothing they needed to do. God said to Moses:

> Tell the people of Israel to go forward. Lift up your staff, and stretch out
> your hand over the sea and divide it, that the people of Israel may go
> through the sea on dry ground. (Ex. 14:15–16)

They were not handed a long list of things to do to accomplish their
own salvation. They were not about to be turned into soldiers. They
would simply be spectators. Someone else was going to do the fighting, and all they needed to do was stand firm in their confidence that
God would fight this battle for them, and watch him accomplish his
saving work.

> Then Moses stretched out his hand over the sea, and the LORD drove the
> sea back by a strong east wind all night and made the sea dry land, and
> the waters were divided. And the people of Israel went into the midst of
> the sea on dry ground, the waters being a wall to them on their right hand
> and on their left. (Ex. 14:21–22)

This was not one of those miracles that happened in an instant. They
were on the west side of the sea and God exerted his authority over the
wind, starting on the east side of the sea. All night the Israelites waited
as the east wind submitted to God's authority, dividing the waters,
creating a wall of water on each side and dry ground in between.
And while it was God doing the saving, their salvation did require a
response of faith. They had to put their faith in what God had said.
Their faith became evident when they took that first step into the Red
Sea behind Moses.

Now, certainly this vast group of likely two million Israelites had varying amounts of faith. Some probably expected the walls of water to let loose on them with every step, while others likely walked through with a sense of confidence and wonder that the God who had just brought down ten supernatural plagues on Egypt would keep the waters of the Red Sea at bay until they were safely across. Yet when they got to the other side, both kinds of people were equally saved.[1]

The Hebrew expression Moses used in verse 13 for "the salvation of the LORD" is "Yahweh-yeshua." So Moses said essentially: "You will see Yeshua."[2] And this makes sense to us, because we know that the salvation of God is bound up

They weren't saved because of their amount of faith or the quality of their faith but by the object of their faith—their Savior.

in a person, the person given the name Yeshua, Jesus himself.

When we hear the word of Yeshua, the salvation of the Lord, and respond in faith, we are united to the greater Moses, and like the Israelites, we pass from death to life. Jesus described salvation in exactly these terms saying:

> Truly, truly, I say to you, whoever hears my word and believes him who sent me has eternal life. He does not come into judgment, *but has passed from death to life.* (John 5:24)

In opening up the Red Sea to make a way through death for his people, God was showing how he would miraculously make a way through death for all those who come to him by faith through his Son, Jesus Christ.

～ While Moses stretched out his hands over the sea to make a way for his people, Jesus stretched out his arms on the cross to make a way for us.

～ While Moses plunged into the waters of the Red Sea and all those who followed him emerged on the other side unscathed, Christ plunged into the waters of death so that following him we might pass through death unscathed to resurrection life.

⮟ While the waters of the Red Sea destroyed Pharaoh and his armies when Moses stretched out his hand, Jesus brought destruction on the Devil, when he was nailed to the cross, "that through death he might destroy the one who has the power of death, that is, the devil" (Heb. 2:14).

The sea the people feared became the means of their deliverance from the Egyptians. Likewise, the physical death we fear becomes the means of our deliverance into the Promised Land of God's presence. We need not fear death. Our Deliverer has raised his rod, and we can pass through on dry ground, unscathed. When the day comes that you stand on that shore, or as you stand with those you love when they come to the end of this life, hear him say to you, "Fear not, stand still, and see the salvation of the LORD."

True Bread

The salvation of God put a song in Israel's heart. But it was quickly crowded out by discontent. Israel's singing and celebration soon turned into sourness and complaining. Of course, if you have ever set out on a cross-country car trip with a couple of toddlers, you can't help but recognize this scene. It does not take long at all for the back seat to descend into grumbling and complaining and needing a drink and something to eat.

I remember when our son Matt was about three or four, and we were heading out on a trip. On the way out of town we stopped at Sam's Club. We had seen there a combo TV-VCR made for the car, but we didn't buy it when we first saw it because it seemed too expensive. But the prospect of six hours in the car with a bored toddler somehow made the price seem insignificant. On that trip, and many that followed, David or I would push Play and one of us would say, "How much did that thing cost?" and the other would respond, "It doesn't matter!"

Imagine traveling with two million toddlers who are already grumbling and complaining when you've barely started the journey. "I need a drink! I need something to eat! When are we going to get there?" That was Moses's plight. It was three days into the wilderness when the people of Israel began to get really thirsty, and there was no water. Now we might expect that people who had seen the water of the Nile turned into blood and the waters of the Red Sea part would rest in knowing that providing water was not an insurmountable problem for their God. Surely the one who had brought them out of Egypt and through the Red Sea would also provide for them in the wilderness. Here was lesson number one in daily provision in the wilderness.

> Then they came to Elim, where there were twelve springs of water and seventy palm trees, and they encamped there by the water. (Ex. 15:27)

This was a place of abundance—one spring for each of the twelve tribes and obviously enough water to nourish seventy palm trees. Perhaps they should have gotten the message that their God intended to provide for them in every way. But as we will see, gratitude is not going to be their strong suit. Instead, the Israelites proved to be world-class whiners.

> And the whole congregation of the people of Israel grumbled against Moses and Aaron in the wilderness, and the people of Israel said to them, "Would that we had died by the hand of the LORD in the land of Egypt, when we sat by the meat pots and ate bread to the full, for you have brought us out into this wilderness to kill this whole assembly with hunger." (Ex. 16:2–3)

What distorted memories they have already of their days in Egypt! What short memories they have of God's abundant provision! God would be right at this point to rain down fire on them. Rather than move forward in their salvation, they wanted to go in reverse and return to slavery. They convinced themselves that there were only two options: dying in Egypt with full stomachs or dying in the desert with empty stomachs. God seemed to have no place in the picture. But instead of raining down fiery judgment, God rained down grace.

> In the evening quail came up and covered the camp, and in the morning dew lay around the camp. And when the dew had gone up, there was on the face of the wilderness a fine, flake-like thing, fine as frost on the ground. When the people of Israel saw it, they said to one another, "What

is it?" For they did not know what it was. And Moses said to them, "It is
the bread that the LORD has given you to eat." (Ex. 16:13–15)

The Hebrew word, *man hu'* means "what is it?" That's what they
called this miraculous food that was sent to them by God every morning for forty years. For forty years the people ate "what is it?" "What's
for supper?" someone would ask, and the answer was always "what is
it?" There was never anything like it before and hasn't been since. This
was nourishment supplied by a miracle of God, a daily miracle that
lasted for forty years. But it was also a daily test. They could never store
up any for the next day but simply had to trust that God would send the
manna they needed again tomorrow.

I don't know about you, but I strongly prefer going to bed at night
knowing that the refrigerator and pantry are stocked for tomorrow. I
want to know that there is enough money in the bank today for tomorrow's bills. I want to know I have built up and stored up enough energy
for tomorrow's challenges, enough good will to get my way, enough
ideas for tomorrow's chapter. This reveals that my natural setting is
not to trust God but to trust in what I can accumulate, what I can create and collect. But to experience the salvation of God is to experience
and rest in his daily provision for all of our needs. God has always been
in the business of giving his people just enough to keep us dependent
on him. This is why we are to pray, "Give us this day our daily bread"
(Matt. 6:11). He wants us to come back and ask him again tomorrow,
because he wants the relationship with us that is fostered through
daily dependence.

Israel's part was merely to receive the bread he provided for them,
eat it, and trust him to provide it again tomorrow. They didn't have
to plant or tend or harvest. There was no to-do list other than to simply gather up what was on the ground right outside their door on a
daily basis.

Now, this idea of having the groceries delivered to the door sounds
pretty good to me. I do not enjoy going to the grocery store and often
put it off until we have only moldy bread and canned tuna, and a trip
to the store can no longer be avoided. I head into a fully stocked store

and pitch boneless, skinless chicken breasts into the cart along with a loaf of any kind of bread and any kind of fresh produce anyone could want (and a brownie mix is always good to have on hand for when that chocolate craving must be satiated).

Clearly it was not that way in the desert. And it was still nothing like that in the days of Jesus, long after the Israelites had entered into the land. Putting food on the table day by day was a much more difficult task then than it is for us today. That's why when Jesus fed five thousand people with five barley loaves and two fish, they followed him to the other side of the Sea of Galilee, hoping to ingest more of his miraculous bread. Of course, Jesus knew exactly what they were after. Having felt the pleasure of a full stomach the day before, they were thinking about how good it would be to have someone to fill their stomach like that every day. They liked what they saw in his miracle-working power, and they wanted more of it.

But they didn't really want him.

And as we read about it in the Gospels, we can't help but feel a bit indicted ourselves, because we know we have been exactly like that. We've come to God again and again with our list of requests and expectations, asking him to be our supplier for the life we've charted out for ourselves. Yet, if we're honest, we realize we have often been more interested in what he can give to us than in who he intends to be to us.

Jesus had the people's attention by satiating their physical appetite, but he wanted to use this desire for food to teach them about what he really had come to do.

> Do not work for the food that perishes, but for the food that endures to eternal life, which the Son of Man will give to you. (John 6:27)

And their initial response was promising:

> Then they said to him, "What must we do, to be doing the works of God?" (John 6:28)

But they didn't particularly like his answer to their question:

> Jesus answered them, "This is the work of God, that you believe in him
> whom he has sent." (John 6:29)

They wanted to know what they needed to do. And Jesus said there
was no work for them to do, that they needed only to eat the bread
right in front of them by believing in him. According to John Piper,
"Believing is seeing Jesus for the Food that he is, and eating. That is,
taking him into your soul, your life, as the all-satisfying, life-giving
Treasure that he is."³

> Jesus said to them, "I am the bread of life; whoever comes to me shall not
> hunger, and whoever believes in me shall never thirst. (John 6:35)

This bread was not a "what is it?" but a "who is it?" Jesus could do
more than multiply the bread; he *was* the bread, the spiritual bread
from heaven that gives life to the world. Jesus was saying, "Come to
me, trust me, feed on me, draw your life from mine." The gospel is not
about what you must do for God. It's about what he has done for you
through the Savior he sent, Jesus Christ. All that is required of you is
to believe that what he has already accomplished is not simply for the
world out there, but for you. When you take and eat, his life pulses
through your life.

Interestingly, when the people heard this, they did exactly what
their ancestors did in the wilderness:

> So the Jews *grumbled* about him, because he said, "I am the bread that
> came down from heaven." (John 6:41)

But they were about to become outright offended when they heard
what Jesus said next:

> Truly, truly, I say to you, whoever believes has eternal life. I am the bread
> of life. Your fathers ate the manna in the wilderness, and they died. This
> is the bread that comes down from heaven, so that one may eat of it and
> not die. I am the living bread that came down from heaven. If anyone eats
> of this bread, he will live forever. And the bread that I will give for the life
> of the world is my flesh. (John 6:47–51)

Wait a minute. This made no sense. The "bread that I will give for the life of the world is my flesh"? Jesus was saying that eating the true bread means nourishing our souls with the benefits of his atoning death. We don't eat this bread simply by listening to his teaching on the hillside or observing his miracles among the masses. To eat the bread of life means that we must savor his sacrificial death as our life.

Jesus offers himself to you and invites you to feed on his death as your life. Maybe you are a bit like the people of his day, and this is not what you were looking for from Jesus. Perhaps you had a different miracle in mind, a miracle that would take care of what you see as your most pressing problem today. Perhaps the order you've placed with God is for the miracle of a body rid of cancer or a bank account filled with money or a house filled with an intact family, and as you see Jesus offering himself to you as the bread of life, if you're honest, you grumble on the inside. So often we want to *use* God to get things from him that we think we need, when *he* is what we need. And he offers himself freely.

> *To eat the bread of life means that we must savor his sacrificial death as our life.*

Here is Jesus offering himself to them, and to us, as true bread that will save and sustain. And what is our part in this? All we need to do is take and eat. But the truth is, many people would rather starve to death than feed upon Christ. Many people simply do not believe that the bread of life will really taste good to them, satisfy them, or sustain them over the long haul, and they refuse to eat it.

> This is the bread that came down from heaven, not like the bread the fathers ate, and died. Whoever feeds on this bread will live forever. (John 6:58)

All who insist on being self-sufficient and feeding themselves will one day find that they have starved themselves to death. But all those who take and eat the bread of life will pass through death and find unending life and satisfaction on the other side.

Living Water

So as they come up with new ways to fix the "what is it?" everyday, the Israelites were learning the lesson that the God who saved them will provide for them, right? Evidently not. It would seem they'd gotten just a few miles down the road when complaints started bubbling up in the back seat once again. This time it was not a lack of food but a lack of water. And rather than go to their divine Provider and ask him for what they needed, they began to complain to Moses. But it was more than simply complaining. We read that they "quarreled" with Moses (Ex. 17:2). The word used here refers to lodging an official complaint or bringing charges against someone, as you would in a court of law. They accused Moses of attempted murder, saying that he had brought them out into the desert to kill them with thirst. They made themselves accuser, judge, jury, and executioner and intended to carry out the death sentence on Moses by stoning.

> So Moses cried to the LORD, "What shall I do with this people? They are almost ready to stone me." And the LORD said to Moses, "Pass on before the people, taking with you some of the elders of Israel, and take in your hand the staff with which you struck the Nile, and go. (Ex. 17:4–5)

More is happening here than may be obvious to us at first. Moses is to "pass on before the people" not as an accused criminal but as the judge of Israel holding in his hand the rod of judgment. The people well understood the symbol of the rod in the hand of Moses. Would he lift up that rod so that God's judgment would come down on them? Certainly that is what they deserved. But then God said to Moses:

> Behold, I will stand before you there on the rock at Horeb, and you shall strike the rock, and water shall come out of it, and the people will drink. (Ex. 17:6)

What is happening here? The Almighty God did not stand before men like a servant; men stood before God. Yet here God says that he will stand before Moses, the judge. Why would God, in the midst of this courtroom scene, identify himself with the rock and instruct Moses to strike it? He will stand in the place of the accused, identifying himself with the rock, and he will bear the judgment the people deserved for their rebellion. Instead of receiving punishment, they will be flooded with the mercy of a gushing stream of water flowing from the rock.[4]

Do you see the picture Exodus is painting here? The apostle Paul did. Paul recognized this Rock. He saw that it was God, in the person of Jesus Christ, who stood on the Rock. It was Christ who was struck with the rod of God's justice in place of guilty people:

> For I do not want you to be unaware, brothers, that our fathers were all under the cloud, and all passed through the sea, and all were baptized into Moses in the cloud and in the sea, and all ate the same spiritual food, and all drank the same spiritual drink. For they drank from the spiritual Rock that followed them, and *the Rock was Christ*. (1 Cor. 10:1–4)

Long ago in the desert, God showed his people how he would execute just judgment against sinful rebellion while also saving guilty sinners—by pouring out the punishment we deserve on Christ. By his substitutionary death, he would become to us a stream of living water, which is exactly what he said when he stood up in the temple on the last day of the Feast of Tabernacles:

> If anyone thirsts, let him come to me and drink. Whoever believes in me, as the Scripture has said, "Out of his heart will flow rivers of living water." (John 7:37–38)

How would he become to us this living water? By becoming thirsty himself. On the cross, as he bared his back to be struck by the rod of God, Jesus said, "I thirst" (John 19:28). There on the cross, certainly he must have been physically thirsty as he hung in the hot sun, but his cry was really about the agonizing spiritual thirst he was experiencing in those hours. There, Jesus experienced the desperate thirst that you and I deserve to experience forever. He experienced that thirst in our place so that we need never experience it but can enjoy a never-ending, always-refreshing stream of living water.

What is your part in this salvation? Drink. Drink. Drink the living water that flows from Christ alone. Believe in him; enter into a trusting, ongoing relationship with him in which he daily fills you with his own overflowing life and joy.

Are you seeing that the physical salvation of the Israelites at the Red Sea provides a picture for us of the spiritual salvation available to all who will trust in Christ? While the Exodus story reveals the salvation of one group of people from their enemies, the Egyptians, in the gospel story we discover the salvation available to all who will come to Jesus. We simply cannot save ourselves or heal ourselves or provide for ourselves the kind of food and drink that will enable us to be satisfied and saved forever. So are you willing to follow the true light who will lead you home through the wilderness of this world? Will you entrust yourself to the strong Savior who will bring you through the waters of death and into life? Will you eat the true bread of the body of the crucified and risen Christ and drink the living water that flows from him?

Lots of people in this world have settled for looking to Christ as an example. But we need much more than an example. We need a Savior.

That day when I was a little girl canoeing on the Current River, I was able to figure out how to save myself, and I emerged from the rushing river on my own. But the day will come when I will stand on the shore of another kind of river. The day will come when each of us will find ourselves relentlessly pursued by that enemy we call death. We will not be able to outrun or overcome it. And when that day comes, we can remember that Christ provides the only way through the waters of death. He has gone through those waters before us and has soundly defeated the enemy of death so that we can be confident that we too will emerge from the waters of death unscathed. We will see the salvation of the Lord. It won't be up to us to save ourselves. Jesus, our Yeshua, will get us safely to the other side.

Looking Forward

The Song of Moses and of the Lamb

When we see the great work of salvation that God has accomplished, and it begins to sink in that we are alive not because of our own strength, wit, or accomplishment but wholly because the LORD has fought for us and won, we simply cannot stay quiet. We break out in song. That's exactly what the Israelites did.

> I will sing to the LORD, for he has triumphed gloriously;
>> the horse and his rider he has thrown into the sea.
> The LORD is my strength and my song,
>> and he has become my salvation;
> this is my God, and I will praise him,
>> my father's God, and I will exalt him. (Ex.15:1–2)

Their sighing has given way to singing; their groaning to praising. They are not celebrating their own prowess or power but the victory accomplished by God and granted to them. It is clear that the God they had heard about from their ancestors is their God. Perhaps for the first time for many of them, they called their forefather's God, "my God."

This celebratory song was really only a foretaste of a coming day when this song of Moses will be sung again. Revelation 15 says that God's people will once again sing the song of Moses, but at that time the song of Moses will be sung with "the song of the Lamb." This new song will tell of a greater redemption for all those who have placed their trust in the Greater Moses and of the final destruction of all God's enemies.

> Great and amazing are your deeds,
>> O Lord God the Almighty!
> Just and true are your ways,
>> O King of the nations!
> Who will not fear, O Lord,
>> and glorify your name?
> For you alone are holy.
>> All nations will come

> and worship you,
> for your righteous acts have been revealed. (Rev. 15:3–4)

Our song will not be about our own victory or greatness but about the greatness of God. It will not be about what we have done but about what God has done.

Just as the Israelites praised God for who he is and what he had done as they stood safely on the other side of the Red Sea, so will all of God's children who are gathered safe on the other side of this earthly existence sing this song. Gathered around the throne of heaven, all who have been rescued from slavery to sin, all who have put their faith in the blood of the Passover Lamb, will sing into eternity with joy.

Discussion Guide

Salvation and Provision

Getting the Discussion Going

1. Try to imagine what this journey of two million people, just released from a lifetime of slavery, must have been like. What do you think they might have been thinking about, enjoying, fearing, or anticipating as they left Egypt? *Hope, possibilities; fear of the unknown + how they would feed themselves.*

Getting to the Heart of It

2. Through the pillar of cloud, God led the Israelites away from the expected route into a place where they were hemmed in on three sides, with the Egyptians bearing down on them. Why do you think he did that? *So there was no choice but to go thru the water → "no turning back"*

3. The Israelites are told to "fear not, stand firm, and see the salvation of the LORD, which he will work for you today" (Ex. 14:13). Yet they had to respond in faith made evident by identifying themselves with Moses and stepping onto the dry ground of the Red Sea. What is the difference between their accomplishing their own salvation and responding in faith to God's salvation? *They could not save themselves. They had to trust Moses & God.*

4. What is the difference for us between responding to salvation offered in Christ and accomplishing our own salvation? (You might bring Acts 16:30–31 and Ephesians 2:8–9 into this discussion.)

Acts: "Sirs, what must I do to be saved?" Believe on the Lord Jesus Christ.

Eph: God saved you by his special favor when you believed... And you can't take credit for it, it is a gift from God.   Perfect precious Gift

111

5. It may seem simple, but certainly it is essential to grasp fully: what does it mean to believe in Jesus? *Believe he is the son of God, sacrificed to free us.*

6. In the Personal Bible Study, you were asked to identify God's part and Israel's part in the crossing of the Red Sea, the provision of manna, and provision of water. What was Israel's part in each and how does this help us understand our part in experiencing salvation and provision in Christ? *They had to risk crossing the sea and they had to trust they would be provided for.*

7. Imagine you are Jesus on the road to Emmaus, working your way through the Old Testament and explaining to Cleopus and his companion how it is really all about you. What do you think Jesus might have said about the pillar of cloud that provided light and guidance, about Moses crossing the Red Sea, about the manna, and about the rock?

Getting Personal

8. In this story we've seen how passing through the Red Sea and emerging from it into new life is analogous to our passing through the waters of death and emerging into new life in the presence of God. Does this picture make you think differently about your own death or that of someone you love? In what way?

Getting How It Fits into the Big Picture

9. Throughout this study we are seeking to grasp how the passage we're studying fits into the bigger story of God's plan for redemption. In numerous places throughout the rest of the Old Testament, God repeatedly identifies himself as "the LORD your God, who brought you out of the land of Egypt, out of the house of slavery," or something similar. When we step back and think about all the ways God could identify or introduce himself, why do you think this is what he often chose? *He is the deliverer, from our sin (slavery). It illustrates that he saved us first. He has been there since the beginning of time.*

Week 5

The Giving
of the Law

Exodus 19–24

3/17

Personal Bible Study
Exodus 19–24

1. Read Exodus 19:1–5. God is about to give Israel his law. What is the foundation he lays in these first verses for commanding obedience to his law?

'You have seen what I did to the egyptians. You know how I brought you to myself & carried you on eagles wings.

2. According to Exodus 19:5–6, what is God's purpose in bringing the Israelites out of Egypt and in giving them his law?

now if you obey me and keep my covenant You will be my own special treasure ... my holy nation.

3. Read Exodus 19:9–15. How is Israel supposed to prepare to meet with God?

purify, wash clothing, abstain from sex Set boundary lines. Ready on the third day.

4. According to Exodus 19:16–18, how did God reveal himself to his people at Sinai?

Thunder, lightning + a dense cloud long blast from ram's horn mtn shook w/ earthquake

115

5. Many people think of God's law as something opposed to grace. Yet the Ten Commandments are given on the foundation of God's grace. How is grace expressed in Exodus 20:2?

I am the Lord your God, who rescued you from slavery in Egypt.

6. What is the appropriate response to God's grace according to Exodus 20:2–17?

To obey his commands & put no other God before him.

7. How did Moses comfort the trembling Israelites in Exodus 20:18–20?

He explained God's need to show his power and they were not to fear as long as they obeyed.

8. First, God gave his people the moral law, found in the Ten Commandments, written in stone with his own finger, which indicated that this law is eternal. Then God gave civil and ceremonial law, which Moses wrote on parchment, signaling that it was for a particular time in history. The Book of the Covenant (20:22–23:33) is a series of laws that flow from the basic principles enunciated in the Ten Commandments. These civil and ceremonial laws were attached as an appendix for the era in which God took Israel under his wing as his special nation. Read Exodus 20:22–26 along with Exodus 23:10–19, which focus on Israel's worship. Which of the Ten Commandments are expounded in these verses?

Worshiping altars, creating altars to God (1) do not worship any other gods (3) remember Sabbath (2) do not make idols

9. Exodus 21:1–23:9 contains basic guidelines for living in community as a just society while also calling the people to live as those who are set apart to the Lord. The civil law provided a series of legal precedents that illustrated basic legal principles drawn from the Ten

Commandments. Skim this section and list several general categories or issues these ordinances address.

Fair tx of slaves, personal injury, protection of property, social responsibility, don't blaspheme, tithing, justice in courts, no oppression

10. Exodus 23:20–33 brings God's law giving to a conclusion with an assurance of blessing. In Exodus 23:20–21 God promises to send an angel to guide the Israelites. But this angel seems to be more than an average angel. He seems to be distinct from God yet also has divine attributes. Perhaps this is the pre-incarnate Son of God, going before God's people to protect them and bring them to the place God has given to them. What signs do you see in these verses that this angel may be the pre-incarnate Christ?

He is my representative + bears my name 'Obey him + follow all his instructions'

11. List several of the additional blessings God promises in Exodus 23:22–33.

Food, water, health, no miscarriages or infertility. Long, full lives.

12. In Exodus 24:1 Moses and Aaron, Aaron's two sons, and seventy elders of Israel (as representatives of the whole nation) were invited to ascend the mountain and meet with God. Read Exodus 24:2–8 and describe what Moses had to do to make it possible for him and the other representatives to enter into the presence of God.

Built altar w/ 12 pillars, sacrifice + sprinkled blood on altar + the men.

13. Near the end of the book of Hebrews, the writer draws upon the passage we are studying, Exodus 19–24, and contrasts what it was like for the people to approach God at Mount Sinai with what it is like for believers to approach God through Jesus. He frames this as the difference between coming to Mount Sinai and coming to Mount Zion. Read

Hebrews 12:18–29. Work your way through the following verses, writing a corresponding statement that reflects the similarities and differences between what the Israelites experienced at Sinai and what we experience as believers who approach God through Jesus Christ.

Mount Sinai	*Mount Zion*
God's people were warned to stay away from and to not touch the mountain of God, or they would die. (Ex. 19:12, 13, 23) *Stay away*	Heb. 4:16; 10:22 *Come boldly to the throne… receive mercy, find grace "come"*
Israel, God's firstborn, assembled in the desert to experience God's presence. (Ex. 4:22; 19:17) *darkness gloom. They were afraid, terrified*	Heb. 12:23 *Mt Zion, city of Living God, thousands of Angels in joyful assembly.*
The LORD descended in fire and spoke, revealing the glory of God. (Ex. 9:18)	John 1:14; Heb. 1:2 *H: God has spoken through his son reflecting his glory. Word became human, glory of Son*
When God came down to give his law, the whole mountain trembled. (Ex. 19:18)	Matt. 27:51 *Jesus died, Temple torn, earth shook rocks split apart*
Moses went up into the presence of God to be the mediator of the old covenant. (Ex. 19:20)	Heb. 12:24 – *Jesus, the one who mediates the new covenant bet God + the people*
The blood of the old covenant was the blood of a sacrificed animal, which spoke of judgment on the disobedient. (Ex. 24:5–8)	Matt. 26: 27–28; Heb. 12:24 *Jesus last supper—this is my blood, seals the covenant. H: and is sprinkled, blood which graciously forgives*
Moses, Aaron, Aaron's sons, and seventy elders beheld God and ate and drank. (Ex. 24:9–11)	Rev. 3:20 *I stand at the door + knock. I will come in a share a meal as friends I will invite everyone*
In the old covenant, the law was written on tablets of stone by the finger of God. (Ex. 24:12)	Heb. 10:14–16 – *thru Jesus. This is new covenant. I will put my laws on their hearts so they will*

understand them. And on their minds so they will obey them.

Clouds on the Mountain

Most of us know what it is like to be shocked or surprised so that we scream out in fear. But do you know what it is like to be truly gripped by fear? Have you ever been convinced that you were about to die?

I can remember only one time when I truly thought I was going to die. Our family had flown in my dad's little four-seat airplane to Phoenix, Arizona, for a family reunion. We took off from the airport to fly home, and as we headed over the mountains, clouds seemed to appear from nowhere and everywhere, closing in around us. I think the reason I was so afraid was that it appeared to me that my dad, who is a very experienced and confident pilot, was unnerved. He tried getting around the clouds, above the clouds, and nothing was working. I remember sitting in the backseat and having what I thought might be my last conversation with God in this life. I told him I was ready to meet him, and, honestly, I thought I was going to.

My dad was able to turn around safely, and we flew back to Phoenix. I had never been so relieved to feel the wheels of that little plane touch down on a runway. I remember getting off the plane, going into the bathroom in the terminal, and bursting into tears of relief.

As we come to Exodus 19–24 today, we enter a scene of absolute terror in which the people thought that they might die. And indeed they had every right to be afraid. God had come down, and his presence on the mountain was terrifying. I'm not sure we get very nervous today at the idea of being in the presence of God. Perhaps our vision of God is too tame to ever instill fear. Some of us see God as more like a cuddly, pushover grandpa than like a demanding judge, or more like a congenial Santa than like a consuming fire. We have come to think of God as someone we can casually consider and skeptically poke at, a deity we can design to our liking. But when we see him as he is, we cannot help but recognize that God is dangerous. Don't let anyone convince you otherwise. Like the guy said in the oft-quoted movie line: "Be afraid. Be very afraid."

Sinai's Terrifying Presence

Three months after emerging from Egypt and crossing the Red Sea, the Israelites reached the mountain of God, the place about which God had told Moses, "When you have brought the people out of Egypt, you shall serve God on this mountain" (Ex. 3:12). Moses went up the mountain to meet with God and then came back down to prepare the people of Israel to hear God speak to them. God was about to come down on Mount Sinai, but they were warned not to approach or even touch the edge of the mountain or they would die. It was as if yellow police tape roped off the base of the mountain and large "Keep Out!" signs were posted all around it. Everything about this scene shouted, "Danger!"

Three days later, a thick cloud came down and shrouded the mountain with crashing thunder and explosive lightening. Moses had led the people to the very place where God had spoken to him from the flaming bush. But this time, it wasn't just a bush that was on fire; the whole mountain was on fire. The whole mountain shook so that rocks split and tumbled down. The sound of a trumpet grew louder and louder. But most dreadful was the sound of the voice of the living God so penetrating and powerful that "all the people in the camp trembled" (Ex. 19:16).

We need Steven Spielberg's special-effects department, or at least an energized imagination, to help us to picture this scene in a way that comes anywhere near what the people of Israel must have seen and to sense the fear they must have felt. Moses writes:

> Now when all the people saw the thunder and the flashes of lightning and the sound of the trumpet and the mountain smoking, the people

were afraid and trembled, and they stood far off and said to Moses, "You speak to us, and we will listen; but do not let God speak to us, lest we die." (Ex. 20:18–19)

To hear God's voice directly was terrifying, so they wanted Moses to listen for them so they wouldn't have to. Why would God have come down in such a terrifying way? Was he trying to scare them? No. God was merely being himself. This is who God is. This is the reality of his presence. And they needed to know who they were dealing with as he was about to spell out the terms of his relationship with them, making a costly claim on their lives.

Sinai's Sin-Revealing Law

When God began speaking at Mount Sinai, he began by describing what he is like, evidenced by what he had done.

> The LORD called to him out of the mountain, saying, "Thus you shall say to the house of Jacob, and tell the people of Israel: You yourselves have seen what I did to the Egyptians, and how I bore you on eagles' wings and brought you to myself." (Ex. 19:3–4)

This was not just anybody about to lay down the law. This was their Redeemer, who had crushed their enemies even as he drew them close to himself. So first he told them who he was and what he had done, and then he told them who they were to be and what they were to do:

> Now therefore, if you will indeed obey my voice and keep my covenant, you shall be my treasured possession among all peoples, for all the earth is mine; and you shall be to me a kingdom of priests and a holy nation. (Ex. 19:5–6)

Wow!

Clearly God did not say, "If you will obey me, you can enjoy relationship with me." He said, "Because I have brought you into a relationship with me, here is how you are to respond to my grace. My grace shown to you has made a claim upon you." So we see that the Ten Commandments he's about to give them are not an abstract code of duty hung in a relational void but the heartbeat of his covenant relationship with his people, his treasured possession. "The law was given to those who had been saved by grace in order to show them how to live in that grace."[1]

While the all-important gospel words found in the opening statement of the Ten Commandments are left out of most artistic depictions of two stone tablets, it is in them that we see the grace of the law of Moses:

> I am the LORD your God, who brought you out of the land of Egypt, out of the house of slavery. (Ex. 20:2)

Using his special covenant name, Yahweh, he told the people not simply that he is the one true God over all the universe but rather, "I am the LORD *your* God," indicating a personal, saving relationship. The basis for his laying down his law for their lives was that he was their God and redeemer. And, my believing friend, this is the basis on which God calls you to obedience. If he is your God and redeemer, he has a legal claim over your life. He doesn't come telling you to obey *so that* you can belong to him. Rather, he comes to you in grace and mercy to bring you out of your bondage to sin by his mighty power. It is on the basis of that saving relationship that you are subject to his covenant law.

> *Clearly God did not say, "If you will obey me, you can enjoy relationship with me." He said, "Because I have brought you into a relationship with me, here is how you are to respond to my grace."*

Have you come yet to the place where you have seen that God's law is his grace toward you? Maybe that doesn't sound right to you. Perhaps it seems that God's unbending law handed down at Sinai has nothing to do with grace and everything to do with meaningless religious ritual or impossible-to-live-by rules. You need to see that it is God's grace to us to reveal his divine nature, which we see in his law. It is his grace to us that he is willing to show us how to live in this world in rich relationship with him and each other. It is his grace that holds up a mirror before us so that we can see the extent of our sinfulness. Until we look into that mirror and see how far we've fallen short of God's righteous standard, we will never see our need for a Savior.

God's exercise of grace is not that he relaxes his demand for full obedience to his law. His grace is shown in opening our eyes to see our desperate need for one who obeyed God's commands fully in our stead. Martin Luther put it this way:

> After the Law has humbled, terrified, and completely crushed you, so that you are on the brink of despair, then see to it that you know how to use the Law correctly; for its function and use is not only to disclose the sin and wrath of God but also to drive us to Christ.[2]

The law was intended to make the people of God long for the coming of Christ. As the people of God placed their hopes not in their own goodness but in God's promise, they were saved by grace through faith in the Savior who *would come*, just as we are saved by grace through faith in the Savior who *has come*. (They looked forward in faith and were given life; we look backward in faith and are given life.)

So the law's demands reveal our need for Christ. In addition, the very content of the Ten Commandments points us to Christ, the one who did not "come to abolish the Law or the Prophets . . . but to fulfill them" (Matt. 5:17).

∼ Why did God forbid the making of images for worship? In time he would send Jesus, who was the "image of the invisible God" (Col. 1:15). Jesus is the only image of God worthy of worship.

∼ Why was God so zealous for his holy name to be honored? God intended to exalt the name of Jesus above every name. His name will be the only name under heaven given among men by which we must be saved.

∼ Why are we to keep the Sabbath? The Sabbath points us to Christ in whom we find ultimate and eternal rest.

∼ Why should we keep our marriage vows? This will picture the faithfulness of our bridegroom, Jesus, who will make us his pure bride.

In his Gospel John writes that "the law was given through Moses; grace and truth came through Jesus Christ" (John 1:17). We might assume that John is contrasting two mutually exclusive realities: the law of God revealed at Sinai and the grace of God revealed in Jesus Christ. However, John does not say, "The law was given through Moses, *but* grace and truth came through Jesus Christ," as if he is comparing two opposite realities (though it is rendered this way in some translations). Instead, he is helping us to grasp a greater revelation, a glorious development in redemptive history. Whereas grace was *given* when "the law *was given* through Moses," John is telling us that now grace has *come* in the Word-made-flesh. It is not that grace has now replaced the law but that a grace greater than that which was given in the law of Moses has been given in Jesus Christ .

There was grace in the law, and Jesus came to fulfill the law, so we know that the law is good. What, then, do we do with the fact that, in several places in the New Testament, we read things that seem, on the surface, to suggest that God's law is not good or no longer applies?

First, we have to understand that the Jews of Jesus's day had misunderstood the originally gracious Sinai covenant and perverted it into a covenant of works, resulting in bondage. Sometimes when we read disparaging comments on the law in the New Testament, it is not the law that is the problem, but the misuse of the law by false teachers—the law being used for a purpose for which it was never intended.

Another "reason the New Testament talks about the law in different ways is because there were several different kinds of law."[3] Along with the moral law summarized in the Ten Commandments found in Exodus 20, God also gave Moses the Book of the Covenant, the civil and ceremonial law found in Exodus 20:22–23:33. Israel was not just a family, but a nation that needed laws to live by.

God's people had begun with one man—Abraham—whom God chose from all of the people of the earth to be the father of many descendants. Abraham's grandson Jacob went into Egypt, and his family multiplied into a huge slave-labor force. But now they were much more than a family. Now they were a nation preparing to enter into the land God would give them. The Book of the Covenant provided a series of legal precedents that illustrated basic legal principles for living in community as the people of God. It provided guidance on how the state needed to operate, how it would wage war with its enemies, how it should look after the land, how to take care of the poor, and so on.

The Book of the Covenant also contained the ceremonial law, which provided regulations for Sabbaths, feasts, festivals, and sacrifices. Since this ceremonial law was given in the same breath as the Ten Commandments, it is clear that God knew the people would not be able to keep his commandments perfectly and would need a provision for their sin. The sacrifices were effective not in atoning for sin but in pointing forward to the once-for-all atoning work of Christ.

Only the Ten Commandments were written on tablets of stone by the finger of God. They were written in stone because they would remain in effect for as long as time endures. But the ordinances of the Book of the Covenant were written on parchment by the pen of Moses, implying that they do not have the same eternal force. When Jesus fulfilled the ceremonial law, it meant that the people of God were no longer required to offer sacrifices in the temple. The sacrifice of Christ fulfilled all that was required. The civil laws were given for the era in which God took Israel under his wing as his special nation, which was a unique, unrepeatable, nontransferrable relationship. The civil law expired because the people of God are no longer a national entity but instead are made up of people from every nation of the earth who place their faith in Christ alone. Our king is Jesus, and his kingdom is not of this world (John 18:36).

So the ceremonial laws pointed toward the cross of Christ, which would bring them to fulfillment and therefore make them obsolete. And the civil laws pointed toward the kingdom of Christ, which has now been established, so they also are obsolete. After Christ came, the civil and ceremonial law were set aside, which is why the New Testament sometimes seems so dismissive of the law.

The New Testament makes it clear that we are no longer "under law" (Rom. 6:14; Gal. 5:18), but it does not declare an end to God's moral law as the standard for our lives. "Jesus commands us to keep it, not as a way of getting right with God, but as a way of pleasing the God who has made us right with him."[4]

In fact, according to Jesus, there is no love for him apart from keeping his commandments (John 14:15). We are kidding ourselves if we think of ourselves as having an intimate relationship with Christ, if we refuse to see our religious hypocrisy, our refusal to rest, our persistent coveting, our belittling of our parents, and our twisting the truth as an ongoing offense to him. Can you see that the way God intends for us to enjoy communion with him is by keeping his commands? This is why the law is an expression of his grace. As you refuse to allow anything else to be a god to you, as you honor his name and honor his day and honor your parents, as you value life and live with your spouse in faithfulness and nurture contentment and integrity, this is not legalism. This is the grace of God at work in your life making you holy and happy in God. "Obedience to the law—from a willing spirit, as made possible by the Holy Spirit—is the proper response to free grace."[5]

Sinai's Promised Obedience

If the Israelites were frightened by the clouds, fire, thunder, and voice of God when God first came down on the mountain, once they heard his law they really began to tremble in fear (Ex. 20:18). God was demanding total allegiance in every aspect of their lives—what they loved and valued, how they used their time, how they related to their parents and their society, how they conducted their sex and thought lives. Evidently their fear generated a quick, and perhaps rash, response.

> Moses came and told the people all the words of the LORD and all the rules. And all the people answered with one voice and said, "All the words that the LORD has spoken we will do." (Ex. 24:3)

We want to tell them to think this through before they commit. But, of course, we're not standing in the presence of a flaming, shaking mountain. God's requirement was perfect obedience, and they bound themselves by their promise to keep his whole law. But they couldn't do it. In fact, less than forty days after the Israelites made this commitment to obey God's commandment to have no other gods and make no idols, they stood pitching their gold jewelry into the smelting pot to become part of the golden calf.

But we can't be too quick to point fingers, can we? Because we are *what do I bow to* people who bow before other gods, such as our investment portfolios and other people's opinions. We take Christ's name, calling ourselves Christians, and then act completely unChristlike when we don't get the service we think we ought to get in a restaurant or store. We inundate ourselves with entertainment that normalizes sex outside the covenant of marriage. We "borrow" things from people that we never intend to return. We shade the truth in our version of events to make ourselves look good at someone else's expense. We covet the better cars in the carpool line, the better figures and physiques in magazines, and the more attractive or attentive spouses of others. We are law-breakers.

Fortunately, Jesus can do for us what the law could not do. He can save us from ourselves. Jesus loves law breakers. He loves us so much that he doesn't leave us that way. He fills us with his Spirit, who writes God's law on our hearts, giving us the want-to to obey. When we come to Christ, he gives the law, which once drove us to him, back to us, so that now we can pursue obedience to the Ten Commandments, not because we have to, but because we get to!

> *Jesus loves law breakers. He loves us so much that he doesn't leave us that way.*

The grace of God at work in us gives us the power to obey "the perfect law, the law of liberty" (James 1:25). We can worship God wholeheartedly and take his name upon ourselves with integrity because Christ liberates us from our slavery to other gods. Our security in Christ frees us to enjoy his Sabbath rest. He fills our hearts with the same love he has for his Father so that we can honor our parents. He fills us with his very own faithfulness so that we can live in sexual purity. He convinces us of all that is ours in him that will last forever so that we can stop coveting the things other people have that will not last beyond this life.

Sinai's Old-Covenant Blood

We've read in chapter 19 that the Israelites agreed to accept the terms of the covenant (v. 8); and in chapters 20–23, the terms of the covenant are written out. Now, in Exodus 24 we're invited into the ratification ceremony for the covenant, a service of worship at the mountain of God.

> Moses came and told the people all the words of the LORD and all the rules. And all the people answered with one voice and said, "All the words that the LORD has spoken we will do." And Moses wrote down all the words of the LORD. He rose early in the morning and built an altar at the foot of the mountain, and twelve pillars, according to the twelve tribes of Israel. And he sent young men of the people of Israel, who offered burnt offerings and sacrificed peace offerings of oxen to the LORD. And Moses took half of the blood and put it in basins, and half of the blood he threw against the altar. Then he took the Book of the Covenant and read it in the hearing of the people. And they said, "All that the LORD has spoken we will do, and we will be obedient." And Moses took the blood and threw it on the people and said, "Behold the blood of the covenant that the LORD has made with you in accordance with all these words."
> (Ex. 24:3–8)

Moses repeated the commands of the Lord, and the people repeated their promise to obey. And if they could have obeyed perfectly, the service would have ended there. But, of course, God knew they were unable to obey fully, so Moses offered sacrifices at the foot of Mount Sinai and sprinkled the blood on the people. The blood put the covenant into effect. It showed his people how serious he was in demanding obedience to his law, a vivid reminder that their obedience was a matter of life or death.

For many people, God is a kindly fellow who winks at indiscretion and goes soft on following through with promised punishments. But that is clearly not the God of the Bible. God is pure and holy and demands perfection. If someone has told you that God accepts you just the way you are, don't believe it. It isn't true.

The day will come when each of us will stand before God, this God who is a consuming fire. And if you're planning to face that day on your own, as you are, presenting your own record of goodness, quite certain that God will grade on a curve, you should be afraid—very afraid.

[handwritten: Is this a place?]

But You Have Come to Mount Zion . . .

But there is a way to come before this dangerous God without fear. You don't have to face God at Mount Sinai. You can go to a different mountain—Mount Zion. The prophets often depicted the restoration of Zion, or the city of Jerusalem, as the manifestation of the kingdom of God. But earthly Jerusalem is really a symbol for the true and heavenly city of God. "Zion is where Jesus reigns now at the right hand of God and where we come by faith in the gospel."[6]

> For you have not come to what may be touched, a blazing fire and darkness and gloom and a tempest and the sound of a trumpet and a voice whose words made the hearers beg that no further messages be spoken to them. . . . But you have come to Mount Zion and to the city of the living God, the heavenly Jerusalem, and to innumerable angels in festal gathering, and to the assembly of the firstborn who are enrolled in heaven, and to God, the judge of all, and to the spirits of the righteous made perfect, and to Jesus, the mediator of a new covenant, and to the sprinkled blood that speaks a better word than the blood of Abel. (Heb. 12:18–19, 22–24)

Mount Sinai was dark and stormy, but Mount Zion is a city of bright and shining joy. Mount Sinai was a dangerous place that inspired fear; Mount Zion is a peaceful place of perfect safety. At Mount Sinai the angels blazed with fire and blasted with noise, but at Mount Zion the angels host a great celebration. While God repeatedly warned the people to stay away from Mount Sinai, he repeatedly invites us to draw near to him at Mount Zion.

How can this be? Is it because at Mount Sinai we have the harsh, scary God of the Old Testament, and in Hebrews we discover the soft and sentimental God of the New Testament? No, not at all. The difference is not in God himself; he is present and the same on both mountains—ablaze in holiness and abundant in mercy. The difference is in the mediator. To come to Mount Zion is to approach God as one who has been made right with him through the finished work of Christ. Because of Christ, we can approach God with nothing to fear and everything to gain.

In his terrifying presence at Mount Sinai, God repeatedly warned the people not to come near. If they had touched the mountain in their sinful state, they would have died instantly. But if you have been joined by faith to Christ, you don't have to be afraid of drawing near to God at Mount Zion. In fact, you are invited, even urged, to draw near rather than stay away. Rather than a terrifying presence, you will find an approachable person.

> Let us then with confidence draw near to the throne of grace, that we may receive mercy and find grace to help in time of need. (Heb. 4:16)

Why can you dare to approach? Not because you have been sprinkled with the blood of an animal, but because you have been washed in the blood of the Lamb. His blood has cleansed you and marked you so that *you don't have to be afraid of drawing near*.

To the Israelites at Mount Sinai, the law was a mirror that revealed their sin, an indictment that convicted them, an obligation set before them that they simply could not meet. But we come to Mount Zion and find not only a sin-revealing law, but a law-fulfilling Savior. This is exactly what Jesus said he came to do when he stood up on a mountain and reaffirmed the law given at Mount Sinai. In the Sermon on the Mount we hear Jesus pressing in on the inner nature of the moral law, increasing rather than diminishing its demands, making us even more aware of our need for him.

~ Jesus said, "Blessed are the pure in heart" (Matt. 5:8). But how can we be pure in heart without the blood of Christ to wash our hearts clean?

~ Jesus said that our righteousness must exceed that of the scribes and Pharisees (Matt. 5:20). But how can our righteousness ever exceed that of the scribes and Pharisees if Christ's righteousness is not imputed to us?

~ Jesus told us to pray for God to forgive our debts as we have forgiven our debtors (Matt. 6:12). But how can we find the footing to forgive without experiencing the generous forgiveness we've received through Christ?

〜 Jesus said our giving to the needy should be done in secret (Matt. 6:4). But how can we give anything away unless we believe that Christ will one day share with us all that he stands to inherit?

〜 Jesus told us to enter by the narrow gate instead of the easy, wide way that leads to destruction (Matt. 7:13–14). But how can we enter into the narrow gate that leads to life if Christ does not show us the way?

Anyone who tells you they live by the Sermon on the Mount clearly has not read it. This sermon forces us to our knees, saying, "I can't do it!" It leads us to turn to one who fulfilled every letter of it and to ask him to transfer to us his perfect record of obedience in exchange for our record of wrong. So while it is true that "all have sinned and fall short of the glory of God" (Rom. 3:23), it is also true that you have been "justified by his grace as a gift, through the redemption that is in Christ Jesus, whom God put forward as a propitiation by his blood, to be received by faith" (Rom. 3:24–25). *You don't have to be afraid of falling short.*

While those who stood at Mount Sinai wanted to obey and pledged to obey all God commanded, there was a problem. They did not have the power to obey. It would seem there was no hope, yet hope is found in Christ:

> For God has done what the law, weakened by the flesh, could not do. By sending his own Son in the likeness of sinful flesh and for sin, he condemned sin in the flesh, in order that the righteous requirement of the law might be fulfilled in us, who walk not according to the flesh but according to the Spirit. (Rom. 8:3–4)

The obedience promised by the people at Mount Sinai was a failure. But all of our failure is forgiven because of the Promised One's perfect obedience. His perfect obedience met the righteous requirement of the law so that "there is therefore now no condemnation for those who are in Christ Jesus" (Rom. 8:1). *So you don't have to be afraid of sin's power to condemn you or control you.*

The old covenant at Mount Sinai was a blood covenant. From the very beginning, that blood pointed toward a wholly sufficient, once-for-all sacrifice. And on the night before that final sacrifice was offered, Jesus said to his disciples gathered in the upper room:

> This is my blood of the covenant, which is poured out for many for the forgiveness of sins. (Matt. 26:28)

God does not demand your blood to pay for your sins. He offers his own. And, therefore, *you don't have to be afraid of sin's penalty.*

All of those who believe that God will invite them into his holy home because they have been a good person—at least better than most people they know—intend to approach this dangerous God on the basis of what they have done. They foolishly intend to meet with God at Mount Sinai and present him with their record of goodness, which they will discover quickly will not be good enough. But those who come to Mount Zion based not on what they have done but on what Christ has done have no cause for fear.

My dad's little airplane is now for sale, and I ride on commercial airliners that have sophisticated systems to guide the pilots safely through the clouds that come down on the mountains. But perhaps there will come a day when I will find myself sitting again on one of those airplanes, having my final conversation with God in this life. If that day comes, I won't have to be afraid, because I have come to Mount Zion. When this life ends, I will open my eyes in the heavenly Jerusalem surrounded by innumerable angels in celebration. I'll be surrounded by the spirits of the righteous made perfect—those in Moses's day who put their faith in the coming Savior, and those from Jesus's day who bowed to him in belief, and those throughout all the centuries who have fled from the ultimate terror of Mount Sinai to the eternal security of Mount Zion. There, we will see God. We will eat and drink in the eternal wedding supper of the Lamb. And we will never have to be afraid again.

Looking Forward

Security in the Shaking

When God spoke on Mount Sinai, revealing himself in the law, the force of his holy presence caused the earth to shake. Exodus 19:18 says:

> Now Mount Sinai was wrapped in smoke because the LORD had descended on it in fire. The smoke of it went up like the smoke of a kiln, and the whole mountain trembled greatly. (Ex. 19:18)

As God laid down the law at Mount Sinai, the force of it shook the earth. And years later when the full force of the law came down on Christ at Mount Calvary, the earth shook again.

From the cross, "Jesus cried out again with a loud voice and yielded up his spirit. And behold, the curtain of the temple was torn in two, from top to bottom. And the earth shook, and the rocks were split" (Matt. 27:50–51). Why did the earth shake? It shook because the judgment of God was falling on Jesus to punish sin. The judgment you and I deserve for our refusal to love the Lord our God, our incessant idolatry, our flippant use of his name, our murderous anger, our uninhibited lust, our little white lies, fell on Jesus that day. And the force of the tremendous weight of that judgment shook the earth.

The writer of Hebrews says that "yet once more" there will be a shaking of the earth (12:26). This is the violent shaking described in Revelation:

> When he opened the sixth seal, I looked, and behold, there was a great earthquake, and the sun became black as sackcloth, the full moon became like blood, and the stars of the sky fell to the earth as the fig tree sheds its winter fruit when shaken by a gale. The sky vanished like a scroll that is being rolled up, and every mountain and island was removed from its place. Then the kings of the earth and the great ones and the generals and the rich and the powerful, and everyone, slave and free, hid themselves in the caves and among the rocks of the mountains, calling to the mountains and rocks, "Fall on us and hide us from the face of him who is seated on the throne, and from the wrath of

the Lamb, for the great day of their wrath has come, and who can stand?" (6:12–17)

The day is coming when Jesus will return, and this time he will come not to bear the judgment for our law-breaking but to bring judgment upon all who persist in their refusal to take refuge in him. Once again the judgment of God will shake the earth, and the only ones who will survive will be those who have hidden themselves in the Lamb.[7]

judgment day

Discussion Guide

The Giving of the Law

Getting the Discussion Going

1. Try to imagine what it must have looked like, sounded like, and felt like, to stand at the foot of Mount Sinai when God came down on the mountain in cloud, fire, and thunder, and the entire mountain trembled. Can you think of any movie scenes or personal experiences that might resemble the sight, sound, or feel of it? *Any futuristic natural disaster movie.*

Getting to the Heart of It

2. God descended in overwhelming power and demanded that the people take three days to consecrate themselves in preparation for seeing God. Look together at Exodus 19:10–15 to note how they were supposed to prepare themselves. If you had been an Israelite, what message would you have understood from this three-day preparation and repeated warnings to not touch the mountain? *Wash clothing, refrain from sex.*

3. Remembering that Exodus is telling us not only the story of the salvation of Israel from slavery in Egypt but also the story of our salvation from sin, what can we learn from this order of events: the people were saved and were made God's treasured possession, and then they were given the law? *reminds me of adam + eve*

4. How is God's law an expression of the grace of God?
he is guiding them in relationship and moral responsibility to keep them safe

5. Many people think that Christianity is living by a bunch of rules. Is it? If not, what role do the Ten Commandments have in the life of a believer? *They are the guide and promise we make to God.*

6. In the Sermon on the Mount, Jesus said, "Do not think that I have come to abolish the Law or the Prophets; I have not come to abolish them but to fulfill them. . . . For I tell you, unless your righteousness exceeds that of the scribes and Pharisees, you will never enter the kingdom of heaven" (Matt. 5:17, 20). In what ways did Jesus fulfill the Ten Commandments? And how can a person's righteousness exceed the meticulous law keeping of the scribes and Pharisees of Jesus's day? *They can't exceed except w/ Christ's intervention*

7. How would you explain to someone why the ceremonial law (laws about the tabernacle, sacrifices, feasts, and festivals) and the civil law (legal precedents for Israel as a nation) are no longer binding on believers? *They preceded Christ. Loving Christ is now the law.*

Getting Personal

8. Both the Old and the New Testaments affirm that our "God is a consuming fire" (Deut. 4:24; Heb. 12:29). Is this how you've pictured God? And do you find yourself afraid of standing before this consuming fire one day, or at rest about it? Why? *Not afraid due to Grace*

Getting How It Fits into the Big Picture

9. Throughout this study, we are seeking to grasp how the passage we're studying fits into the bigger story of God's plan for redemption. How does God's revelation about himself through his giving of the law point us toward and prepare us to embrace Christ?

words became flesh
laws become Jesus' example

Week 6

The Tabernacle

Exodus 25–40

Personal Bible Study

Exodus 25–40

The tabernacle is the most important building in the history of the world. While Moses devoted two chapters in Genesis to the creation of the heavens and the earth, fifty chapters in the Bible are given to explaining the tabernacle's pattern, construction, and service. It is the only building ever constructed with the specific purpose of communicating how sinful people can have a relationship with a holy God. It is also, perhaps, the most comprehensive revelation of God's plan of salvation through Jesus Christ in the entire Old Testament.

1. Read Exodus 25:1–9. What does the Lord instruct his people to make for him and why?

a sacred residence to live among the people of Israel.

2. Read Exodus 25:10–22, which describes the one piece of furniture that will be in the Most Holy Place. What does this passage reveal regarding: *Ark of Acacia wood*

What it will be overlaid with:

Pure gold

What it will contain:

stone tablets of the covenant

What will be on top of it:

Arks Cover - pure gold
a cherabim

What will happen there:

God will meet them there between the 2 cherubim + atonement cover

3. Read Exodus 25:23–40 and Exodus 30:1–10, which give instructions for the construction of three pieces of furniture to go in the Holy Place. What were they, and what was their function?

Table — holds bread + dishes   *altar - incense*

lampstand - decorations

4. Read through Exodus 26, which contains the instructions for constructing the curtains, frames, bars, and coverings of the tabernacle. The entire tent was 45 feet long, 15 feet wide, and 15 feet high. Think through or perhaps measure out various rooms in your home or church or some other building. What space are you familiar with that would be roughly the same size as the tabernacle?

B's studio

5. Read Exodus 27:1–8 and Exodus 30:17–21, which describe two pieces of furniture that were to be made to go in the courtyard surrounding the tabernacle. What were they, and what was their function?

altar — incence

wash basin — to clean hands before entering

6. God's intention and purpose for the tabernacle echoes God's grand purpose, which was stated to Abraham (Gen. 17:7–8), and also earlier in Exodus (6:7). It will be repeated again and again throughout the Bible. What is it, according to Exodus 29:45–46?

To live among them.

7. There was a time when God dwelt with his people in the garden of Eden. And if we look carefully, we can see that God has built reminders of Eden into his design for the tabernacle. Read through the following descriptions of Eden in the first column, and write a corresponding statement about the tabernacle from the verses given in the second column.

Eden	Tabernacle
There was bdellium and onyx stones. (Gen. 2:12)	Ex. 25:3, 7 *onyx, yarn, linen, leather, acacia wood*
Two cherubim guarded the entrance. (Gen. 3:24)	Ex. 25:17–22 *2 cherubim on top of the ark*
A tree of life stood. (Gen. 2:9)	Ex. 25:31–33 *lampstand w/gold branches*
God dwelt there with his people. (Gen. 3:8)	Ex. 29:45–46 *I will live there*
The seventh day was set aside for rest and made holy. (Gen. 2:1–3)	Ex. 31:12–18 *people must keep Sabbath or die*
Human rebellion spoiled its beauty and perfection. (Genesis 3)	Ex. 32:1–7 *They made a gold calf & sacrificed to it.*

8. John 1:14 reads: "The Word became flesh and dwelt among us, and we have seen his glory, glory as of the only Son from the Father, full of grace and truth" (John 1:14). The word used there, "dwelt," is the same word that is used for "tabernacle." John was making the point that just as God's presence descended into the tiny room of the tabernacle long ago so that he could live with his people, God's presence

had now descended in human flesh to live with his people. Read the following statements about various aspects of the tabernacle and write a statement about Jesus in the second column that describes how Jesus fulfilled that aspect of the tabernacle.

Aspects of the Tabernacle	The Person and Work of Christ
The Ten Commandments inside the ark of the covenant represented God's perfect character and law.	Matt. 5:17; 2 Cor. 5:21 *Christ was perfectly righteous and fulfilled the law of God in our place.*
The ark of the covenant represented the throne of God.	Luke 1:32; Heb. 4:16 *Lord will give Jesus the throne of God. Come boldly to throne of God*
The mercy seat represented the mercy of God.	Rom. 3:25; 1 John 4:10 *We are made right w/ God when we believe in Jesus' sacrifice, living water*
The curtain in the tabernacle barred access to all except the priest.	Matt. 27:51; Heb. 10:19–20 *Jesus' blood opened the curtain*
The incense burned on the altar of incense represented the prayers of the priests on the people's behalf.	Heb. 7:25 *Jesus pleads w/ God on our behalf.*
The bread of the Presence represented God's commitment to feed and provide for his people.	John 6:32–33, 52–58 *Bread from heaven was Jesus. Live forever*
The lampstand, fashioned after a tree, provided light that leads to life.	John 1:4–5; 3:19–21 *Life was light, shining in darkness*
The washing in the bronze basin represented the washing away of uncleanness to enter God's presence.	1 Cor. 6:11; Titus 3:5 *Sins washed away*
Sacrifices were offered on the brazen altar to atone for sin.	Heb. 9:12–14; 10:11–12 *Christ perfect sacrifice for our sins.*

9. Read Hebrews 8:1–7. The writer says that our high priest, the risen and ascended Jesus, now ministers in "the true tent" of which the tabernacle erected by Moses was merely a "copy and shadow." What does this tell us about what was being pictured in the design and furniture and activity of the tabernacle? Consider the colors and designs of the curtain.

Shadow of heaven

10. We have seen that God has always intended to dwell with his people, and we know that one day we will see him face-to-face. According to the following verses, where has God chosen to dwell?

Genesis 3:8:

Walking in the Garden of Eden

Exodus 40:34:

Inside the tabernacle

2 Chronicles 7:1–3:

Inside the temple (solomon)

Matthew 3:16–17:

Gods spirit descended upon Jesus baptism

Colossians 1:19:

God was pleased to live in Christ

11. According to the following verses, where does God choose to dwell now?

Romans 8:9; 1 Corinthians 3:16:

R: spirit of God living in you. C: you are the temple of God & he lives in you

Ephesians 2:22:

Believers joined together to be a temple where God lives by his spirit.

12. According to the following verses, where does God intend to dwell?

2 Peter 3:13:

new heaven & earth, a world where everyone is right w/ God

Revelation 21:3:

Look! the home of God is now w/ his people. No more death, sorrow or pain

Teaching Chapter

At Home, at Last Together

Recently David and I drove to Knoxville to move our college-student son, Matt, from last year's old house to this year's cool condo, and I found myself hoping he will live there next year too, so we don't have to do that again. I could make a long list of things I hate about moving, but for sure the worst thing has to be cleaning the old place, when all you can think about is getting settled in the new place. But once you've moved your stuff out of the old place, you have to deal with the dust bunnies that multiplied under your bed along with the coins, paperclips, salt packets, and screws that collected in the backs of drawers, wiping out the refrigerator, and wiping down the bathroom. I think we can all agree that this is definitely not the fun part.

When I think about the drudgery of cleaning out the old place, I can't help but remember what may have been the best wedding gift I received. One of my coworkers, Carrie Matthews, came over to the old (and I mean old!) duplex that I lived in and helped me clean it that week before my wedding. I can still see her scrubbing down that awful bathtub. Now, that's a good friend.

My heart had already moved ahead of me to that little apartment on Alford Road that David and I dubbed "Avocadoland." Everything from the shag carpet to the countertops to the entry-door light fixture was 1970s avocado. And we loved it. Because this was going to be our home, where we would live together and love each other.

When you love someone, you want to live together in commitment to each other. In fact, this is what we were made for. Human history began with the home that God created where he could live together with those he loved. In the garden of Eden, God's original earthly sanctuary, Adam and Eve lived naked and unashamed, enjoying perfect intimacy with God and each other. But then an interloper entered, turning their hearts away from God. Their sin transformed the beauty of life lived in perfect oneness in the garden into the brokenness of life lived expelled from God's sanctuary and personal presence, in a world that had been corrupted by the curse. In Genesis we read that God "placed the cherubim and a flaming sword" at the entrance to the garden so that Adam and Eve could not come back in their sinful state (3:24).

But God has never been content to live with this separation from those he loves. So right there in the garden, even before he expelled them from it, he promised One who would come and destroy all that brought strife and alienation and separation and would restore the perfection and intimacy that God has always intended to share with his people. Then he began working out his plan to bring us back to him by setting his love on one particular man, Abraham, from whom the Promised One would come. As Abraham's descendants multiplied into what became a nation, God set his love on them, not because of anything wonderful or unique about them but because he loved them and chose to make them his own. They were to be his representatives in the world, making him known throughout the entire earth and to every generation. And to these people, he began revealing more and more about himself and his intentions to one day dwell with his people again in perfect beauty, purity, and intimacy. God intended to implant within the hearts of his people a longing to live with him in his home as we once did in the garden.

Do you have that longing? Or are you content here, so absorbed in our current culture and surroundings that you have little longing for a future at home in God's presence? In the passages we are looking at in this chapter, we see what God, long ago, set before his people that would remind them of how things once were in Eden as well as point them forward to the way things will be one day in the new heavens and the new earth, which will be even better than Eden once was. What was this picture of the perfection of the past as well as the promise of the future? The tabernacle.

Because this tabernacle was intended to picture Eden as well as heaven, it had to be constructed to exact specifications and decorated in particular ways and in spectacular colors. This is the tabernacle that foreshadowed "the city that has foundations, whose designer and builder is God" (Heb. 11:10), so it is God himself who drew up the blueprints that Moses and the Israelites were to follow to a T.

That is what God was doing in the passages in Exodus that we are studying this week. God provided very specific instructions for the tabernacle. Why was he so particular? It was because this tabernacle was not an end in itself. It served to point toward a greater tabernacle and a greater way of dwelling with God that was to come.

When we left Moses, in Exodus 24, "the appearance of the glory of the LORD was like a devouring fire on the top of the mountain in the sight of the people of Israel. Moses entered the cloud and went up on the mountain. And Moses was on the mountain forty days and forty nights" (vv. 17–18). Moses went up into the presence of God to listen to God speak to him. This is the first time we've read something like this in the Bible. God had appeared before and spoken, but this was different. What would you imagine God would want to communicate to Moses to take back to his people whom he had rescued from Egypt? What would be on the tip of his tongue, of primary importance?

God showed Moses a visual prototype and delivered verbal blueprints for building a tent in which he intended to live among his people. Rather than appearing to his people from time to time, God intended to move into the neighborhood to live among them. God gave Moses detailed designs for the tabernacle, saying,

> Let them make me a sanctuary, that I may dwell in their midst. Exactly as
> I show you concerning the pattern of the tabernacle, and of all its furni-
> ture, so you shall make it. (Ex. 25:8–9)

The Pattern for God's Dwelling Place

What kind of dwelling did God instruct his people to make for him? Interestingly it was not large, or ornate, or especially beautiful. Certainly we can think of much more remarkable homes, such as the Taj Mahal, Buckingham Palace, Versailles, or Hearst Castle. The tabernacle was not even a building but rather a giant tent, a portable sanctuary for God's presence. It was only about 15 feet wide by 45 feet long and was divided into two rooms—an outer room, which was called the "Holy Place," and the inner room, called the "Most Holy Place" or the "Holy of Holies." It was surrounded by a tall fence enclosing an area of a little more than 10,000 square feet (about the size of two basketball courts) creating a courtyard outside the tabernacle where there was a bronze altar for making sacrifices and a bronze basin for ceremonial cleansing.

What gave this structure its significance was not its size, but its designer—the Maker of heaven and earth—as well as its detail. This structure said something significant about how God intended to make it possible for a holy God to dwell with sinful people as it pointed to numerous aspects of the saving work of Jesus Christ.

This structure said something significant about how God intended to make it possible for a holy God to dwell with sinful people as it pointed to numerous aspects of the saving work of Jesus Christ.

We don't usually start a construction project with what goes inside, but God began his detailed instructions for the tabernacle from the inside out, beginning with the piece of furniture that would be at its heart—the ark of the covenant. *Ark* is an Old English word for "chest" or "box." Why would God begin his grand design with instructions regarding a rectangular box a little smaller than 4 feet by 3 feet? He did so because this was the most important thing in the whole tabernacle. This ark was the exact place where God would descend to dwell with his people. This would be his earthly throne.

> They shall make an ark of acacia wood. Two cubits and a half shall be its
> length, a cubit and a half its breadth, and a cubit and a half its height.

> You shall overlay it with pure gold, inside and outside shall you overlay
> it, and you shall make on it a molding of gold around it. . . . And you
> shall put into the ark the testimony that I shall give you. You shall make
> a mercy seat of pure gold. Two cubits and a half shall be its length, and a
> cubit and a half its breadth. And you shall make two cherubim of gold; of
> hammered work shall you make them, on the two ends of the mercy seat.
> (Ex. 25:10–11, 16–18)

There was something inside this box and something on top of it.
Cherubim formed out of hammered gold were at each end of the box's
solid-gold lid. What are cherubim? Are they the plump, little, naked
baby cherubs like those we see in so much angelic artwork? That's not at
all how the Bible portrays cherubim. Remember that it was two cherubim who were placed at the entrance to the garden of Eden when Adam
and Eve were expelled from it, charged with guarding the entrance with
swords. So certainly these are fierce creatures. Here we see the cherubim serving as guards of God's dwelling place once again as they are
depicted on the ark of the covenant protecting the throne of God.

The space above the cherubim was empty, as it was to be filled
only with the living presence of God. Inside the ark would be the Ten
Commandments written on stone tablets by the finger of God. But, of
course, this was the law that exposed Israel's sinfulness. If God were
to interact with his people based only on his law, they would be condemned. That is why what God prescribed to go between his presence
on the throne and the law was so important. Between God's presence
and God's law was the atonement cover or the mercy seat. When we call
this the "mercy seat," we're not talking so much about a chair but rather
a location, as in "the seat of power." The atonement cover symbolized
the center and source from which God showed mercy to sinners. But
the atonement cover alone was not sufficient. It had to be sprinkled
with the blood of a sacrifice. The high priest, once a year, sprinkled
the blood of an animal sacrifice on the mercy seat, demonstrating that
atonement had been made (Leviticus 16). In this way, "when God came
down to dwell with his people, he would not see first of all, the law that
they had broken, but the saving blood of an atoning sacrifice."[1]

Outside the Most Holy Place, in the Holy Place, there were three pieces of furniture: the table for the bread of the Presence, the golden lampstand, and the altar of incense. The tabernacle's true magnificence was in its message, not in its massive size or ornamental grandeur, and its furnishings were not large. The table was about the size of a common coffee table: 3 feet long, 1.5 feet wide, and less than 3 feet tall. What was most important about the table was what was on it: twelve loaves of sacred bread as well as various plates, dishes, pitchers, and bowls. What was this bread there for? Was this bread for God to eat, like when we leave a plate of cookies for Santa Clause on Christmas Eve? No, this bread was not there to meet some need in God but to symbolize our need for him. Twelve loaves of bread consumed by the priests and then replaced weekly served as a reminder of God's promised provision for the twelve tribes. It whispered reminders of God's constant awareness of their daily needs and his intentions to provide for them. It spoke not only of the source of their provision but the substance of their provision, because more than needing God to feed them, they needed to feed on God. This is exactly what Moses would make clear later in Deuteronomy where he wrote:

> Man does not live by bread alone, but man lives by every word that comes from the mouth of the LORD. (Deut. 8:3)

The second piece of furniture in the Holy Place, the golden lampstand, had a practical as well as symbolic purpose. The tabernacle was a tent, four layers thick. It had an inner lining made of linen, which was covered with cloth woven from goats' hair. This was covered with rams' skins, and over the top went a waterproof tarp made from the thick hides of sea cows. Underneath those layers it must have been very, very dark. So surely the golden lampstand was there to provide light to the priests who entered so they could see what they were doing. But there is more here that becomes clear as we examine the careful instructions God gave to Moses for its design:

> Make a lampstand of pure, hammered gold. Make the entire lampstand and its decorations of one piece—the base, center stem, lamp cups, buds, and petals. Make it with six branches going out from the center stem,

three on each side. . . . Make the seven lamps for the lampstand, and set
them so they reflect their light forward. . . . Be sure that you make everything according to the pattern I have shown you here on the mountain.
(Ex. 25:31–32, 37, 40 NLT)

The lampstand was made in the shape of a tree, echoing the tree of
life in Eden. And from the beginning it showed God's people that, as
 we approach God, we are coming into the light, that God alone is the
source of all life and light, and that anywhere apart from him is utter
darkness.

The small altar of incense went in the middle of the Holy Place
directly in front of the ark of the covenant, with the thick curtain that
separated the Holy Place from the Most Holy Place in between. Burning
incense on this altar was part of the priests' daily routine. Every morning they would trim the wicks and replenish the oil in the golden lampstand and would burn fragrant incense on the altar, and the same routine
was repeated in the evening. So each morning and evening as the priest
offered incense on the golden altar, he was, in a sense, approaching the
mercy seat, the throne of grace from which God answers the prayers of
his people.

As we move into Exodus 26, we learn about the various layers of
the tent that housed the Holy Place and the Most Holy Place, culmi-
nating in these instructions for the curtain that would separate the
two rooms:

> Make a special curtain of finely woven linen. Decorate it with blue, pur-
> ple, and scarlet thread and with skillfully embroidered cherubim. Hang
> this curtain on gold hooks attached to four posts of acacia wood. Overlay
> the posts with gold, and set them in four silver bases. Hang the inner cur-
> tain from clasps, and put the Ark of the Covenant in the room behind
> it. This curtain will separate the Holy Place from the Most Holy Place.
> (Ex. 26:31–33 NLT)

If you were a priest who stood in the tabernacle and looked around
at what was woven into the linen fabric in the inner layer, you would
see a deep blue background with cherubim looking as if they were sus-
pended in midair. So when you walked into the tabernacle you would

be symbolically transferred from an earthly location to a heavenly one. The tabernacle was a vivid portrayal of heaven, the dwelling place of God. It simultaneously pointed back to when heaven was on earth, when God walked with Adam and Eve in the garden in the cool of the day, as well as forward to the day when heaven will once again come to earth, when God will once again dwell with his people with the intimacy we once enjoyed in the garden.

God's Presence in His Dwelling Place

Over and over again throughout the following chapters of Exodus we read that the tabernacle's design and creation were just the way that God had instructed. And when we come to the end of Exodus, we read:

> [Moses] erected the court around the tabernacle. . . . So Moses finished the work. (Ex. 40:33)

Everything was set into place as God had instructed, and only one thing was needed: the glorious presence of God to fill it up:

> Then the cloud covered the tent of meeting, and the glory of the LORD filled the tabernacle. (Ex. 40:34)

A spectacular display of the radiance of God's being descended from Mount Sinai into this little tent in the middle of the camp. This would now be the place for God's people to meet with the living God, the fulfillment of God's earlier promise of Exodus 29:45, "I will dwell among the people of Israel and will be their God."

But immediately after this we read:

> Moses was not able to enter the tent of meeting because the cloud settled on it, and the glory of the LORD filled the tabernacle. (Ex. 40:35)

The whole book of Exodus has been moving toward the moment when God's people would worship him at his mountain. Yet when God finally descended into the tabernacle, even Moses, their mediator who had met with God on the mountain, couldn't enter in. Perhaps in that

moment the reality of God's holiness and the people's sinfulness sank
a little deeper into everyone's understanding.

Let's try, for a moment, to put ourselves in the sandals of the
Israelites out in the desert, if we can. Here is this tent in the center of
camp, built to exact specifications. We know that God, who brought
us out of slavery through the Red Sea and gave us his law, designed
this tabernacle to communicate something significant and specific. So
what is it we are supposed to see as we look at it? What are we supposed
to understand?

When average Israelites looked at the tabernacle and thought
through its meaning, they were confronted with a difficult reality—
they were never allowed to go inside. Here was God in their midst, but
most Israelites never had a chance to see past the door, let alone go
inside and meet with God. Everything about the tabernacle declared
to the Israelites: *No access. Do not enter.* If you were a man, you were
allowed only into the courtyard. If you were a woman, you weren't
even allowed in the courtyard. Only a select few priests ever served in
the Holy Place during their lifetime. And even they were confronted
with a curtain—a curtain that the Jewish Talmud says was four inches
thick and took more than a hundred priests to move![2] Only one priest,
once a year, went beyond the veil into the Most Holy Place, where
God's presence dwelt.

So, as we stood outside the tabernacle complex or in its courtyard examining and thinking it through—as we watched the priests
carrying out their duties and wondered at the cloud of God's glory
radiating from the Most Holy Place—perhaps we would recognize
that this was not all that God intended when he said that he would
dwell among us. Perhaps we would grasp that it was merely a shadow
of a greater reality to come, a greater access, a greater intimacy that
God intended to share with his people. And perhaps as we stood outside day after day, year after year, it would implant in our hearts a
longing for God to fulfill his promise to send a better mediator, a
better sacrifice, a true tabernacle in which we could have unfettered
access to our God.

The Person in Whom God Was Pleased to Dwell

John announced the arrival of the true tabernacle when he said:

> And the Word became flesh and dwelt among us, and we have seen his
> glory, glory as of the only Son from the Father, full of grace and truth.
> (John 1:14)

The word John used for "dwelt" is the Greek word for "putting up a
tabernacle," *skēnoō*. He was saying that Jesus became flesh and "tab-
ernacled" among us. Certainly no Jewish person reading these words
of John's Gospel would have failed to grasp what was being said. They
understood that God in his glory had dwelt in the tabernacle. John was
saying that God's glory had now descended not to a place in the tabernacle or the temple but in the person of Jesus Christ.

The book of Hebrews calls the tabernacle "a copy and shadow of
the heavenly things" (8:5), "symbolic" (9:9) of "the greater and more
perfect tent" (9:11). Imagine if Jesus himself were to take us on a tour
of the tabernacle, showing how he was the substance that cast the tabernacle's shadows. We would see that everything about the tabernacle
pointed to some aspect of his character and work, and that, in fact, the
tabernacle had no meaning apart from him.

When he took us through the courtyard, perhaps he would point
to the bronze altar and say that when he offered himself as a perfect
once-for-all sacrifice, he put an end to the sacrifices of bulls and goats,
which never had the power to take away sin (Heb. 10:4). Perhaps he
would point to the bronze basin and say for we need no longer wash
ourselves to come into God's presence, for he has cleansed us with the
only cleansing agent that can wash away the stain of sin and purify our
conscience—his own blood (Heb. 9:14).

As Jesus entered into the Holy Place, perhaps he would point
toward the lampstand and say, "I am the light of the world. Whoever
follows me will not walk in darkness, but will have the light of life"
(John 8:12). Perhaps he would point to the table of the bread of the
Presence and say, "For the bread of God is he who comes down from
heaven and gives life to the world. . . . I am the bread of life; whoever

comes to me shall not hunger. . . . The bread that I will give for the life of the world is my flesh" (John 6:33, 35, 51). Perhaps he would point to the altar of incense and say that he "always lives to make intercession" for those who draw near to God through him (Heb. 7:25).

For hundreds of years the curtain hung in the tabernacle and then in the temple for generations of priests to see as they ministered at the table and the golden altar. It announced to them that the way to approach God was not yet made known. And yet, because the curtain was made of fabric rather than stone or metal, it was obviously temporary. A way of access into the presence of God would one day be revealed.

Matthew tells the dramatic story of when the curtain was finally opened. It happened on the day Jesus hung on the cross, when Jesus shouted out again, and he released his spirit. At that moment the curtain in the sanctuary of the temple was torn in two, from top to bottom (Matt. 27:50–51). So, in giving us a tour of the tabernacle, surely Jesus would point to the torn curtain and say, "Now you can have confidence to enter the holy places by my blood, by the new and living way that I opened for you through the curtain, that is, through my flesh" (see Heb. 10:19–20).

The cross of Christ is our mercy seat. It is the place where the blood of an atoning sacrifice reconciled us to God by coming between God's holiness and our law breaking.

As we entered the Most Holy Place, perhaps he would point to the mercy seat, covered in blood, and say, "I entered once for all into the holy places, not by means of the blood of goats and calves but by means of my own blood, thus securing an eternal redemption" (see Heb. 9:12). This is love: not that you loved God, but that he loved you and sent his Son as an atoning sacrifice for your sins" (see 1 John 4:10).

The cross of Christ is our mercy seat. It is the place where the blood of an atoning sacrifice reconciled us to God by coming between God's holiness and our law breaking. "For all have sinned and fall short of the glory of God, and are justified by his grace as a gift, through the redemption that is in Christ Jesus, whom God put forward as a propitiation by his blood, to be received by faith" (Rom. 3:23–25)

Perhaps, if Jesus were giving us a tour of the tabernacle, he would remind us of how the cloud covered the tabernacle, filling it with his glorious presence, and then he might repeat the words that the angel Gabriel spoke to his mother about his conception: "The Holy Spirit will come upon you, and the power of the Most High will overshadow you; therefore the child to be born will be called holy—the Son of God" (Luke 1:35). This was the glory of God descending to fill Mary's womb with his glorious presence. From the moment of his conception, Jesus was the one in whom the fullness of God was pleased to dwell (Col. 1:19).

Perhaps Jesus could go on to point out to us that the tabernacle was outwardly humble and unattractive, just as the prophet Isaiah had said about Messiah: "He had no form or majesty that we should look at him, and no beauty that we should desire him" (Isa. 53:2). Perhaps he would help us to see that the tabernacle was the center of Israel's camp, a gathering place for God's people, and then turn to us and say, "When I am lifted up from the earth, [I] will draw all people to myself" (John 12:32).

Surely he would help us to see that his death was a means to an end, and that end is what God states again and again throughout the Old and New Testaments: "I will be your God, you will be my people" (see Gen. 17:1–8; Ex. 6:7, 29:45; Lev. 26:12; Jer. 31:33; Ezek. 11:20).

The Place Where God Will Dwell with His People

The people of God will one day gather around the throne of God. He will be our God, and we will be his people, and there will be no barriers, no sin to separate, no symbols—only glorious substance. We will approach God not through a mediator but face-to-face, not only one day a year but for all eternity.

On that day there will be no need for a brazen altar for offering sacrifices. The Lamb who was slain, our all-sufficient sacrifice, will be on the throne, and we will be singing, "Worthy is the Lamb who was slain, to receive power and wealth and wisdom and might and honor and glory and blessing!" (Rev. 5:12).

There will be no need for a washing basin. All of those around the throne will have "washed their robes and made them white in the blood of the Lamb" (Rev. 7:14).

There will be no need for the table of the bread of the Presence. He will have fulfilled his promise to anyone and everyone who has heard his voice and opened the door to "come in to him and eat with him, and he with me" (Rev. 3:20).

There will be no need for a golden lampstand, not even for a sun or moon, "for the glory of God gives it light, and its lamp is the Lamb" (Rev. 21:23)

There will be no need for an altar of incense. The prayers of a suffering church will have been answered, and its people will stand clothed in white robes, with palm branches in their hands and crying out with a loud voice, "Salvation belongs to our God who sits on the throne, and to the Lamb!" (Rev. 7:10).

There will be no curtain that will separate us from the presence of God. We will be close enough to see his face (Rev. 22:4), close enough that he will reach out and wipe away every tear from our eyes (Rev. 21:4).

I told you about that place my heart had moved to even before I moved myself and my stuff to Avocadoland. I remember well what it was like in those days leading up to our wedding. We were planning and merging our lives together, but we weren't living together or sleeping together. As our wedding day got closer, it got harder and harder to go home to my little dingy duplex at night. We wanted to be together. When we returned from our honeymoon and drove up to our apartment, David said, "It's getting late. I guess I better drive you home." And we looked at each other and smiled, knowing it wasn't true, because we didn't have to be separated anymore. This was our home, and now we lived together. We could share everything.

This is a picture of what it means when we read John's vision of that day when all that the tabernacle pointed to becomes reality. Finally, we'll be together with our God forever. There will be no more relating from a distance; faith will have become sight. Shadows will fall away, and only glorious substance will remain.

Do you find yourself longing for the separation and distance to give way to togetherness? Has your heart moved ahead of you to a place of intimacy with the Almighty? Or do you find yourself content where you are in this old place, perhaps even so convinced that this is where the good stuff is that you see making your move into the dwelling place of God as a tragedy, something to put off as long as possible?

Is your true longing to have a few kids and a nice house, not be too sick and live on this earth a long time, maybe build a little business, watch your sports team win a few seasons, and have some fun vacations? Can't you see that you were made for more? More beauty, more wonder, more joy, grander purposes, greater glory, deeper relationship? We were made for so much more than a few years on this earth and then turning back to dust. We were made to live forever in God's perfect place, enjoying his perfect rule in perfect relationship with him.

Won't you welcome God to implant within you a longing for that day, for that greater reality of living in his presence? Will you allow your heart to move ahead of you to that place, that day, when we will hear the loud voice from the throne declaring the best news anyone could ever hear: "Behold, the dwelling place of God is with man. He will dwell with them, and they will be his people, and God himself will be with them as their God" (Rev. 21:3).

Looking Forward

Christ Will Appear a Second Time

On the Day of Atonement, the high priest would enter the the Most Holy Place with the blood of sacrifice, first to make atonement for himself, and then to make atonement for the people of Israel:

> Then he shall kill the goat of the sin offering that is for the people and bring its blood inside the veil and do with its blood as he did with the blood of the bull, sprinkling it over the mercy seat and in front of the mercy seat. Thus he shall make atonement for the Holy Place, because of the uncleannesses of the people of Israel and because of their transgressions, all their sins. And so he shall do for the tent of meeting, which dwells with them in the midst of their uncleannesses. (Lev. 16:15–16)

Just as the instructions for building the tabernacle had been detailed, so the instructions for the Day of Atonement with its ceremonial cleansing and sprinkling of sacrificial blood were detailed. If the high priest failed to follow the prescribed instructions from God, he was subject to death. So when the high priest disappeared behind the curtain of the Most Holy Place on the Day of Atonement, the people waited and watched for him to come out alive and well. When he did, they knew that the sacrifice had been accepted by God and their sin had been effectively atoned for. It is this imagery of the high priest disappearing into the Most Holy Place, and then reappearing to declare that sin had been atoned for, that the writer of Hebrews had in mind when he wrote:

> For Christ has entered, not into holy places made with hands, which are copies of the true things, but into heaven itself, now *to appear in the presence of God on our behalf*. Nor was it to offer himself repeatedly, as the high priest enters the holy places every year with blood not his own, for then he would have had to suffer repeatedly since the foundation of the world. But as it is, *he has appeared once for all at the end of the ages* to put away sin by the sacrifice of himself. And just as it is appointed for man to die once, and after that comes judgment, so Christ,

> having been offered once to bear the sins of many, *will appear
> a second time,* not to deal with sin but to save those who are
> eagerly waiting for him. (Heb. 9:24–28)

In this passage the writer uses the Greek word for "to appear" three times. He points to the past, when Christ "appeared once for all at the end of the ages to put away sin by the sacrifice of himself." Why is this described as the "end of the ages," when it happened two thousand years ago? Because this was the turning point, or climax, of history. The death of Jesus was not just one event in a line of similar historical events but rather the decisive act that will bring an end to life in this broken world as we know it.

The writer also speaks of the present, the time in which Christ has entered the heavenly Most Holy Place "to appear in the presence of God on our behalf." Jesus is, even now, appearing before the throne of God to intercede for us before the Father.

Then the writer speaks of a second appearing of Jesus on this earth, when Jesus will return to usher in a new era of perfect restoration and righteousness. If God's people in the Old Testament looked eagerly to see the high priest reappear from behind the curtains of the Most Holy Place, how much more should we look eagerly to see our Great High Priest pull back the curtain of heaven to reappear from the heavenly Most Holy Place? When Christ appears a second time, it will be one more confirmation that the Father is satisfied with his sacrifice. And while he appeared the first time to deal with sin once and for all, when he comes again it will be to deliver the salvation that we have set our hopes upon—complete deliverance from this fallen, sinful world into the bright and beautiful, heavenly holy place.

Discussion Guide

The Tabernacle

Getting the Discussion Going

1. Have you ever bought a piece of furniture or a playset that came in a box and required you to put it together, carefully following the instructions and diagrams? That gives us a bit of a sense of what Moses and the people of Israel were doing as they followed God's careful, detailed instructions for building the tabernacle. Try to put yourself in the sandals of the typical Israelite on the work crew. What kinds of things do you think might have gone through your mind as you studied the plans, collected materials, and crafted the structure and furniture?

Getting to the Heart of It

2. Why do you think God gave, and Moses recorded, such detailed instructions about the design and building of the tent in which he would dwell?

3. As you read about the various pieces of furniture in the Most Holy Place, the Holy Place, and the courtyard of the tabernacle and saw how they each pointed to the person and work of Christ, what was most interesting or meaningful to you?

4. How does a greater understanding of the tabernacle help us better understand the significance of what the writer of Hebrews wrote when he said, "Let us then with confidence draw near to the throne

of grace, that we may receive mercy and find grace to help in time of need" (Heb. 4:16)?

5. How does the background of the tabernacle also make the following verses more meaningful? "Therefore, brothers, since we have confidence to enter the holy places by the blood of Jesus, by the new and living way that he opened for us through the curtain, that is, through his flesh, and since we have a great priest over the house of God, let us draw near with a true heart in full assurance of faith, with our hearts sprinkled clean from an evil conscience and our bodies washed with pure water" (Heb. 10:19–22).

6. In what way would you say that the tabernacle "preached the gospel" to the Israelites, and how did it answer the basic question of how a sinful person can approach a holy God?

7. If we're honest, many of us would have to admit that our hearts do not long for this dwelling place with God. Our hearts are content with and set on this earthly life. Why do you think that is, and what do you think we can do to nurture our longing for our future home with God?

Getting Personal

8. In the Personal Bible Study questions, we looked at where God has chosen to dwell in the past and where he dwells now—in believers and in his church. Considering how important cleansing and purity was in the tabernacle that God designed, what thoughts does that give to you about God's Spirit dwelling within you?

Getting How It Fits into the Big Picture

9. Throughout this study, we are seeking to grasp how the passage we're studying fits into the bigger story of God's plan for redemption and helps us to understand how God is working out that plan. What does the fact that the tabernacle both hearkened back to Eden and provided a copy and shadow of heavenly things tell us about what we can expect in our eternal future?

The Priesthood

Exodus 28–29

Exodus 28–29

In Exodus 28 and 29, we find the instructions God gave to Moses about the establishment of the priesthood, those set apart to serve him in his tabernacle. Specifically in these two chapters we find out who will serve him as priests, the clothing the priests are to wear for this service, the content of their service, and the ceremony by which the priests will be commissioned for their service.

1. Read Exodus 28:1. What do we know about Aaron, who, with his sons, was appointed by God to serve as priest? (If you need some help, see Ex. 4:12–16; 7:1–7).

Moses brother, spoke for him.

2. What three words do you find in Exodus 28:2 that define what should mark the high priest's clothing?

Beautiful, lend dignity, show his separation to God.

honor
glory
beauty

3. List the garments to be made for the priest, detailed in Exodus 28:4.

Chestpiece   sash
ephod
robe
emb tunic
turban

165

4. Compare Exodus 26:1 to Exodus 28:5. What do you think might be the significance of the similarity you see here?

TAB > linen, blue, purple & scarlet yarn.
Garments same. Both are to glorify God:

5. Read through Exodus 28:6–43, noting a detail or two regarding the color, materials, or design of each garment.

~ ephod (vv. 6–14)
linen, emb w/ gold, scarlet, blue, purple
2 pieces joined @ shoulders
~ breastpiece (vv. 15–30) *2 onyx stones engraved*
for God's will, same mt'l as ephod, pouch, gemstones
~ robe (vv. 31–35) *braided Gold ropes*
Blue, one piece w/ reinforced hole for head
~ turban (vv. 36–39) *fringe + bells*
I set apart as holy to the Lord!
~ coat (v. 39)

~ sash (v. 39)
Same mt'l as ephod

6. The garments of the other priests are far simpler than those of the high priest yet still set apart from ordinary clothing. What instruction does Exodus 28:40 provide for them?

for dignity + respect
Make tunics, sashes + headpieces
+ linen underclothes

7. In Exodus 29 we move from the clothing of the priests to the consecration of the priests. Read verses 4–7 and describe three aspects of the consecration of Aaron and his sons to the priesthood that you find there.

1. *Young Bull - blood*

2. *Burn sacrifice (fat from Bull)*

3. *annoint w/ oil*

8. Exodus 29:10–34 describes six offerings involved in the priest's ordination. Most of these will be explained more fully next week, when we move into Leviticus. Read through these verses and note a brief detail or observation about each of the offerings.

Sin offering (vv. 10–14)

Young Bull + 2 rams, w/o defects
Slaughter + smear blood on alter

Burnt offering (vv. 15–18)

Born bill after slaughter

Ram of ordination (vv. 19–21)

· mix blood w/ oil &   *earlobes*
sprinkle on Aaron + sons.   *thumbs*
                                 big toes

Wave offering (vv. 22–24)

take fat from spec parts and bread +
give to Aaron to provide as special gift to lord.

Food offering (v. 25)

after wave offering, + bread burnt for lord
+ the priests can keep some meat

Peace offerings (vv. 26–28, 31–34)

Boil remaining meat

9. In Exodus 29:38–43 God gives instructions regarding the daily duties of the priests for generations to come. What are they?

2 one yr old lambs sacrificed daily
offer at the entrance, where I will
meet you + speak.

10. Aaron, as the first high priest, revealed important aspects of what our Great High Priest, Jesus, would be and do. Every aspect of his clothing pointed to specific aspects of the ministry of Christ. Read the following statements about the clothing of the Old Testament priests and write a corresponding statement in the second column about the priestly ministry of Jesus.

The Old Testament Priest's Clothing	Jesus, Our Great High Priest
The priest carried the sins of the people on his shoulders as represented by the precious stones on the shoulder of his ephod engraved with their names. (Ex. 28:6–14)	Heb. 9:28 *died to take away the sins of all people*
The priest carried the concerns of the people of God near his heart as represented by the twelve precious stones on his breastpiece engraved with their names. (Ex. 28:15–30)	John 17:9–10 *Jesus prayed for his disciples, all belonging to God. He guarded them so not one was lost except Judas*
The priest wore a royal robe in his role of chosen mediator for the people of God. (Ex. 28:31–35)	John 19:2, 23 *Soldiers put a purple robe on him. They took his robe, which was one piece + cast lots for it.*
The priest wore a turban, which, by its engraved gold plate, crowned his head with the proclamation "Holy to the LORD." (Ex. 28:36–39)	Heb. 7:26 *God appointed his son who was made perfect forever.*

11. The consecration of the priest also pointed to specific aspects of the person and ministry of Christ. Read the statement about the Old Testament priests in the first column below and write a corresponding statement in the second column about the priestly ministry of Jesus.

The Old Testament Priest's Consecration	Jesus, Our Great High Priest
Priests were washed with water. (Ex. 29:4)	Matt. 3:13–15 *Jesus Baptised in Jordan River by John the Baptist.*
Priests were anointed with oil. (Ex. 29:7)	Matt. 3:16–17 *Came out of water, Spirit of God descended + voice This is my beloved son, and I am fully pleased w/ him*

Priests offered sacrifices for their sin. (Ex. 29:10–21)	John 10:18 *Jesus said No one can take my life from me, I lay it down Voluntarily.*
Priests ate a meal of that which had been sacrificed. (Ex. 29:31–34)	1 Cor. 11:23–25 *Lord's supper – Bread – body Wine – blood*

12. The writer of Hebrews especially draws upon his readers' understanding of and dependence upon the priesthood to help his readers see the superiority of the ministry of Jesus. Read the following statements about the Old Testament priests in the first column below and write a corresponding statement in the second column about the priestly ministry of Jesus from Hebrews.

The Old Testament Priesthood	**Jesus, Our Great High Priest**
The high priest passed through the curtains of the tabernacle to enter the earthly dwelling place of God. (Leviticus 16)	Heb. 4:14 *Jesus, in heaven, trust him (understands our weakness)*
The priests struggled with the same temptations as the people, and sinned. (Heb. 5:3)	Heb. 4:15
The people were not invited to come anywhere near the throne room of God in the Most Holy Place and could have expected to die if they did. (Num. 4:20)	Heb. 4:16 *Let us come boldly to the throne of our gracious God. There we will receive his mercy + we will find grace...*
Priests were appointed by God. (Ex. 28:1)	Heb. 5:1–5 *A priest is chosen to represent other humans in their dealings w/ God. He offers sacrifices for their sins. Called by God, as Aaron was*

Priests in the order of Aaron were appointed on the basis of ancestry. (Heb. 7:14–17)	Heb. 7:16 (Jesus) He became a priest not by the old rea... but by the power of a life that cannot be destroyed.
Many priests interceded for the people for a limited number of years. All of these priests died. (Heb. 7:23)	Heb. 7:24–25 Jesus remains a priest forever, his priesthood will never end.
The priests repeatedly failed by falling into sinful idolatry and abuse of their privilege. (2 Chron. 36:14)	Heb. 7:26 Jesus is Holy & blameless
The priests offered daily animal sacrifices year after year. (Heb. 7:27)	Heb. 7:27 He does not offer sacrifices every day ... Jesus did once + for all when he sacrificed himself on the cross
The priests served before God's throne that dwelled temporarily in a tent made by men, a copy and shadow of the realities of heaven. (Heb. 8:5)	Heb. 8:1–2 Jesus sat at God's right hand, per permanently. "Tent" bu, it by Lord not by human hands
The priests entered into a tent made by hands on the basis of the blood of an animal. (Ex. 39:42)	Heb. 9:11–14 He took blood into the most Holy place, his own blood.
The high priest entered the Holy Place every year with the blood of a sacrifice. (Heb. 9:25)	Heb. 9:25–26 He died one time, the ultimate sacrifice. Jesus did not need to die again & again
The priest repeatedly offered the same sacrifices that could never take away sins. (Heb. 10:11)	Heb. 10:12–14 Sacrificed one time, good for all time.

Teaching Chapter

Category and Context

Do you remember what you thought when you first heard people talking about surfing the Internet? I remember wondering what it meant to surf, and why anyone would want to. What would you find if you surfed, and who put that stuff up there, and where exactly did they put it? And who is in charge of this thing called the "Internet" anyway? I had no categories to help me make sense of it until someone used the term *bulletin board*. Then it started to become clearer. To see it as an electronic bulletin board in cyberspace where information was posted gave me a category and helped me begin to make sense of it. (Although I admit that I still wonder exactly where the Internet is in the universe and who's in charge of it.)

Similarly, I can remember when the secretary in our department at the publishing company where I worked at the time got that blessed little box called a "Mac Plus" with its slot for floppy discs. What helped me most as I was learning to use it was to think of the hard drive as a file cabinet, and the desktop as similar to the desktop on my real desk. I created documents and stored them in file folders inside larger file folders. The filing cabinet standing there in my office provided me with something familiar and tangible that gave me a category for making sense of what was happening on the screen and inside that little box, which now I'm quite sure I couldn't live without.

Today we're going to look at something familiar and tangible that God provided to his people that would give them a category for making sense of who Jesus is and what he came to do. Throughout the history of his dealings with Israel, God provided his people with context and categories they would need to understand Jesus. When he gave instructions for the tabernacle, the priesthood, and the sacrifices, he was not simply setting up a religious system that would be an end in itself. They were not means of worship that were replaced because they didn't work out. They were always meant to be temporary. In the tabernacle, priesthood, and sacrifices, God was providing a framework, a set of categories, that would help his people to understand the ministry of Jesus when he came. In every aspect of the priesthood—its calling, its clothing, its consecration and commission—we see shadows cast backward into Israel's history by our Great High Priest, Jesus himself. So let's look together at God's instructions for the establishment of the priesthood in Exodus 28 and 29.

> *In every aspect of the priesthood—its calling, its clothing, its consecration and commission—we see shadows cast backward into Israel's history by our Great High Priest, Jesus himself.*

But before we begin, we have to deal with the aversion many of us have to the whole idea of priests. Many of us have a cynicism about organized religion, and, frankly, that is what the word *priest* conjures up in our minds. When we think about priests, many of us see ordinary men in ornate robes, images that bring to mind empty religion, or errant doctrine, or even sexual abuse. Some of us simply see priests as irrelevant to real relationship with God. Others of us, on the other hand, feel rather desperate to have a priest, wanting a professional religious person nearby to be holy and serious about God because we know we are worldly and distracted.

Clearly we are going to need to let go of our idea of the priesthood in its modern-day sense so that we can enter into and embrace the priesthood as God originally designed it. God set the Old Testament priesthood in place as the way for his people to meet with him for centuries. It was important to him, and therefore we want it to be important to us. If we want to see Jesus as he truly is, we must recognize that our personal history and frame of reference are simply too limited to interpret Jesus in all of his glory and fullness. We need the frame of reference, or categories, that God has given to us. So we want to examine the priesthood as given by God. Along the way, we'll discover that though we may not have recognized it before, we need a priest. We'll also discover the only priest we'll ever need.

We Need a Priest

Earlier in Exodus, we saw that God called his people out of Egypt for the very purpose of worshiping him. Under the Mosaic covenant, they were to be a "kingdom of priests" (Ex. 19:6) demonstrating God's standard of holiness in a world that had little knowledge of God. This is how they would fulfill their calling to be a blessing to the nations. But this privilege was conditional: Israel had to obey the law of God. And of course they flagrantly disobeyed almost immediately and therefore couldn't come anywhere close to God. How were they going to worship him if they couldn't come anywhere near him in their sinful state? This is why God ordained the priesthood. The priests would enter into God's presence on their behalf.

The Priests' Calling

> Then bring near to you Aaron your brother, and his sons with him, from among the people of Israel, to serve me as priests—Aaron and Aaron's sons, Nadab and Abihu, Eleazar and Ithamar. (Ex. 28:1)

No man could appoint himself to be a priest. No one took a spiritual gifting self-test and determined that he had the skill set to be a priest, and applied for the position. The Old Testament priesthood was grounded in God's divine choice and call of the tribe of Levi to serve in this holy capacity. Aaron, a Levite, would serve as high priest. Aaron was Moses's brother and had served as Moses's spokesperson; he had done miraculous signs, held the prophet's hands up in prayer, and went up the mountain to see God. But, of course, Aaron is also the one who led Israel in its false worship of the golden calf (Exodus 32), so it is

clear from the outset that being a priest, a spiritual leader to the people
of Israel, will be a matter not of Aaron's aptitude but of God's grace.

The Priest's Clothing

While there were a large number of priests, there was only one high
priest. And as the high priest, Aaron could not wear ordinary clothing.
God's instruction to Moses was:

> You shall make holy garments for Aaron your brother, for glory and for
> beauty. (Ex. 28:2)

So we see that the Bible uses three important words to describe the
garments the priest wore: *holy, glorious,* and *beautiful.* We recognize
that these three words are actually used throughout the Scriptures to
describe God himself. Because God is holy and glorious and beautiful,
the only way to approach him is to be adorned with holiness, glory,
and beauty. The holiness or sacredness of the priest's special garments
demonstrated that he had been set apart by God for his role as high
priest. The glory or weightiness of the clothing reflected the gravity of
his priestly office. The beauty of his garment reflected the splendor and
beauty of the God he approached. The high priest was the best-dressed
man in Israel in robes made of pure white linen decorated with gold,
blue, purple, and scarlet yarn.

In this way, the priest represented God to the people. But the priest
also represented the people to God. The priest was a mediator who
represented each side to the other. Whenever the priest performed his
sacred duties, he was acting not for himself alone but for all the people,
and his clothing vividly pictured this reality.

He wore an ephod, which was likely a long, sleeveless apron or
vest with two straps that went over his shoulders. Two semiprecious
stones were mounted on the shoulder straps and were inscribed with
twelve names—the names of the twelve tribes of Israel. So when the
high priest entered the Holy Place, he wore the tribal names of Israel on
his shoulders. It was as if he lifted the people onto his shoulders and
carried them into the presence of God.

Attached to the front of the ephod was a breastpiece made of fabric with twelve precious stones mounted on it, one for each of the twelve tribes of Israel, signifying that these people were precious to God. Fastened to the ephod with braided chains of gold, the stones were kept close to the priest's heart. So he carried God's people on his shoulders and close to his heart. He was not only to bear the people's burden on his shoulders but also to have their interests at heart. If you were an Israelite in those days, no matter what tribe you were in, when you saw the name of your tribe on the breastplate of the high priest, you could be sure that as he carried out his work before God in the tabernacle, he was doing that work on your behalf.

The high priest also wore a robe made of blue or violet, a seamless garment that went under the ephod and hung down at least to the knees, that had fringe decorated with pomegranates and little bells that made a tinkling sound whenever the high priest moved. He wore a turban of fine linen with a gold plate affixed to the front that was engraved with the words "Holy to the LORD" signifying that he and the people he represented before God were set apart by God and to God to be a holy nation.

The Priest's Consecration

Before the priest could be clothed in these holy garments and enter into God's presence, he had to be consecrated for service by being washed and anointed and by offering sacrifices.

> You shall bring Aaron and his sons to the entrance of the tent of meeting and wash them with water. (Ex. 29:4)

So, first, he was washed with water, which was symbolic of spiritual purification.

> Then you shall take the garments, and put on Aaron the coat and the robe of the ephod, and the ephod, and the breastpiece, and gird him with the skillfully woven band of the ephod. And you shall set the turban on his head and put the holy crown on the turban. (Ex. 29:5–6)

Once they were washed, Aaron and the other priests were dressed in the holy garments designed for them by God himself. Then the high priest was anointed with oil, which indicated he was chosen by God for a special task:

> You shall take the anointing oil and pour it on his head and anoint him. (Ex. 29:7)

This special blend of oil and spices prepared specifically for this occasion was poured over the high priest's head and ran down onto his garments. It was a visual representation of God pouring out his Spirit on the man, empowering him for his holy duties.

At this point, the priests looked good, but there was a significant gap between their outward appearance in holy, glorious, and beautiful garments, and their inward spiritual condition, which was unholy and unclean. Something had to be done about their guilt, so sacrifices were made—three kinds of sacrifices spread out over seven days. The sin offering showed that the priests needed to have their sins forgiven just like everyone else. The burnt offering, which was completely consumed by fire, symbolized their need for total dedication to God. And the third sacrifice, the blood sacrifice, sanctified the priests for their sacred duties.

> You shall take the other ram, and Aaron and his sons shall lay their hands on the head of the ram, and you shall kill the ram and take part of its blood and put it on the tip of the right ear of Aaron and on the tips of the right ears of his sons, and on the thumbs of their right hands and on the great toes of their right feet, and throw the rest of the blood against the sides of the altar. (Ex. 29:19–20)

The blood was applied to the lobe of the priest's ear, indicating that what he heard was to be devoted to God, and then to his thumb, indicating that what he did was to be done in dedication to the Lord, and then to his big toe, indicating that all of his work and walk was to be dedicated to the Lord. The priests belonged to God from head to toe. Their thoughts, words, and activity were to be all for God.

Finally, Aaron and his sons ate an ordination meal, sharing the remainder of the ram, the ram of ordination; the second ram; and finally three types of bread, which had been put in the basket.

The Priests' Commission

Then God commissioned the priests, detailing their ongoing daily duties:

> Now this is what you shall offer on the altar: two lambs a year old day by day regularly. One lamb you shall offer in the morning, and the other lamb you shall offer at twilight. . . . It shall be a regular burnt offering throughout your generations at the entrance of the tent of meeting before the LORD, where I will meet with you, to speak to you there. There I will meet with the people of Israel, and it shall be sanctified by my glory. (Ex. 29:38–39, 42–43)

The heart of the daily worship at the tabernacle, and later the temple, was perpetual blood sacrifice. If you grew up observing the daily activity of the priests, the daily slitting of the throats of animals would have impressed upon you that sin has consequence, and the consequence is death. You could not have missed the message that the sacrifice of an innocent substitute was necessary to obtain forgiveness and approach God. And you would have been grateful that there was a priest offering sacrifices and prayers on your behalf, and instructing you in the truths of God. Aaron was told, "You are to distinguish between the holy and the common, and between the unclean and the clean, and you are to teach the people of Israel all the statutes that the Lord has spoken to them by Moses" (Lev. 10:10–11). The priest had the day-to-day responsibility to offer sacrifice as well as to instruct God's people in the law and ways of God.

So the priest was a mediator, saying on behalf of God's people to God, "Will you accept me on the basis of this blood sacrifice?" And likewise, the priest said on behalf of God to his people: "Will you be holy?"

The Priests' Corruption

Leviticus 8 and 9 tell us about the day Aaron and his sons were consecrated, and at the end of chapter 9 we read:

> Then Aaron lifted up his hands toward the people and blessed them,
> and he came down from offering the sin offering and the burnt offer-
> ing and the peace offerings. And Moses and Aaron went into the tent of
> meeting, and when they came out they blessed the people, and the glory
> of the LORD appeared to all the people. And fire came out from before
> the LORD and consumed the burnt offering and the pieces of fat on the
> altar, and when all the people saw it, they shouted and fell on their faces.
> (vv. 22–24)

This is a glorious beginning to the Levitical priesthood. But it was
shortlived. When we turn the page to Leviticus 10 we read:

> Now Nadab and Abihu, the sons of Aaron, each took his censer and put
> fire in it and laid incense on it and offered unauthorized fire before the
> LORD, which he had not commanded them. And fire came out from before
> the LORD and consumed them, and they died before the LORD. (vv. 1–2)

As modern readers we're not sure what to make of this. Honestly, at
first blush this penalty seems rather harsh for such a small infraction.
We want to give these two guys the benefit of the doubt that they were
compelled by good instincts. But we must remember that every detail
about the priest and his service to God in the tabernacle was designed
by God. God was setting down a pattern that would point to the one who
would fulfill everything the priesthood and tabernacle were created to
display, so strict adherence was essential. Nadab and Abihu decided to
offer worship according to their preference rather than according to
God's clear instruction.

So, from the very outset, the Aaronic priesthood was shown to be
inadequate. It was like a newly christened ship that sank the moment
it hit the water. And it didn't really improve over time. The sad reality
is that none of Israel's high priests ever lived up to what God intended
for those he set apart to serve him in his temple. As we continue reading through the history of Israel in the Old Testament, we discover that,
as much as anything else, it was the corruption of the priests that led
Israel into exile, and eventually the priesthood broke down altogether.
In 2 Chronicles 36:14 we read that "all the leaders of the priests and
the people became more and more unfaithful. They followed all the

pagan practices of the surrounding nations, desecrating the Temple of the LORD that had been consecrated in Jerusalem" (NLT). Hosea prophesied that "the children of Israel shall dwell many days without king or prince, without sacrifice or pillar, without ephod or household gods" (Hos. 3:4). The day would come when, because of Israel's rebellion, there would be no one to wear the ephod, no one to bear the tribal names before God, no one to offer sacrifice for sins.

The priests that God had called and clothed and consecrated and commissioned became completely corrupt. They refused to listen to God's word; they had no heart for glorifying God, no interest in the ways of God. They used their position to enrich themselves, and led those they were responsible to care for astray. Clearly a better priest was needed—a priest who would love God's word and walk in God's ways and would faithfully teach and lead God's people. This would be the priest God promised when he said to Eli, "I will raise up for myself a faithful priest, who shall do according to what is in my heart and in my mind" (1 Sam. 2:35). Surely this is the priest we need.

The Priest We Need

If you had lived in the days of Jesus and were looking for the priest that God had promised to raise up for himself, you likely would have been quite sure that Jesus could not be that priest. Everyone knew that priests came only from the tribe of Levi, and Jesus was from the tribe of Judah. What the people of Jesus's day did not understand was that Jesus did not come to fit into the established system of priestly ministry and simply improve upon it. Jesus came to put an end to that earthly priestly system and become, as the writer of Hebrews calls him, our "great high priest" (Heb. 4:14). Jesus was a priest because of who he is, not because of the family he came from.

The writer of the book of Hebrews leaned heavily on the people's understanding of the Old Testament priesthood as he wrote to convince them of the superiority of Jesus. Clearly the Old Testament priesthood provided them with a category that would help them to understand the ministry of Christ, who, like the priests in the Old Testament, was called by God himself, clothed in holiness, consecrated, and commissioned to serve God's people, yet was far superior to any of the priests in the Aaronic order.

Our Great High Priest Called

The writer of Hebrews says of the priesthood:

> No one takes this honor for himself, but only when called by God, just as Aaron was. So also Christ did not exalt himself to be made a high priest, but was appointed by him who said to him, . . . "You are a priest forever, after the order of Melchizedek." (Heb. 5:4–6)

The writer of Hebrews quotes Psalm 110, a psalm about the priest God promised to send who, rather than being "after the order of" or, we might say, "along the lines of" Aaron, would be "along the lines of" Melchizedek. Who was Melchizadek and what was the "order of Melchizedek"? Melchizedek was a priest of God who was appointed by God and respected by Abraham hundreds of years before Aaron was appointed as a priest. So Jesus was not a priest by human ancestry, like the Aaronic priests, but a priest by divine appointment, like Melchizedek.

Our Great High Priest Clothed

Jesus was robed in royal righteousness and had written across every aspect of his life, "Holy to the Lord."

Jesus was also clothed as a priest, just as Aaron was. Certainly he did not wear the ornate ephod, bejeweled breastpiece, and "Holy to the Lord" headpiece. These were merely outer garments the priests wore that were designed to point to him who was truly holy, glorious, and beautiful through and through in his person. Jesus was robed in royal righteousness and had written across every aspect of his life, "Holy to the Lord."

There was one incident recorded in John's Gospel, however, in which his clothing spoke to his priesthood. John writes that the Roman soldiers arrayed Jesus in a purple robe and that

> when the soldiers had crucified Jesus, they took his garments and divided them into four parts, one part for each soldier; also his tunic. But the tunic was seamless, woven in one piece from top to bottom. (John 19:23)

Why would John include this detail except that he is helping us see Jesus's identity as priest? By mentioning the seamless robe, which is what the priests uniquely wore, John was pointing to the reality that as Jesus hung on the cross, he was doing the high-priestly work of bearing our sin and offering sacrifice. We were being carried on his shoulders as he took our sin upon himself in order to deal with it in the presence of God. It was our great need for salvation that was close to his heart. In doing his greatest priestly work, our Great High Priest hung not in ornamental finery but in naked glory—glory that emanated from who he is, not from what he wore.

Our Great High Priest Consecrated

Just as washing with water was the first step in the ordination of an Aaronic priest, so Jesus was washed when he entered the Jordan River to be baptized. This washing took place not because he was unclean, but so that he could be set apart as a priest for sinners. His anointing also took place at his baptism. Luke records that when Jesus had been baptized and was praying, the heavens were opened and he saw the Spirit of God descending like a dove and settling on him (Luke 3:21–22). While the oil poured over the priests in the Old Testament was symbolic of the Spirit's setting them apart for God's service, Jesus was anointed with the Spirit himself. This was God anointing his Great High Priest, so that Jesus could one day open the scroll of Isaiah in the temple and read: "The Spirit of the Lord is upon me, because he has anointed me" (Luke 4:18).

In addition to being washed with water and anointed with oil, Aaron and his sons offered a series of sacrifices for their sins. Jesus, too, offered a sacrifice for sin, a singular sacrifice that was wholly sufficient to atone for the sins of all God's people. This sacrifice wasn't for his own sin, but for ours. And it wasn't the blood of innocent animals that was shed, but that of the innocent Son.

For it was indeed fitting that we should have such a high priest, holy, innocent, unstained, separated from sinners, and exalted above the heavens. He has no need, like those high priests, to offer sacrifices daily, first for his own sins and then for those of the people, since he did this once for all when he offered up himself. (Heb. 7:26–27)

Our Great High Priest Commissioned

Aaron and his sons were commissioned to offer sacrifices, to intercede for the people, to lead in the worship of God, to distinguish between what was clean and unclean, and to teach the people the truths of God. Likewise Jesus, our Great High Priest, was commissioned to this same service, but he accomplished it in far greater ways than any Aaronic priest.

∼ When Jesus, our Great High Priest, stood up and taught the people, "the crowds were astonished at his teaching, for he was teaching them as one who had authority, and not as their scribes" (Matt. 7:28–29).

∼ Jesus taught what truly made a person clean and unclean saying, "'Do you not see that whatever goes into a person from outside cannot defile him, since it enters not his heart but his stomach, and is expelled?' (Thus he declared all foods clean.) And he said, 'What comes out of a person is what defiles him'" (Mark 7:18–20).

∼ Jesus led the people in worship, receiving to himself the worship reserved for God alone. In fact when the Pharisees told Jesus he ought to rebuke a multitude of people who cried out as he entered the city, "Blessed is the King who comes in the name of the Lord!" Jesus said, "I tell you, if these were silent, the very stones would cry out" (Luke 19:38–40).

∼ And just as Aaron and his sons interceded for the people of God, pronouncing on them God's intention to bless them (Num. 6:22–27) and also intervening between God and the people when they deserved judgment (Numbers 16), so did Christ intercede for the people of God. Jesus has ascended into heaven, where he is, even now, continuing to intercede for us as our Great High Priest. He serves as our heavenly worship leader (Heb. 2:12) and prays for our sanctification (John 17:17).

Our Great High Priest Corrupted ?

So we see that just as the Aaronic priests were called, clothed, conse-crated, and commissioned, so was Jesus. Our Great High Priest was also corrupted. But not in the same way the Aaronic priests became corrupt. It was not his own sin—his own greed or idolatry or apathy toward the things of God—that corrupted him. It was ours. He who was infinitely holy, glorious, and beautiful became marred, not with his own compro-mise or shallowness or disfigurement of sin, but with ours. He who was singularly beautiful became, on the cross, "as one from whom men hide their faces. . . . He poured out his soul to death . . . ; yet he bore the sin of many, and makes intercession for the transgressors" (Isa. 53:3, 12).

Our Great High Priest Continues

There is one key way, however, in which Jesus was not at all like the Old Testament priests.

> The former priests were many in number, because they were prevented by death from continuing in office, but he holds his priesthood perma-nently, because he continues forever. (Heb. 7:23–24)

Whereas the Aaronic priests died, Jesus will never die. Forever, he will be our Great High Priest. He "always lives to make intercession" for us (Heb. 7:25). He will always be securing our place before God and sus-taining our life for God. For all eternity he will be saving us.

In the Old Testament tabernacle and temple, only the high priest could go anywhere near the throne room of God in the Most Holy Place, and only once a year. But now, all those who belong to Christ are invited in, based not on our inherent adequacy but on our neediness. So what are we to do?

> Let us then with confidence draw near to the throne of grace, that we may receive mercy and find grace to help in time of need. (Heb. 4:16)

To be a Christian is not merely to have Jesus as your example to follow; it is to have Jesus as your priest to intercede for you before a holy God, your mediator to intervene in what would otherwise be a hopeless situation, your advocate who asks the Father to treat you not as you deserve but as he deserves.

Do you need to humbly acknowledge your need for this priest? You can have all the suspicion you'd like about the religious establishment, but you simply cannot ignore your desperate need for this priest. He who is clothed in holiness, glory, and beauty will represent you before God so that when God looks at you, he will see only absolute holiness, radiant glory, and rapturous beauty. When Jesus is your priest, you can enter in the very throne room of God with great confidence—confidence that you will find just what you need when you need it—mercy for your past failures and grace for your present and future needs. You will be accepted and loved and provided for. Your Great High Priest has gone before you to see that it is so.

Looking Forward

A Kingdom of Priests

John's "revelation of Jesus Christ" (Rev. 1:1) begins with his vision of Jesus "clothed with a long robe and with a golden sash around his chest" (Rev. 1:13). This clothing, which is similar to the clothing the high priest in the Old Testament temple wore, tells us that into eternity Jesus remains our Great High Priest.

John praises him "who loves us and has freed us from our sins by his blood and made us a kingdom, priests to his God and Father" (Rev. 1:5–6). So we also immediately see that Jesus is not the only priest revealed in Revelation. Throughout Revelation we see that what God intended all along—for the people of God to be a kingdom of priests (Ex. 19:6) representing him and displaying his glory throughout all of his creation—has come to full fruition. All of those who have been purchased by the blood of Christ are priests in the eternal kingdom of God. They do not come only from the Israelite tribe of Levi, like the Old Testament priests, but "from every tribe and language and people and nation" and have been made into "a kingdom and priests to our God" (Rev. 5:9–10). Christ calls people of any and all nationalities and races and languages into his holy eternal priesthood.

The priests in this priesthood are clothed just as the Old Testament priests were clothed. Throughout Revelation, all of the people of God, not just a select few, are clothed in white (3:5, 18; 4:4; 6:11; 7:9, 13) and linen (18:2, 16; 19:8, 14). This purity is not put on as a garment over an otherwise sinful self; it is an inner purity made possible by being washed by the blood of the Lamb (Rev. 7:14). These priests do not enter the Most Holy Place once a year, but all of the earth will have become God's throne room, where all "will see his face, and his name will be on their foreheads" (Rev. 22:4). "Holy to the Lord" is not merely an ornament on a turban that we will put on and take off. Our belonging and beauty will be written into our very being.

The same precious gems that once decorated Eden (Gen. 2:12) and later the priest's garments will have become the beautiful foundation of the eternal city of God, marking it as paradise restored. Access to the tree of life will no longer be barred, but this tree will bring healing to the nations (Rev. 22:2). By this we see that God's wardrobe for his Old

Testament priests was really part of God's plan, stretching from creation to glory.

> And the wall of the city had twelve foundations, and on them were the twelve names of the twelve apostles of the Lamb. . . . The wall was built of jasper, while the city was pure gold, like clear glass. The foundations of the wall of the city were adorned with every kind of jewel. The first was jasper, the second sapphire, the third agate, the fourth emerald, the fifth onyx, the sixth carnelian, the seventh chrysolite, the eighth beryl, the ninth topaz, the tenth chrysoprase, the eleventh jacinth, the twelfth amethyst. (Rev. 21:14, 18–20)

Rather than the names of the twelve tribes engraved upon stones on the priest's shoulders and breastpiece, here the names of the Lamb's apostles are engraved on the city's foundation. God's people are defined not by descent from Israel but by fidelity to the gospel as passed on by the apostles.

There is no need for this priesthood to offer sacrifices, because on the throne, at the center, stands the Lamb "as though it had been slain" (Rev. 5:6). Into eternity, the once-for-all sacrifice of our Great High Priest will still be the source of celebration and the grounds of worship for all of God's kingdom of priests.

The Priesthood

Getting the Discussion Going

1. When it is suggested to you that you need a priest, do you easily agree or do you find yourself challenging the suggestion? Why?

I associate priests w/ catholic priests

Getting to the Heart of It

2. Through your study this week, what have you come to see as reasons that God ordained the Old Testament priesthood? *To go before the multitudes and represent them to God.*

3. One thing we are learning, and will continue to see as we work our way through the writings of Moses, is that details that might seem tedious to us are actually quite significant. How is that the case in the detailed instructions God gave regarding the clothing for the priests and high priest? *They match the tabernacle, represent Jesus to God.*

4. Look back at Exodus 28:12, 29, and 38. What key concept was being communicated by the high priest's clothing, and why is this significant? *Aaron was carrying representations of the tribe of Israel to God.*

5. How does an understanding of the ordination of the priests as outlined in Exodus 29 help us to understand why Jesus was baptized, since we know he was not a sinner who needed to be cleansed? *It was the accepted manner and & fulfilled prophesy*

6. Look back at question 12 in the Personal Bible Study, in which you compared aspects of the Old Testament priesthood to the priesthood of

Jesus from Hebrews. Would several of you share an aspect of his superior priesthood that has particular meaning to you? In other words, what difference does it make that we are represented by Jesus, our Great High Priest, rather than by an Old Testament–era priest?

He took it all, one time, and permanently

7. In two places in Hebrews, the "so what?" of having Jesus as our priest is emphasized, telling us that because he is our priest we can "with confidence draw near to the throne of grace, that we may receive mercy and find grace to help in time of need" (4:16), and we can "draw near with a true heart in full assurance of faith" (10:22). Certainly the Israelites knew what it was like to be unable to "draw near" to God in the temple. What do you think it means in very tangible terms to draw near to God? What do you think it means to do this with confidence?

Getting Personal

8. Do you find it difficult or easy to believe that Jesus represents you before God and carries your needs and concerns close to his heart when he does? Do you think Christ can be trusted to intercede for you in the way you most need it? *Yes, Jesus knows my heart and my needs.*

Getting How It Fits into the Big Picture

9. Throughout this study, we are seeking to grasp how the passage we're studying fits into the bigger story of God's plan for redemption. What did you see in the "Looking Forward" section that helps you to see how our Great High Priest and we, as a kingdom of priests, will minister before God into eternity?

Christ calls people from all nationalities into his priesthood.

Sacrifice and Sanctification

Leviticus

Personal Bible Study

Leviticus

1. Leviticus 1–7 contains instructions God gave to Moses regarding five offerings or sacrifices to be offered at the tabernacle. Read or skim Leviticus 1–7, noting a detail or two that seems significant to you following the example provided.

Offerings	*Observations*
Burnt offering (Leviticus 1)	*Cattle, sheep, goats, or birds without blemish* *Offerer put hands on animal* *Blood poured on altar sides* *Completely consumed by fire*
Grain offering (Leviticus 2)	
Peace offering (Leviticus 3)	
Sin offering (Lev. 4:1–5:13)	
Guilt offering (Lev. 5:14–6:7)	

We might, at first, wonder why we need to study the details of these sacrifices, since we know that Christ put an end to the sacrificial system by fulfilling it. But studying Leviticus helps us to see the breadth and fullness of what Christ did for us in offering himself as a sacrifice for sin. In fact, without Leviticus we would not understand what the New Testament means when it says that Christ was a sacrifice for sin.

2. Each of the sacrifices outlined in Leviticus 1–7 tells us something unique about the sacrifice of Christ. Look up the following New Testament passages and compose a statement about Christ that compares or contrasts the sacrifice prescribed in Leviticus with the sacrifice of Christ.

Offering	Fulfilled by Christ
Burnt offering (propitiation)	1 Pet. 1:18–19 *Just as the burnt offering that atoned for our sin was a lamb without blemish, so was Jesus, our ransom, without blemish.* Rom. 3:23–26 *While the burnt offering satisfied God's anger toward some sin, the sacrifice of Jesus satisfied his wrath against all of our sin.*
Grain offering (dedication)	John 6:48–51
Peace offering (fellowship)	Eph. 2:13–14
Sin offering (purification)	Heb. 1:3 Heb. 13:11–12
Guilt offering (restitution)	Isa. 53:10 Phil. 3:9

We might think that people in the Old Testament era were saved by offering animal sacrifices (which would be works) and that we are saved by faith in Christ. But it is important for us to remember that people in the Old Testament times were saved in the same way we are saved. Here is how Vern Poythress explains it in his book *The Shadow of Christ in the Law of Moses*:

> As they looked ahead through the shadows, longing for something better, they took hold on the promises of God that He would send the Messiah. The promises were given not only verbally but symbolically, through the very organization of the tabernacle and its sacrifices. In pictorial form God was saying, as it were, "Look at My provisions for you. This is how I will redeem you and bring you into My presence. But look again, and you will see that it is all an earthly symbol of something better. Don't rely on it as if it were the end. Trust Me to save you fully when I fully accomplish My plans." Israelites had genuine communion with God when they responded to what He was saying in the tabernacle. They trusted in the Messiah, without knowing all the details of how fulfillment would finally come. And so they were saved, and they received forgiveness, even before the Messiah came. The animal sacrifices in themselves did not bring forgiveness, but Christ did as He met with them through the symbolism of the sacrifices.[1]

3. How are both Old Testament era saints and New Testament era saints saved, according to Romans 3:25–26?

The writer of Hebrews affirms that it was God's plan all along for the Old Testament sacrifices to point to the sacrifice of Christ and then fade away: "We have been sanctified through the offering of the body of Jesus Christ once for all. . . . Where there is forgiveness of these, there is no longer any offering for sin" (Heb. 10:10, 18). It isn't that the animal sacrifices failed in their divinely appointed function. They were not plan A that didn't work. They served their function, which was to serve as a symbol of the sacrifice God would accept; the sacrifices were not the reality of it. And once the reality came, there was absolutely no further need for the symbol.

But this does not mean that the sacrificial laws outlined in Leviticus no longer apply to God's people. They still apply because God still demands an adequate sacrifice for our sins. But we observe those laws today not by offering animals according to the Mosaic system but rather by trusting Christ as our sufficient sacrifice.

4. Read through the biblical statements about the Levitical sacrifices in the left column below and write a statement in the right column that describes the superiority of the sacrifice of Christ.

Old Testament Animal Sacrifices	Sacrifice of Christ
Sacrifices could not perfect the conscience of the worshiper but dealt only with regulations. (Heb. 9:9–10)	Heb. 9:14
The high priests entered the holy places every year with the blood of a sacrificed animal. (Heb. 9:25)	Heb. 9:26
The law was a shadow of good things to come. (Heb. 10:1)	Heb. 10:1
Continual sacrifices could never make perfect those who drew near. (Heb. 10:1)	Heb. 10:14
The animal sacrifices reminded people of sin but couldn't take away sin. (Heb. 10:3–4)	Heb. 10:17

Leviticus 11–15 records purity laws defining what is clean and unclean. Clean does not equal sinless, and unclean does not equal sinful. For example, if someone had died and you were preparing the corpse for burial, that would make you unclean. It wasn't wrong or sinful to touch the person's body, but it did make you ceremonially

unclean. You would need to take certain measures to remedy your ceremonial uncleanness. Similarly, other things that we regard as good and right, such as sexual intercourse in marriage, menstruation, and childbirth, all made you unclean, but that did not mean that they were sin. "Uncleanness indicated something that deviated from what is normal."[2]

The purity laws can't be explained in terms of general wisdom for hygiene, sanitation, and gastronomic health. They focus attention on God's act of separating clean Israel from the unclean nations. They also serve to demonstrate the effects of sin on our bodies and the environment we live in. To make sense of Leviticus 11–15, we have to have firm in our minds the events of Genesis 3, which tell us how humanity and all of creation went from being perfectly good to thoroughly broken, from clean to unclean. We also need to remember that along with the curse God pronounced that day in the garden came the promise of redemption and renewal—the seed of the woman would one day crush the head of the Serpent. That happened when Christ rose from the grave, conquering sin, death, and the Devil. And the day is coming when we will live in bodies and an environment that will be perfectly restored and even better than it once was in the garden. What is now imperfect and unclean will become perfectly clean. So, as we read the purification laws in Leviticus, rather than seeing them as random or even ridiculous, we can see that God is helping us to get a picture of the impact sin has had on us and the world we live in and his intentions to make all things new (Rev. 21:5).

5. Read or skim Leviticus 11–15, noting how the content is reflected in the middle column of the chart below. Then look up the reference in the third column and write down the biblical phrase from the passage that states how each aspect of our unclean world will be cleansed when Christ returns.

Clean at Eden	Declared Unclean in Leviticus	Cleansed at the Consummation
All of the animals in Eden ate green plants for food. (Gen. 1:30)	Leviticus 11: Primarily, animals that are predators and feed on the death of another animal since the fall are unclean.	Isa. 11:6
Childbearing, which should have brought only pleasure, was made painful by the curse. (Gen. 3:16)	Leviticus 12: The pain of childbirth since the fall, illustrated by the blood loss that accompanies it, made a woman unclean.	Rev. 21:4
Adam and Eve went from abundant life and health to impending death. (Gen. 3:19)	Leviticus 13, 15: Chronic skin diseases and bodily discharges that demonstrate the systemic nature of death and dysfunction in our physical bodies caused by the fall made a person unclean.	Rev. 21:4
All that God had made was perfect, with no deformity or decay. (Gen. 1:31)	Leviticus 14: Mold and mildew in the home were indicators of the decaying nature of the world since the fall and therefore were unclean.	Rev. 21:27 Rev. 22:3

When I Grow Up, I Want to Be . . .

"What do you want to be when you grow up?," we like to ask little children. And they give us the name of a profession that seems interesting or exciting. "What are you studying?," we ask those same kids when they go off to college. They tell us their major, and we comment on what we've observed about that profession. However, if you ask most mothers what they want for their child, they likely won't name a particular profession or pursuit. More likely they will say, "I don't really care what he does; I just want him to be happy."

Imagine a little child saying, "When I grow up I want to be holy," or a college student saying, "I'm studying holiness because I want to live a holy life." Imagine a mom saying, "I don't really care what she does; I just want her to be holy." It sounds a little strange to us, doesn't it? Perhaps that's because we don't see holiness as all that important or interesting. Or perhaps we don't really think it is possible. Yet if we were to ask God what he wants most for us, his children, surely he would say, as he has already said, "Be holy, for I am holy." (Lev. 11:44).

For most of us, there is a part of us that wants to say in response, "Yeah, like that could happen." We want to tell God, "I'm sorry, but you have set the bar too high. Couldn't you just settle for me being a really nice person, trying really hard to be good? Couldn't you just be like other parents and simply want me to be happy? Because I think I know how to pursue happiness. But holiness? I don't know about that." But God does not back down. God told Moses:

Speak to all the congregation of the people of Israel and say to them, You shall be holy, for I the LORD your God am holy. (Lev. 19:2)

Knowing that your Father wants you to be holy, as he is, do you find within yourself any desire to be holy? Perhaps we need to ask ourselves, Have I come to the place that, more than merely being happy, what I really want is to be holy? Do I really believe that holiness is what will make me truly and eternally happy?

If we're really interested in holiness, we're going to want to turn to the book of the Bible that is all about holiness. But it is a book most of us have likely avoided—the book of Leviticus. Every year when we've had such good intentions of reading through the Bible, around mid-February, when we get to Leviticus, we have started running out of steam. Let's be honest: we find Leviticus boring—chapter after chapter of slaughter this and sacrifice that, wave this and wash that, eat this and don't eat that. Leviticus can seem redundant, remote, and, frankly, irrelevant. It's also very bloody—drain the blood, pour the blood, sprinkle the blood—which feels primitive. We don't sacrifice animals in the temple anymore, so, when we read it, we want to ask the same question our kids ask when they're studying algebra: "Do I really need to know this? How am I ever going to use this in real life?"

The big-picture message of Leviticus is this: God is holy. We hear that and want to say, "Yeah, I get that." We hear one sermon on the holiness of God and think, *What's next?* Of course, this reveals that we have not yet begun to grasp the infinite holiness of God. The primary meaning of the word *holy* is "separate." It comes from an ancient word that means "to cut" or "to separate." To say that something is "holy" meant that it was a cut above. So when the Bible calls God "holy," it means primarily that God is a cut above—in fact, so far above and beyond us that he seems almost totally foreign to us.[3] When we say that God is "holy," we also mean that his character is unimpeachable, that he cannot be charged with any wrong."[4] Throughout the Bible we read that God is not just holy but that he is "holy, holy, holy," which means he is holy to an infinite degree. Now we're starting to see that grasping the holiness of God is not going to be as simple as we might have thought.

It might help us to do a quick review of where we've been thus far in Scripture, which has brought us to this revelation of God's holiness in Leviticus. In Exodus we witnessed God delivering his people out of slavery in Egypt for the very purpose that they might worship him and become "a kingdom of priests and a holy nation" (Ex. 19:6). He made clear to the Israelites that he would be their God and they would be his people, separated from evil and sin, and devoted to him. And because he did not want this to be a long-distance relationship, he instructed his people to build a tent in which he would live, in the center of their camp. At the end of Exodus we read that the very presence of God descended to dwell in that tent. He who is infinitely holy came down to live among people who were not holy.

The book of Leviticus picks up where Exodus left off, saying that "the LORD called Moses and spoke to him from the tent of meeting" (Lev. 1:1). What God said to Moses became the content of the book of Leviticus and provided, in practical terms, a "user's manual" for the tabernacle so that the people of God would know how to approach God and interact with him. God had come to dwell amongst his people, and he wanted them to know him by entering into an experiential understanding of his holiness. For God's people to really "get" God will require more than simply giving them the information, "I, the Lord your God, am holy." To really know God is going to require that the reality of his holiness become a part of every aspect of their lives. Everywhere they turn and everything they do will need to serve as a lesson on God's infinite holiness.

At the same time, they are going to need to see God's holiness in stark contrast to their sinfulness. Once again, they need more than simply to be told that they are sinful. They need for the reality of their sinfulness to become unavoidable and undeniable. They need to experience it in a way that will engage all of their senses and their entire schedule. Perhaps as they understand the holiness of God and their sinfulness, they will see their need for a savior who will save them from their sin and make them acceptable to their holy God. That is the essence of the book of Leviticus.

Provision of Sacrifice

Lesson number one on God's holiness and the people's sinfulness was delivered in the form of instructions for offering sacrifices at the tabernacle. Now, today when we say that something was "a real sacrifice," rarely do we mean that blood was shed. For us, *sacrifice* means giving something up or taking something on that costs us a little money or comfort or convenience. *Sacrifice* in the Bible, however, is the bloody reality of a bellowing animal being butchered on an altar. Imagine the sensory overload of this experience—the violent resistance of the animal, the spurting of blood, the feel of pulling the animal apart, the smell of its burning flesh and bones. Imagine the emotional and spiritual impact of offering this sacrifice, knowing that it was your sin that made this death necessary. And imagine the frustration in knowing that you'll be back tomorrow or next week because you will sin again.

In Leviticus chapters 1–7 we find detailed instructions for offering sacrifices—five regular offerings that will invade all of the Israelites' senses, informing their minds and engaging their hearts in regard to the seriousness of sin as well as the possibility and provision of a substitute. Why should we study these details of the various sacrifices in Leviticus, since we are no longer required to offer sacrifices? We should do so because they help us to understand *how* the work of Christ saves people like us from our sin. Each of the sacrifices points to a different aspect of Christ's sacrifice of himself.

The burnt offering was the most important sacrifice at most Israelite festivals and was offered once every morning and once every evening. Bringing the burnt offering was a very personal experience, intended most certainly to make an impression on the Israelite offering his sacrifice:

> He shall lay his hand on the head of the burnt offering, and it shall be accepted for him to make atonement for him. Then he shall kill the bull before the LORD, and Aaron's sons the priests shall bring the blood and throw the blood against the sides of the altar that is at the entrance of the tent of meeting. (Lev. 1:4–5)

To make atonement for his sin and to gain God's acceptance, the offerer identified himself with the animal by laying his hand on the animal's head. When the animal died, it died for the offerer's sins. Neither the offerer nor the priest ate any of the meat; it was all burned in the fire. This was sacrifice in its purest form—a valuable animal given up wholly to God.

Along with the burnt offering, offered twice each day, was the grain offering of fine flour, oil, frankincense, and salt, which expressed gratitude to God and served as a way of asking the Lord to remember the offerer with favor (Leviticus 2).

The fellowship or peace offering was more than a sacrifice; it was a festive meal. A bull, a sheep, or a goat was shared by the Lord, the priests, and the one who offered it (Leviticus 3). In fact, the worshiper was allowed to bring family and friends along to spend a couple of days enjoying the meat in the presence of God at the tabernacle. The act of the offering reminded the worshiper that the only way he had been able to come back into the fullness and joy of fellowship and communion with God was through the blood of a perfect substitutionary sacrifice.

Sin pollutes and corrupts. The sin offering was offered to cleanse away the filth of sin. In this offering, something unusual was done with the blood:

> The priest shall dip his finger in the blood and sprinkle part of the blood seven times before the LORD in front of the veil of the sanctuary. And the priest shall put some of the blood on the horns of the altar of fragrant incense before the LORD that is in the tent of meeting, and all the rest of the blood of the bull he shall pour out at the base of the altar of burnt offering that is at the entrance of the tent of meeting. (Lev. 4:6–7)

By using the blood of the animal in this way, God was demonstrating in dramatic fashion that it was the blood that atoned for Israel's sin. The blood cleansed the tabernacle, the priests, the people, and the land from the defilement caused by the sin of the people. There was blood on the veil, blood on the horns of the altar, and blood poured out. Everywhere the sinner looked was an unavoidable statement about the pervasive nature of sin and need for atonement.

The guilt offering asked for something beyond sacrifice; it required restitution. The guilty person had to confess his sin publicly, offer the blood sacrifice, and also make full restitution of what was defrauded, adding an additional 20 percent. Rather than a cheap or easy repentance, this dearly cost the person who sinned.

> *By offering these sacrifices in faith, the people of the Old Testament demonstrated their faith in Christ, the superior, once-for-all sacrifice, the Lamb of God who takes away the sin of the world.*

None of the animals offered in these sacrifices could, in themselves, take away a person's sin or truly pay the debt for sin. But by offering these sacrifices in faith, the people of the Old Testament demonstrated their faith in Christ, the superior, once-for-all sacrifice, the Lamb of God who takes away the sin of the world.

Principle of Substitution

The sacrificial provisions in Leviticus taught the Israelites that God can be approached with the blood of a worthy substitute. And while all of these sacrifices might seem like an unbearable burden to us, wouldn't you be relieved, as an Israelite, to know that, instead of paying the penalty for sin yourself, God would accept a substitute in your place?

Yes, there was certainly a cost to these sacrifices. Imagine the expense of taking the best animal in your herd down to the temple in Jerusalem just to be burnt up. That was the animal that would have produced the best offspring, and it wasn't easy to give up. Imagine the time burden, especially if you didn't live in Jerusalem. You would have to travel and find a place to stay. Imagine the emotional or spiritual burden as you made this trek, knowing that you would have to identify and confess your sin to the priest in offering your sacrifice. But also imagine the burden rolling away. When you slit that animal's throat and watched it burn, and the priest declared your sin forgiven, imagine the sense of relief you felt. You would think, *It should be me. I am the one who deserves to die. But this innocent animal has become my substitute. This animal has died so I can live.* This was good news.

Promise of Cleansing

If you were an ancient Israelite, Leviticus would have helped you to understand how the death penalty you deserved for your sin could be dealt with by a substitutionary sacrifice. It would also have helped you to grasp how God would make it possible for the Israelites, as sinful people, to approach a holy God and to be made holy as he is. To impress this upon his people, God set up a system of symbols so that everything in their ordinary lives was classified into one of three categories: holy, clean, or unclean.

But to grasp what God was intending to teach, we have to understand that Leviticus uses the language of *clean* and *unclean* differently than we do today. When we use these terms, we're usually talking about health or hygiene—about whether something is dirty and germ-infested or free of such contaminants. When our hands are clean, we don't want to dig down into the trashcan to get something, because we don't want them to get dirty. Or when we're covered with dirt from working in the yard, we don't want to sit down on the couch and get it dirty. But in Leviticus, rather than referring to health or hygiene, *holy*, *clean*, and *unclean* refer to ritual states or categories. What makes these categories hard for us to grasp is that many of the laws presented in Leviticus concerning cleanness and uncleanness don't offer an explicit rationale for why something or someone is clean or unclean. But the big-picture story of the Bible can help us to make sense of this. When we set the clean and unclean laws in the big story of the Bible—that God created everything clean and beautiful in the garden, that Adam and Eve's sin ruined that perfection, that Christ took the curse and uncleanness of the world upon himself, and that the day is coming when all of creation will be purified and made whole—what may have seemed random or ridiculous or even cruel becomes purposeful and powerful and precious.

The laws for clean and unclean begin in Leviticus 11 with what might seem at first like a random designation of animals that were unclean, animals that were clean, and animals that could be sacrificed (holy). The unclean animals were those that came into contact with carcasses, and, therefore, just as contact with a dead body made a person unclean, this contact made these animals unclean, according to the law.

The clean animals were those that "chew the cud" or were vegetarian, which is what all animals were in the garden of Eden. In chapter 12, we discover that a woman was unclean for a number of weeks after she had a baby, which is a very bloody experience. In chapter 13, we're told that chronic skin diseases—the kind of diseases that are not temporary but indicate something is wrong systemically—made one unclean. Similarly, we find in chapter 14 that mold and mildew exhibited in the walls of a house made a house unclean. And in chapter 15, we are told that any bodily discharge made a person temporarily unclean.

Do you see a pattern here of disease, decay, and death? And do you see that all of these disorders provide a graphic demonstration of the effects of the curse on all of humanity and the entirety of creation? Disease and decay are a major feature of living in a fallen and cursed creation. By selecting certain examples of disease and decay and labeling them unclean, we learn that all disease, decay, and death are unacceptable to the one who created heaven and earth and pronounced it good. "The Living God sees all these intruders into His wonderful creation and reassures us, through these laws, that one day he will certainly drive these squatters out."[5]

> *Leviticus is a living picture of God's rejection of the effects of sin on humanity and creation and his intention to one day set everything right.*

Food laws didn't have to do with a healthy diet or food safety. And the isolation and washing of those with diseases didn't have to do with preventing the spread of infectious diseases. Leviticus is not an ancient guidebook for a healthy diet and disease prevention, though many people have tried to reduce it to that. Leviticus is a living picture of God's rejection of the effects of sin on humanity and creation and his intention to one day set everything right. Every day, as you avoided what would make you unclean or dealt with what had made you unclean, it would be a reminder to you that the Lord had not forgotten how he made the world before human sin and that he will not forget his promise to make all things new.

Everything designated as unclean pointed out the effects of the curse of sin on this world. Animals fed on other animals only after the curse. Childbirth became painful and bloody only after the curse, and sexual relations between men and women became infected with sinful passions only after the curse. Bodies bled and developed disease only after the curse. Children were born with birth defects only after the curse. Mold and mildew, the visible evidence of decay, came into being only after the curse. So these things were unclean.

But God will not abandon our world to its uncleanness. He will make it clean. The way the world will become clean will be by the blood of a sacrifice sufficient to atone for the world's sin.

Are you beginning to see that all of the laws of Leviticus were a visual aid to present the gospel of Christ? And can you see what this system of symbols would have impressed upon you if you had lived every day working out its demands? Everything you ate, everything and everyone you touched, and everything you did had to be run through the grid of clean and unclean. You would have known that God was interested in your whole life, not just your religious activity. You would have known that what is holy cannot and must not come in contact with what is unclean, which would have motivated you to reject the unclean lifestyle of the Canaanites around you. You also would have had hope knowing that things that were unclean could become clean. A person with a skin disease or discharge could become clean by offering the appropriate sacrifice and ceremonial washing. The priest and the instruments he used in the tabernacle could be consecrated, or be made "holy to the Lord," by the sprinkling of the blood of an acceptable sacrifice. And this would have made it possible for you to put your faith in the sacrifice to which all of the animals slaughtered on Israelite altars pointed, believing that his blood would not only cleanse you but make you holy and acceptable to God.

Disparity of Conduct

"By constantly calling the Israelites to *ritual* purity in all aspects of life, the Lord was reminding them of their need for . . . seeking after *moral* purity in all aspects of life."[6] He intended that they live in such a way that would set them apart from all of the people around them who had no desire to reflect God's holy nature—they would be distinct, distinguishable, and different from the nations, for the sake of the nations. Having this holy God as their god placed a claim on their lives that would make a difference in what they would and wouldn't do.

> You shall therefore keep all my statutes and all my rules and do them, that the land where I am bringing you to live may not vomit you out. And you shall not walk in the customs of the nation that I am driving out before you, for they did all these things, and therefore I detested them. . . . You shall be holy to me, for I the Lord am holy and have separated you from the peoples, that you should be mine. (Lev. 20:22–23, 26)

The Egyptians who had enslaved the Israelites lived lives that reflected the gods they worshiped. The Canaanites who surrounded the Israelites lived in accord with the gods they worshiped. Likewise, the one true God, who is holy, holy, holy, said to his people that their lives should reflect the innate quality of the God they served. They should be uncontaminated by the ways of the world around them, unimpeachable in character, exquisite in beauty, and perfect in love like their God.

And it is the same for us. Our lives should reflect the holiness of the God we serve. And so I have to ask you: does your belonging to Christ make a difference in what you will or will not do? Do you have a longing for holiness—for Christlikeness—that compels you to draw the line where many of those around you really have no lines? Where have you drawn the line in what you will let your eyes see and not see, what you will consume and reject, and what you will walk away from and walk toward? I'm not just talking about moral lines or setting yourself apart *from* the world. I'm also asking about your being set apart *to* the Lord. Does your longing to be holy to the Lord have any impact on your Saturday night and Sunday morning schedule so that you will be prepared, body and soul, to worship on the Lord's Day? Does your willingness to be different mean that your Facebook updates and photos reflect an innate desire to know and be pleasing to God in a way that is quite different from that of your unbelieving friends? Or are your life and calendar, your priorities and passions, really pretty much the same as those around you who do not belong to Christ—but with a little church activity added in?

If you belong to God through the saving work of Jesus Christ, are you being made holy by the ongoing sanctifying work of Christ through the Word of God? If you have been cleansed by the blood of Christ, are you now living a clean life? This is the very purpose for which God has poured out his grace on you—to empower you for your pursuit of holiness.

> For the grace of God has appeared, bringing salvation for all people, training us to renounce ungodliness and worldly passions, and to live self-controlled, upright, and godly lives in the present age, waiting for our blessed hope, the appearing of the glory of our great God and Savior Jesus Christ, who gave himself for us to redeem us from all lawlessness and to purify for himself a people for his own possession who are zealous for good works. (Titus 2:11–14)

Leviticus showed the people of God what it was going to mean to live with a holy God in their midst and what it was going to take to be able to approach him. But while Leviticus provided a good start, it did not provide the whole picture. "The only reason we do not have to keep every detail of the God-given revelation of the book of Leviticus is *not* that we live in a modern world and that was a primitive age. It's that what Jesus Christ has done is so breathtakingly superior and sufficient, these regulations have become unnecessary."[7] Our pursuit of holiness centers not on what we touch or what we eat, but on whom we are resting for our righteousness.

But we must read and understand Leviticus even though we are not required to follow all of its regulations, because the more we understand about what Christ has replaced, surpassed, and fulfilled, the deeper and sweeter our love for and worship of him becomes. Every sacrifice and sanctification law in Leviticus reveals to us the beauty of Christ from yet another angle.

Perfection in Holiness

The people of the Old Testament looked forward to one who would be completely holy in a way they never could be, which is why so much excitement surrounded that day when, as Luke recounts it, the angel announced to the virgin Mary, "The Holy Spirit will come upon you, and the power of the Most High will overshadow you. Therefore the child to be born will be called holy—the Son of God" (Luke 1:35). The holy one of God entered into the filth of this world in order that he might offer himself as a sacrifice for sin; to shed his blood so that we might become fully and finally clean.

～ *Jesus was God's provision of a sacrifice* that put an end to the need for all of the sacrifices prescribed in Leviticus. "He has appeared once for all at the end of the ages to put away sin by the sacrifice of himself" (Heb. 9:26). It is not that a sacrifice for our sin is no longer required. It is that the sacrifice of Christ is good enough, perfect enough, to cover your sin and my sin and the sin of all who will put their faith in the sufficiency of his once-for-all sacrifice.

～ *Jesus was the pleasing aroma* in the nostrils of his Father. "Christ loved us and gave himself up for us, a fragrant offering and sacrifice to God" (Eph. 5:2). Christ's sacrifice was pleasing to the Lord because it was a tangible, unmistakable, worldwide demonstration of the sacrificial way in which God loves sinners.

～ *Jesus was our substitute.* Just as the people of God put their hands on the head of the bull or the sheep and their sins were transferred to that innocent animal, so when by faith we lay hold of Christ, our guilt is transferred to him, our substitute.

～ *Jesus alone is our promise of cleansing.* Jesus, the ultimate clean thing, was continually touching unclean things.[8] Perhaps this is exactly what Mark wants us to see in chapter 5 of his Gospel, where we read about Jesus touching unclean thing upon unclean thing—a man with an unclean spirit who lived among the dead near a herd of pigs and cut himself. This man was exponentially unclean. What did Jesus do? He cleansed him so that when the people came out to see him, he was "clothed and in his right mind." Next, a woman who had a discharge of blood for twelve years came up behind Jesus in a crowd and touched his clothing. When he asked who had touched him, Mark tells us she came "in fear and trembling." Why was she afraid? She was afraid because she had made him ceremonially unclean just by her touch. But Jesus recognized this for what it was—reaching out to take hold of the health and wholeness found only in him—in other words, faith. In the same chapter, Mark tells us that Jesus went to the home of the ruler of the synagogue, someone in charge of enforcing the rigid cleanliness laws of his day. When he got there, people were weeping and wailing loudly because the synagogue ruler's daughter was dead. Jesus took the girl by her hand, touching this dead body, which made him ceremonially unclean, and infused her with his own resurrection life. Throughout the Gospels Jesus reaches out to touch lepers and make them clean, and each one shows us a picture of the way Jesus makes sinners clean. He reaches out to touch us, taking upon himself our sin sickness and uncleanness, imparting to us his health, wholeness, and acceptance. We are cleansed because the Holy One of God became unclean for us.

～ Finally, *Jesus is our only hope for dealing with the disparity of our conduct.* The entire law is still applicable because the entire law reflects God's unchanging character. Nevertheless, the way in which we are to obey the law has changed significantly, due to the coming of Christ.

The sacrificial laws still apply because God still demands an adequate sacrifice for our sins. Nevertheless, we observe those laws today not by offering animals according to the Mosaic system but by trusting Christ as our sufficient sacrifice. The cleanliness laws still apply because God still demands that we be cleansed of all unrighteousness in order to be in his presence. But we observe those laws today not by going to the priest to be sprinkled with blood but by going to our Great High Priest, who showers us with the forgiveness he purchased for us at the cross. "If we confess our sins, he is faithful and just to forgive us our sins and to cleanse us from all unrighteousness" (1 John 1:9).

Jesus has freed us from following the regulations of Leviticus. It's not that he has thrown them out; rather he has fulfilled them in himself so that Leviticus no longer has mastery over those who come to him. As you are joined to him, you find that your heart beats with his very heartbeat, igniting in you a passion for personal holiness. You find yourself saying, "When I grow up, I want to be holy" because "you were cleansed; you were made holy; you were made right with God by calling on the name of the Lord Jesus Christ and by the Spirit of our God" (1 Cor. 6:11).

Looking Forward
Nothing Unclean Will Ever Enter It

In Leviticus 21, we read the very stringent guidelines for those who will serve as priests in his holy sanctuary:

> And the LORD spoke to Moses, saying, "Speak to Aaron, saying, None of your offspring throughout their generations who has a blemish may approach to offer the bread of his God. For no one who has a blemish shall draw near, a man blind or lame, or one who has a mutilated face or a limb too long, or a man who has an injured foot or an injured hand, or a hunchback or a dwarf or a man with a defect in his sight or an itching disease or scabs or crushed testicles. No man of the offspring of Aaron the priest who has a blemish shall come near to offer the LORD's food offerings; since he has a blemish, he shall not come near to offer the bread of his God. He may eat the bread of his God, both of the most holy and of the holy things, but he shall not go through the veil or approach the altar, because he has a blemish, that he may not profane my sanctuaries, for I am the LORD who sanctifies them." (Lev. 21:16–23)

When we read this, we can't help but feel a bit offended on human terms—especially those of us who have dealt with the pain of disability, disfigurement, or birth defects. It can appear that those who have physical defects are not "good enough" for God or that he has no desire to have them in his presence. But we must set those instinctual feelings of offense aside so that we can hear and understand what God is really doing and saying here, which, rather than being offensive, provides the answer we have looked for our whole lives to the pain of physical disfigurement and defect. We need eyes to see the hope in what may at first seem harsh.

When the priest went into the tabernacle, he was entering into the holy abode of God. As we remember from our earlier study of the tabernacle, the tabernacle provided a reminder of Eden and the hope of heaven. So when the priest entered into the Holy Place it was as if he was entering into heaven itself. And God is too good to allow disease, deformity, defect, and death to enter into heaven. When we read that God will not allow a priest with any defect or deformity to enter into the Holy Place, that is not bad news for those of us who have felt the pain of such things in this world, but good news. God is saying that he is not willing to make peace with effects of sin on this world. He will not forever tolerate disease and deformity and death. He intends to put an end to them. They will not be allowed into his holy heaven. This means that if you have been touched by the pain of such things, you can be sure that when you enter into his presence, you will be healed and whole. All of the effects of the brokenness of this world that have brought you pain will be gone for good. In Revelation we read:

> Nothing unclean will ever enter it, nor anyone who does what is detestable or false, but only those who are written in the Lamb's book of life. (Rev. 21:27)

Here in Leviticus, as God lays out the system of clean and unclean, he is helping his people to understand that what is unclean because of the effects of sin can be made clean because of the blood of an all-sufficient sacrifice. What is impaired will be made right. What is deformed will be made whole. And all that is made clean, right, and whole through the sacrifice of Christ will one day be made holy to live with him in the fullness of his holy presence.

Discussion Guide

Sacrifice and Sanctification

Getting the Discussion Going

1. In Nancy's teaching she said that many people who intend to read through the Bible start to slow down or give up altogether when they get to Leviticus. Why do you think that is, and have you ever had that experience?

Getting to the Heart of It

2. Nancy mentioned three reasons that people are often uninterested in Leviticus: they see it as boring, bloody, and irrelevant to their lives. After spending time studying Leviticus, would you agree or disagree? Why?

3. Just like last week, when we studied the establishment of the priesthood, we see that details that might seem tedious to us are actually quite significant. How did your study of the five offerings add to your understanding of Christ's sacrifice of himself?

4. Some churches and church leaders suggest that some traditions and theological approaches put too much emphasis on the atonement of Christ and should instead put more emphasis on the teachings of Christ as found in the Sermon on the Mount. How would you use Leviticus to argue with this viewpoint?

Without atonement you would not have the foundation

5. What would you say to someone who says the purity laws in Leviticus appear to be random or harsh?

6. Would you say that the sacrifices and purity laws of Leviticus were a blessing or a burden to the children of Israel? Why?

7. Holiness is the opposite of worldliness. What do you think it means to be worldly? What are some examples of worldliness?

Getting Personal

8. God instructs his people in Leviticus to be holy, to be set apart from the people around them, and Peter reiterates that command in the New Testament (1 Pet. 1:14–16). Nancy challenged us to consider if we have come to the place where we truly want to be holy, set apart from the world around us to the Lord. Are there some practical ways you could pursue holiness in your life that you would be willing to share with the group?

Getting How It Fits into the Big Picture

9. Throughout this study, we are seeking to grasp how the passage we're studying fits into the bigger story of God's plan for redemption. How does God's designation of clean and unclean actually help us to see the big picture of the Bible from Eden all the way to the new heaven and the new earth?

In the Wilderness

Numbers

Numbers

"Numbers" is not the original title of this book. It was given that name when it was translated into Greek, because the first few chapters describe a census taken at Sinai to establish the number of fighting men as they prepared to take the land. Chapter 26 records a second census taken forty years later to determine territories for the various tribes. The original title of this book in Hebrew is "In the Wilderness." The book of Numbers tells the story of the forty years spent traveling in the harsh desert toward the eastern border of the land God had promised to give to his people. It tells of one generation that rebelled against God and died in the desert and the second generation that God would lead into the land.

1. Compare Exodus 19:1 with Numbers 10:11. How long did the Israelites spend at Sinai, and what did they do during that time (from your recollection of Exodus and Leviticus)?

2. Read Numbers 10:33–36. What divine assistance and assurance did the people of Israel receive on their journey to the Promised Land?

3. Read Numbers 11:1–19 and 12:1–9. What three things did the Israelites complain about as they set off toward the Promised Land?

4. Read Numbers 13:1–33 along with Deuteronomy 1:20–22. What key phrase in Numbers 13:2 should have made clear to the scouts sent into Canaan that they weren't on a mission to determine whether to take Canaan but were merely gathering information for moving in?

5. How would you summarize the report given by the majority of the spies?

6. Read Numbers 14:21–23. What judgment did the Lord pronounce against those ten spies and why?

7. Read Numbers 13:30 and 14:6–9. How would you summarize the minority report given by Caleb and Joshua, and what was their reasoning?

8. Read and compare Numbers 14:1–3 with 14:26–35. What did the people say they would rather do than risk being killed by the Canaanites? And what happened to them because they wouldn't trust God to give them victory over the Canaanites?

9. Read Numbers 21:1–3, which is about the second generation of Israelites, as all of the previous generation had died in the wilderness. What do you see in these verses that indicates they are different from the previous generation?

10. Read Numbers 21:4–9. What do you see in these verses that indicates that this second generation is also very much the same as the previous generation?

There are several key places in the New Testament that offer us insight into the Israelites' time in the wilderness and what we should learn from it. Let's look at a couple of them.

11. Read 1 Corinthians 10:1–5. What does this tell us about what is possible even for people who experience miracles from God?

12. Read 1 Corinthians 10:6–13. Why did the events in the wilderness happen, and why were they recorded by Moses?

13. What "evil" things did Israel do, according to these verses?

14. What are we intended to learn from their example?

15. Read Hebrews 3:7–4:3. What was the problem with the Israelites in the wilderness, and what did it lead to?

16. According to Hebrews 3:14 and 4:3, what gives evidence in our lives that our relationship to Christ is authentic?

17. According to Hebrews 4:6–7, what is the appropriate response to hearing the gospel?

Road Trip

I spent a year in a college singing group that traveled to promote the school most weekends during the school year and for the entire summer. We crisscrossed the country in a van carrying five singers and a soundman, pulling a trailer behind us with our gear. Over the many miles we traveled, we developed lots of inside jokes and made plenty of good memories. But we also got tired of each other's stories, picky food preferences, and grumpy moods.

There's nothing like a road trip to really get to know people—except maybe a camping trip. The rigors of an extended road trip or camping trip make it pretty hard to hide what we're really like. Can we agree that it is pretty hard to keep the ugly side of ourselves hidden on a long trip? In the book of Numbers, Moses provides an account of what was perhaps the world's longest road trip—one that lasted for forty years. Forty years of packing and unpacking. Forty years of following directions and facing difficulty. Forty years of whiney voices calling out from the back seat, "Are we there yet?" and "I'm hungry!"

This was not six college students in a van on the interstate but two million former slaves on foot in the desert. They were carrying everything they owned, everything they walked away with from Egypt. They are not freshly showered and coming out of comfy hotel rooms but are dirty and dusty as they emerge from their wind-blown tents. All of the older folks are more than a little cranky because they know that they will never actually arrive at their destination but are destined to die in

221

the desert. Their children, the next generation, will get there, and that's the only thing that keeps them going.

To this point in our study, we've witnessed the Israelites freed from slavery in Egypt, led by the pillar of cloud away from the most direct route to the land of Canaan, delivered from death crossing the Red Sea, and instructed at the foot of Mount Sinai. That is where they've been for many months now, receiving the law that is going to shape them as a nation, constructing the tabernacle where they will meet with God, ordaining the priests who will mediate for them with God, and instituting the sacrifices and sanctified way of life their holy God requires. And now it is time for them to move forward into Canaan, the land God promised to give them long ago when he spoke to their father, Abraham, saying:

> I will give to you and to your offspring after you the land of your sojourn-
> ings, all the land of Canaan, for an everlasting possession. (Gen. 17:8)

This promise is what has brought them out into the wilderness. It was—or ought to have been—the most important thing in their lives. Would they trust God to bring about all that he promised, and would they trust him take care of them while they waited for it? Or would they rebel, resist, and refuse to believe? And really, the questions are the same for us. We who have been adopted as God's children are people who have been given a promise from God regarding an inheritance that awaits us in the heavenly land. Peter wrote:

> Blessed be the God and Father of our Lord Jesus Christ! According to his
> great mercy, he has caused us to be born again to a living hope through the
> resurrection of Jesus Christ from the dead, to an inheritance that is imper-
> ishable, undefiled, and unfading, kept in heaven for you. (1 Pet. 1:3–4)

This promise ought to be the most important thing in life to us. God has brought us out of slavery to sin and promised us abundance and rest in his promised land. But here we are, in this in-between time, wandering through the wilderness we call "life in this world." And the questions for each of are, Will I trust God to bring about all that he has promised and to take care of me while I wait to inherit it? Will I spend my life learning all that God wants to teach me about his provision, his holiness, and his ways here in the wilderness of this world, knowing that he is preparing me for life in his presence? Or will I spend these years called "my lifetime" simply seeking satisfaction for my cravings, grumbling, and complaining when I do not get everything he has promised here and now?

Paul wrote in 1 Corinthians that the experiences of the children of Israel in the wilderness were written "as examples for us, that we might not desire evil as they did" (10:6). So let's open up the book of Numbers to see how God's people responded to God's promise and provision in the wilderness and learn from it so that our desires might be retrained away from evil and toward God's goodness.

In Numbers 10 we get our first glimpse of Israel on the march through the wilderness, about a month after the glory of God had come down to rest on the tabernacle in a cloud.

> In the second year, in the second month, on the twentieth day of the month, the cloud lifted from over the tabernacle of the testimony, and the people of Israel set out by stages from the wilderness of Sinai. And the cloud settled down in the wilderness of Paran. (Num. 10:11–12)

This is a good start, following the lead of the presence of God in their midst. If all continues to go well, they should be in the Promised Land within a few short weeks. But immediately we see that things are not going all that well.

They Grumbled about God's Provision

> Now the rabble that was among them had a strong craving. And the people of Israel also wept again and said, "Oh that we had meat to eat! We remember the fish we ate in Egypt that cost nothing, the cucumbers, the melons, the leeks, the onions, and the garlic. But now our strength is dried up, and there is nothing at all but this manna to look at." (Num. 11:4–6)

Evidently the grumbling started with those who lived on the fringes of the camp—the mixed multitude of people of various nationalities who came out of Egypt with God's people. But this grumbling worked its way inward, spreading its infectious discontent throughout the rest of the camp. What were they complaining about? They were complaining about the same thing you and I complain about when the "Food at this exit" signs on the interstate don't display the familiar logo we're looking for. It's not that they had *nothing* to eat. It's that they wanted something *else* to eat besides the manna God rained down on them every day.

For some reason, perhaps because I believed their complaints, I've always assumed that this manna was tasteless and bland. But if we look closely, we realize that manna was less like the porridge slopped into Oliver's bowl and more like a croissant from a fine French bakery. One translation reads, "It tasted like a pastry cooked with the finest oil" (Num. 11:8 HCSB). The psalmist describes manna as the "grain of heaven" (Ps. 78:24). What do you think the bread made in heaven tastes like? Heavenly, right? Yet it wasn't good enough for these grumblers.

Often people say that if God would do a miracle, then they would believe in him. But the whole history of Israel is the story of people who experienced miracles on a massive scale, including the daily miracle of manna waiting for them outside their tents, yet they did not trust God. Instead of believing in him, they rebelled against him. They became one-dimensional people who thought about life only through the knothole of their craving.[1] Their desire for more variety in their diet, which was not evil in itself, became a demand that blinded them to anything and everything else. God spectacularly delivered them from slavery without asking them to fight a battle. He supernaturally fed them in the desert without asking them to work. He gave them the most humble and faithful leader imaginable. But they couldn't see any of it because they were consumed by their craving.

Isn't discontent with God's provision really as old as the garden of Eden? There Adam and Eve were invited to eat of any tree in the garden except for one. But Eve was unsatisfied with God's provision and had to indulge her craving for the fruit of that one tree.

And isn't discontent with God's provision also as modern as today? Many of us have a craving that blinds us so that we can't see all that God has done for us and all that he has given to us. Yes, we appreciate salvation and all that, but what we *really* crave is to be thin, to have a nicer house in a better neighborhood, to be elevated to a position with more authority and opportunity, to have a child, or to be able to change the child we've got. For the Israelites, everything was about food. What is everything about for you? Are you going to allow that craving to be the knothole through which you view all of life, causing you to lose sight of God's goodness?

They Discounted God's Power

When we come to Numbers 13, it would appear that the Israelites had made good time in the wilderness, and they were on the southern outskirts of Canaan.

> The LORD spoke to Moses, saying, "Send men to spy out the land of Canaan, which I am giving to the people of Israel. From each tribe of their fathers you shall send a man, every one a chief among them." (Num. 13:1–2)

These twelve men weren't so much sneaking around like military spies to judge the odds of defeating the enemy or the advisability of Israel's moving forward. They were sent in to procure information for developing a move-in strategy. They were also sent to collect samples of local produce that would give the Israelites back in the camp a preview of what lay ahead for them to enjoy. This was the land that God had promised to give them. The question of "should we?" shouldn't have even been on the table. And when the scouts returned to camp, all twelve agreed on two things. First, they agreed that what they had been told about this land was true; it was fertile and prosperous. They also agreed that the people living in the land were a force to be reckoned with. But for ten of the scouts, there was also bad news in their report. Listen for their huge "however":

> We came to the land to which you sent us. It flows with milk and honey, and this is its fruit. *However*, the people who dwell in the land are strong, and the cities are fortified and very large. . . . We are not able to go up against the people, for they are stronger than we are. . . . The land . . . devours its inhabitants, and all the people that we saw in it are of great height. (Num. 13:27–28, 31–32)

The majority report left God and his promise completely out of the equation. They seemed to have developed amnesia regarding all of God's protection and provision over the previous months since they had walked out of Egypt and across the dry ground of the Red Sea. But Joshua and Caleb's report and response is very different.

> Caleb quieted the people before Moses and said, "Let us go up at once and occupy it, for we are well able to overcome it." (Num. 13:30)

What was the foundation of Joshua and Caleb's confidence? Was it the military prowess of the people? Not even close. While ten of the scouts focused on the power of the opposition, Joshua and Caleb focused on the power of God, saying in essence, "Let's trust God's promise."

If we were to fast-forward into Israel's story, we would see, many years later, a short little shepherd boy facing one of these Canaanite giants that the scouts saw—Goliath—with nothing but a slingshot, five stones, and confidence in the power of God. He will say, "The LORD who delivered me from the paw of the lion and from the paw of the bear will deliver me from the hand of this Philistine" (1 Sam. 17:37). Once again the Israelite majority will discount the promise of God and inflate the power of their enemy, but God's man will go forward in faith.

They Questioned God's Purpose

The majority report seemed to take the road-trip-weary Israelites past their tipping point.

> Then all the congregation raised a loud cry, and the people wept that night. And all the people of Israel grumbled against Moses and Aaron. The whole congregation said to them, "Would that we had died in the land of Egypt! Or would that we had died in this wilderness! Why is the LORD bringing us into this land, to fall by the sword? Our wives and our little ones will become a prey. Would it not be better for us to go back to Egypt?" And they said to one another, "Let us choose a leader and go back to Egypt." (Num. 14:1–4)

It is actually a pretty good thing to ask the question, "Why is the LORD bringing us into this land?" But, of course, they were not asking the

question out of a desire to fulfill God's purpose but questioning if he
really had one, and suggesting that if he did, it was not working for
them. It's not that they didn't know what God's purpose was. His purpose in his promise had been clear. It's just that they refused to believe
it. They refused to trust God.

My friends, it is not an insignificant thing to know the promise of God and refuse to believe it. But that is what these people did.
They were already thinking through what they'd say to Pharaoh to get
their old jobs back at the brick factory when four men—Moses, Aaron,
Joshua, and Caleb—fell on their faces and tore their clothes, begging
them to trust God's promise, saying: *Joshua + Caleb*
                                                      went ahead

> If the LORD delights in us, he will bring us into this land and give it to us, a
> land that flows with milk and honey. Only do not rebel against the LORD.
> And do not fear the people of the land, for they are bread for us. Their
> protection is removed from them, and the LORD is with us; do not fear
> them. (Num. 14:8–9)

At this point the Israelites were so resistant to this encouragement
to trust God that they took up stones to kill the four men. And this made
God angry. He saw it not solely as a rejection of these men but also as a
rejection of him. He determined to put an end to their misery and start
fresh with Moses to father a greater and mightier nation of people who
would trust him. But Moses, their mediator, appealed to the Lord on
the basis of the glory of God's name and the integrity of God's character,
and the Lord relented. But there would be consequences.

> As I live, declares the LORD, what you have said in my hearing I will do to
> you: your dead bodies shall fall in this wilderness, and of all your num-
> ber, listed in the census from twenty years old and upward, who have
> grumbled against me, not one shall come into the land where I swore that
> I would make you dwell, except Caleb the son of Jephunneh and Joshua
> the son of Nun. But your little ones, who you said would become a prey,
> I will bring in, and they shall know the land that you have rejected. . . .
> Your children shall be shepherds in the wilderness forty years and shall
> suffer for your faithlessness, until the last of your dead bodies lies in the
> wilderness. (Num. 14:28–31, 33)

"Would that we had died in this wilderness!" they complained. Well, now they will. "God will drive Israel into the wilderness because of its unfaithfulness, and he will also transform that same wilderness by an unsurpassed revelation of his grace." [2]

They Presumed upon God's Protection

One would think that this sentence of forty years in the wilderness would get the Israelites' attention in a way that would foster fresh eagerness to obey God. We read that the people "mourned greatly" (Num. 14:39). But clearly their great sadness did not reflect genuine repentance over their refusal to trust and obey God, because immediately they refused to trust and obey God again. God had instructed them to "turn tomorrow and set out for the wilderness by the way to the Red Sea" (v. 25). But they determined to go the other direction, to try to move forward into the Promised Land, in defiance of God's instructions, yet presuming upon his protection (v. 40).

> And they rose early in the morning and went up to the heights of the hill country, saying, "Here we are. We will go up to the place that the LORD has promised, for we have sinned." But Moses said, "Why now are you transgressing the command of the LORD, when that will not succeed? Do not go up, for the Lord is not among you, lest you be struck down before your enemies. For there the Amalekites and the Canaanites are facing you, and you shall fall by the sword. Because you have turned back from following the LORD, the LORD will not be with you." (Num. 14:40–43)

Having taken matters into their own hands, they were thoroughly routed by those who lived in the hill country on the southern edge of the Promised Land and were driven back into the wilderness. I suppose there was something positive here in that they were acting on their desire to experience what God had promised, but they were unwilling to submit to his disciplining judgment and wait on his timing. They saw no sense in spending forty years wandering in the wilderness. But God did not intend for those years to be a waste. God intended to use those years not only to weed out the unbelieving generation but also to train up the new generation to be a people who would obey his word and trust his promise.

Do you ever wonder why God is taking so long to bring about all that he has promised to provide to you? Do you sometimes find yourself impatient with God's plan that can seem like a sentence of meaningless suffering in the wilderness? Just as God intended to use those forty years in the wilderness to teach and train his people, God intends to teach and train you as you walk through life in the wilderness of this world. In the wilderness, we're given the opportunity to work the gospel into our lives in the midst of difficult circumstances. We're forced to reckon with who we are and what we believe and don't believe. In the wilderness we get to learn what it means to live by faith. Over our lifetimes in the wilderness, God intends for us to become people who say to him, "It's not just your blessings I'm after; it's you I really want."

They Were Impatient with God's Plan

The story of the new generation that will enter the land begins in Numbers 21, and we are introduced to them as they experience their first military victory against the Canaanites in Hormah, the same place where the first generation was defeated many years before. They were ready to keep going forward that way into Canaan but instead were instructed by God to

> *Just as God intended to use those forty years in the wilderness to teach and train his people, God intends to teach and train you as you walk through life in the wilderness of this world.*

go around the land of Edom via the route by the Red Sea. The Red Sea? Isn't this going backward instead of forward? Impatient with this plan that would delay their entrance in the land, they began to grumble, just as their parents had. It may be a new generation, but family patterns are hard to break. See if this doesn't sound annoyingly familiar:

> From Mount Hor they set out by the way to the Red Sea, to go around the land of Edom. And the people became impatient on the way. And the people spoke against God and against Moses, "Why have you brought us

up out of Egypt to die in the wilderness? For there is no food and no water, and we loathe this worthless food." (Num. 21:4–5)

What an insult to the God who had freed them and led them and sustained them and provided for them. As we have seen before in Israel's story, God will save them, but it will be a salvation that comes through judgment:

> Then the LORD sent fiery serpents among the people, and they bit the people, so that many people of Israel died. (Num. 21:6)

Snakes, snakes, and more snakes. Not your harmless garden snakes, but poisonous snakes. People are being bitten; they are swollen and fever-filled, feeling as if their insides were on fire. Why would God send snakes? Was God just pulling something creative out of his bag of judgments, or was it a matter of convenience with so many snakes to work with in the desert? Remember that the people were complaining about being brought up out of Egypt. And what was the symbol of Egyptian power featured on the Pharaoh's crown? The serpent. So these serpents said with every hiss: "Is this really what you want? Do you want to be inflicted with suffering by the mighty serpent of Egypt again?"

Of course the serpents were also a reminder of the ancient Serpent who slithered into the garden of Eden and caused Adam and Eve to be ejected from the garden and into the wilderness. These serpents served as a vivid reminder that they were in the wilderness instead of in the Promised Land as a result of their sinful disobedience and unbelief. And evidently the snakes had their intended effect.

> The people came to Moses and said, "We have sinned, for we have spoken against the LORD and against you. Pray to the LORD, that he take away the serpents from us." So Moses prayed for the people. And the LORD said to Moses, "Make a fiery serpent and set it on a pole, and everyone who is bitten, when he sees it, shall live." So Moses made a bronze serpent and set it on a pole. And if a serpent bit anyone, he would look at the bronze serpent and live. (Num. 21:7–9)

Why would God instruct Moses to mount the very image of their misery on a pole and tell the people to look at it to be healed? Up on this pole hung the symbol of Israel's mortal enemies—Egypt and Satan— lifeless and defeated. It was a picture of how the power of sin would one day be defeated for good when the seed of the woman would crush the head of the Serpent. Fixing their gaze and thereby putting their faith in the One who will defeat the ancient Serpent is what brought life and healing.

They Were Faithless in the Wilderness

So there we have it: a few snapshots taken along the way of Israel's forty-year journey in the wilderness. And frankly, it does not create a pretty picture. God brought his people out of Egypt so that they would be his treasured possession, a kingdom of priests, and a holy nation (Ex. 19:5–6). But instead of being a kingdom of priests, they were a collection of complainers. Rather than being a holy nation, they were a holy terror every step of the way. Clearly, for Israel to be accepted by her holy God, she needed someone who would fulfill all that she was meant to be—someone who, in her stead, would be faithful even in the harsh discomforts of the wilderness, someone who would not presume upon God's power, complain about God's provision, or impatiently quarrel against God's plan.

This is why Matthew, in his Gospel, takes such care to make sure his readers see that Jesus is the embodiment of all that Israel was meant to be. Matthew, who was trained by Jesus himself in how to understand the writings of Moses (Luke 24:27), presents Jesus as the true and better Israel.

He Was Faithful in the Wilderness

As we read through the early chapters of Matthew's Gospel, we recognize that Matthew is retracing the history of Israel, helping us to see how its story is echoed in Jesus's life. In chapter 1, the genealogy establishes Jesus as an Israelite. In chapter 2 Matthew writes that Jesus went to Egypt and remained there until Herod died, quoting the prophet Hosea's words that are clearly about Israel, "Out of Egypt I called my son" (see Hos. 11:1). Yet as far as Matthew is concerned, Jesus is the fulfillment of all that Israel pointed to, and in that sense, he is the ultimate people of God and the final Son of God. In chapter 3 we see Jesus walk through the waters of baptism like the Israelites walked through the waters of the Red Sea. And then, in chapter 4, we see Jesus led into the wilderness by the Spirit of God for forty days to face temptation, in the same way the children of Israel were led into the wilderness by God's presence in the cloud for forty years. Just as Israel experienced a lack of food and water in the desert, so did Jesus. Matthew writes:

> And after fasting forty days and forty nights, he was hungry. And the tempter came and said to him, "If you are the Son of God, command these stones to become loaves of bread." (Matt. 4:2–3)

The Israelites were tempted to live a life detached from dependence upon God, and so was Jesus. But while Israel grumbled and complained about God's provision, Jesus remained confident that God was feeding him the very best of food—his own word.

> But he answered, "It is written, 'Man shall not live by bread alone, but by every word that comes from the mouth of God.'" (Matt. 4:4)

Evidently Jesus was thinking through this temptation in the wilderness in light of his identity as the true Israel, and so three times, in response to each of Satan's temptations, he drew from the instructions God gave to the children of Israel in the wilderness. Israel had never seemed to learn that all of her cravings could be entrusted to her great Provider. But Jesus trusted in God's provision.

In the second temptation, Satan quoted from Psalm 91, misusing it for his own purposes:

> Then the devil took him to the holy city and set him on the pinnacle of the temple and said to him, "If you are the Son of God, throw yourself down, for it is written, 'He will command his angels concerning you,' and 'On their hands they will bear you up, lest you strike your foot against a stone.'" (Matt. 4:5–6)

But Jesus would not be manipulated by this twisting of Scripture. He knows that you can make the Bible say anything you want if you do not interpret Scripture with Scripture. Psalm 91 encourages us to trust God, not to test him.

> Jesus said to him, "Again it is written, 'You shall not put the Lord your God to the test.'" Again, the devil took him to a very high mountain and showed him all the kingdoms of the world and their glory. And he said to him, "All these I will give you, if you will fall down and worship me." (Matt. 4:7–9)

The Devil suggested that Jesus prove that he is the Messiah by putting on a show of his sonship for all to see. But Jesus refused to presume upon God's protection as the Israelites had done when they tried to take Canaan in defiance of God's instructions.

> Then Jesus said to him, "Be gone, Satan! For it is written, 'You shall worship the Lord your God and him only shall you serve.'" (Matt. 4:10)

Satan knows that Jesus is slated to be the King of kings and Lord of lords, that he is set to inherit the whole world. What Satan offered was a shortcut to this destination that would not include the cross, "perhaps because he knows the cross is not so much Jesus' doom, as it is his."[3] But whereas the Israelites were impatient with God's route, which took them through the wilderness, Jesus refused to resent God for what his plan would require and "for the joy that was set before him endured the cross" (Heb. 12:2).

Jesus left the ultimate land of milk and honey—heaven itself—to enter into the wilderness of this world with us. Here he showed us what it means to be faithful, to obey, and to be pleasing to God in the midst of hardship and temptation. He showed us what it looks like to depend upon God to provide in his timing and in his way. But he didn't do this merely to serve as our example. He did this to serve as our substitute. On the cross, Jesus entered into the ultimate wasteland of death *in our place* so that we might enter into the abundant life that God has promised.

How Will You Walk through the Wilderness?

John records a conversation between Jesus and Nicodemus, a Pharisee, someone steeped in the writings of Moses, who came to him in the middle of night. He had witnessed Jesus's miracles, and he wondered what he should do, how he should respond. To answer him, Jesus drew upon a story that Nicodemus would be familiar with, a story that pictured exactly what Nicodemus needed to do. Jesus said:

> As Moses lifted up the serpent in the wilderness, so must the Son of Man be lifted up, that whoever believes in him may have eternal life. For God so loved the world, that he gave his only Son, that whoever believes in him should not perish but have eternal life. For God did not send his Son into the world to condemn the world, but in order that the world might be saved through him. (John 3:14–17)

Maybe you have never heard John 3:16 before in this context. But doesn't this background of the scene from Numbers 21 make it clear what Jesus was saying when he talked about believing and not perishing? To believe is to look to Jesus, fully aware that apart from him, you will die in the wilderness. To believe is to look to Jesus, confident that only in him will you find healing from the poison of sin.

Jesus became what was killing us—sin itself—when he was lifted up on the cross and thereby became the remedy for sin.

The Israelites had to look at an image of the thing that was killing them on the pole as a remedy for their sin. Jesus became what was killing us—sin itself—when he was lifted up on the cross and thereby became the remedy for sin. "For our sake he made him to be sin who knew no sin, so that in him we might become the righteousness of God" (2 Cor. 5:21).

If you have looked to Christ and been healed, you can be sure that you will not die out in the desert apart from God's blessing but will one day cross over the river Jordan into the Promised Land. You have this promise as the foundation of your hope. And to the degree that this promise works its way through your entire being, you will live differently here in the wilderness. Instead of complaining, you'll be content with God's provision. Instead of questioning God's purpose, you'll be convinced that all the difficulty in the wilderness of this life is purposeful. Instead of presuming upon God's protection here and now, you'll be confident in his eternal protection. Instead of being impatient with God's plan, you'll be willing to wait to receive all that God has promised.

Don't waste your years in the wilderness, my friend, complaining, questioning, and rebelling against God. But on those days when you do complain or question or rebel, remember this: there is one who has faced every temptation that you have faced and is yet without sin. He has gone before you and will one day welcome you into the land. His welcome will not be based on your record of obedience in the wilderness, but on his. You need only look to him and live.

Looking Forward

The Trumpet Call of God

It was time for the Israelites to begin their journey toward the Promised Land led by the cloud that would lift from over the tabernacle. But how would this massive group of two million travelers make their way forward in any organized fashion?

> The LORD spoke to Moses, saying, "Make two silver trumpets. Of hammered work you shall make them, and you shall use them for summoning the congregation and for breaking camp. And when both are blown, all the congregation shall gather themselves to you at the entrance of the tent of meeting." (Num. 10:1–3)

Instructions to move out were to be mediated through the priests by means of the silver trumpets. Rather than musical instruments, they were more like military bugles that would signal the various tribes to set out on their journey. These trumpets would be used not only during Israel's time in the wilderness but also later to call the people to warfare and worship, after they entered into the land.

> The trumpets shall be to you for a perpetual statute throughout your generations. And when you go to war in your land against the adversary who oppresses you, then you shall sound an alarm with the trumpets, that you may be remembered before the LORD your God, and you shall be saved from your enemies. On the day of your gladness also, and at your appointed feasts and at the beginnings of your months, you shall blow the trumpets over your burnt offerings and over the sacrifices of your peace offerings. They shall be a reminder of you before your God: I am the LORD your God. (Num. 10:8–10)

The prophet Isaiah spoke of a future day when "a great trumpet will be blown" to gather God's people to "worship the LORD on the holy mountain at Jerusalem" (Isa. 27:13). Evidently, the Spirit enabled the prophet Isaiah to see beyond the day when Christ would come the first time, humbly and quietly, and into the day when he will come again. He will not come quietly the second time.

> For the Lord himself will descend from heaven with a cry of command, with the voice of an archangel, and with the sound of the trumpet of God. And the dead in Christ will rise first. Then we who are alive, who are left, will be caught up together with them in the clouds to meet the Lord in the air, and so we will always be with the Lord. (1 Thess. 4:16–17)

If you are in Christ, one day you will hear the trumpet call of God, gathering his people for entrance into his Promised Land:

> Then will appear in heaven the sign of the Son of Man, and then all the tribes of the earth will mourn, and they will see the Son of Man coming on the clouds of heaven with power and great glory. And he will send out his angels with a loud trumpet call, and they will gather his elect from the four winds, from one end of heaven to the other. (Matt. 24:30–31)

This will not be a call to warfare, because the battle will be over. Our great enemy of sin and death will have been defeated and destroyed. This trumpet will call us to resurrected life.

> For the trumpet will sound, and the dead will be raised imperishable, and we shall be changed. . . . Then shall come to pass the saying that is written: "Death is swallowed up in victory." (1 Cor. 15:52, 54)

When that trumpet sounds, we will break camp here and gather before our greater Joshua. He will lead us into the heavenly land. Our wandering and warfare will finally be over, replaced forever by worship.

In the Wilderness

Getting the Discussion Going

1. Tell us about the most rigorous or memorable road trip you've been on. What did you learn about yourself and your companions along the way? *memorable - vac w/ Brinton camping when pregnant w Audrey.*

Getting to the Heart of It

2. We don't tend to think about grumbling and complaining as a very big deal. Yet it seems clear in the book of Numbers that it is a sin God takes seriously. Why do you think that is? *They were not trusting God or grateful*

3. Interestingly, the twelve scouts spent much of their time around Hebron (Num. 13:22). Can you remember anything about Hebron and what happened there in the lives of the patriarchs? (See Gen. 23:9; 25:8–10; 35:27–29.) Why should just standing in Hebron have encouraged them to move forward with taking Canaan? *Cave to bury Sarah + Abraham, Isaac lived there*

4. While years spent in the desert was a judgment on Israel's unbelief, God also used the time in the wilderness to teach and train Israel for living in the land. What aspects of their life in the desert should have taught them significant things about God and life under his care?

5. Just as God provided the cure to his people in the desert, the bronze serpent on the pole, so God has provided a cure to us—Jesus lifted up

on the cross. But the cure requires something of us. The Israelites were told to look at the bronze serpent and live. What does the cure for sin require of us? *Accepting Christ's gift & repenting of our sin.*

6. Matthew subtly contrasts Christ's obedience in the wilderness to Israel's disobedience in the wilderness. Why does it matter that Jesus obeyed in the wilderness? And does it matter if we obey in the wilderness? *His obedience led him to the cross. There was no shortcut.*

7. Nancy said that the promise of God should have been the most important thing to Israel and likewise it should be to us. What is the promise of God, and how do you think we can nurture our treasuring and trusting in this promise? *He will provide for us. We can trust him*

Getting Personal

8. We read in 1 Corinthians 10 that the events in Numbers have been written down as an example for us to instruct us. As you observed Israel's unbelief, disobedience, ingratitude, and rebellion as well as their repentance and faith, in what way has it instructed you? *God punished their behavior*

Getting How It Fits into the Big Picture

9. Remember that our study in Exodus began with a recognition that Israel's story of salvation from slavery is really our story. And we are familiar with talking (and singing) about heaven in terms of crossing over the Jordan River into the land. How does what the Israelites experienced in between salvation and entering into the land picture our lives in between being called out of our old life of slavery to sin and entering into eternity in God's presence?

Love and Obey

Deuteronomy

Personal Bible Study

Deuteronomy

1. Read Deuteronomy 1:1–8. Verses 1 and 5 describe the content of the entire book of Deuteronomy. What is it, and what is the setting in which it was presented?

2. Skim the rest of chapter 1 through chapter 3 and write two or three sentences that summarize the highlights of Moses's recounting of Israel's history in the wilderness.

3. An important word throughout the book of Deuteronomy is *remember*. Summarize in a short phrase from each of the following verses in Deuteronomy what Moses wants the Israelites to remember when they enter into the land:

4:11–14

4:15–20

4:32–40

5:1–21

6:1–9

6:20–25

7:1–11

8:1–20

9:4–6

4. Read Deuteronomy 10:12–13 and list what God requires of his people.

5. What does Deuteronomy 10:14–22 reveal about God and how God's people should respond to him?

6. Mark Dever writes, "We can summarize the message of Deuteronomy with two very simple statements. First, God chooses his people. Second, God's people must choose him."[1] Make note of key phrases in the verses in Deuteronomy listed below that evidence this truth:

4:37

5:10

6:5

7:6

7:7

30:1

7. Repeatedly in Deuteronomy the Israelites are told that they should respond to God's love toward them in love. In fact, they are commanded to love the Lord, a command that Jesus sets forth as "the greatest commandment." What do you think it means to love the Lord with all your heart, soul, mind, and strength, and how do you think it happens?

8. In Deuteronomy 10:16, God commands the Israelites to do something that he says, in Deuteronomy 30:6, he will do. What is it, and what do you think it means?

9. In Galatians 3:10–14, Paul quotes Deuteronomy 27:26 and Deuteronomy 21:23. Try to put what Paul is saying in these verses into your own words.

Teaching Chapter

Something Has to Happen In Your Heart

Does any mother ever really feel ready for that day when she drops her child off at college, or boot camp, or the first apartment, and then drives away? Eighteen or more years of teaching and training have been focused toward this goal of training the child to live successfully away from home. But when that day comes, we suddenly we find ourselves wishing we could roll back the clock and go over the basics again. We wonder if our children will eat right and get the sleep they need and be considerate of their roommates. We wonder what choices they will make with so much freedom and so many new opportunities. We wonder if the things we have sought to instill in them have become a part of who they are and who they will want to become, or if they will simply shed that skin once they are on their own. With so much we want them to remember, we can't help but give them a few final reminders before we drive away.

~ Remember to eat a green vegetable once in a while.

~ Remember to wash the sheets on your bed at least once or twice this semester.

~ Remember that you don't have to do something just because it seems like everybody else is doing it.

~ Remember where you came from and who you belong to and all we've taught you—*and give us a call sometime, would you?*

As parents, we often feel fear rising up in us, because we all know of kids—or perhaps have had kids or have been kids—who exited their parents' homes to head off to college or some other life outside those four walls only to jettison all that was modeled and taught to them. In those cases it seems that all of the rule keeping at home was just that— external adherence to rules that never became part of them.

Oh how we wish that there were some magic elixir we could sneak into the meatloaf that would ensure that our children would truly embrace Christ and develop a desire to please him. But we know we don't have the power in our parenting to make that happen. Our example, our rules, and our reminders simply won't do it. Deep down we know that something has to happen in their hearts. To live differently from the world around them will require something more than a list of rules and reminders. If something does not happen in their hearts— the deepest part of who they are—either all of the rule-keeping will be discarded for a life of rebellion or apathy toward God, or the rules will be coldly kept but with no genuine spiritual life.

Today, as we open the book of Deuteronomy, we get to listen in on Moses's final words to Israel, spoken as they stood on the brink of the Promised Land.

> In the fortieth year, on the first day of the eleventh month, Moses spoke to the people of Israel according to all that the Lord had given him in commandment to them. . . . Beyond the Jordan, in the land of Moab, Moses undertook to explain this law, saying, "The Lord our God said to us in Horeb, 'You have stayed long enough at this mountain. . . . Go in and take possession of the land that the Lord swore to your fathers, to Abraham, to Isaac, and to Jacob, to give to them and to their offspring after them.'"
> (Deut. 1:3, 5–6, 8)

Picture Moses like a parent standing on the curb outside the college dorm. His people are moving out of the wilderness home they have shared with him for forty years and are moving into Canaan. He will not be going in with them; instead he will be heading home. He has spent forty years preparing them for this day, but he wonders, will they remember all that they have learned during these years spent under his guidance? Has any real love for God and passion for his holiness developed in their hearts so that they will remember the Lord in this new land? Have all of the sacrifices and feasts and worship services in the wilderness bound them to God and his promises, or has it all been empty of any real devotion?

In the three speeches that make up the book of Deuteronomy, Moses does not say a bunch of new things he has never said before. Instead, Moses reminds the Israelites of all he has told them and what has gone on before. He reviews the experiences that must remain imprinted on their memory and be part of their identity, the ways of life and habits of the heart that must become intrinsic to their way of life. He sets out, on the edge of this new life in the land, to remind them of all they need to remember if they want to enjoy everything that God has promised.

Remember What You've Done

In the first three chapters of Deuteronomy, Moses recounts the unhappy history of what took place the last time the Israelites stood on the edge of entering into the land.

> You would not go up, but rebelled against the command of the LORD your God. And you murmured in your tents and said, "Because the LORD hated us he has brought us out of the land of Egypt, to give us into the hand of the Amorites, to destroy us. Where are we going up? Our brothers have made our hearts melt, saying, 'The people are greater and taller than we. The cities are great and fortified up to heaven. And besides, we have seen the sons of the Anakim there.'" Then I said to you, "Do not be in dread or afraid of them. The LORD your God who goes before you will himself fight for you, just as he did for you in Egypt before your eyes, and in the wilderness, where you have seen how the LORD your God carried you, as a man carries his son, all the way that you went until you came to this place." Yet in spite of this word you did not believe the LORD your God. (Deut. 1:26–32)

God's people have been here before, on the threshold of the Promised Land, only to be banished to the wilderness because of their rebellious refusal to trust that God would empower them to defeat the enemies in the land and give it to them. They need to remember this sad history so it will not be repeated, so that instead of rebelling and murmuring and refusing to enter, they will believe, obey, and enter in. So Moses warned them with reminders of past failures but also encouraged them with reminders of recent victories. By recalling their recent victories over the king of Sihon and the king of Bashan, Moses assured them that God will give them many more victories over those who now control the land.

Just as the Israelites waiting to enter into the Promised Land needed to remember what they had done in the past, we too need to remember what we have done in our past. We need to look squarely at the fear and unbelief that has led us into sin in the past so that we don't walk that way again. We need to remember the victories God has given us over sins that we thought had too much power in our lives to be overcome. Remembering our past failures as well as our past victories prepares us for the future victories over sin God intends to give to us.

Remember What You've Heard

Having reminded them of what they had done, Moses then began reminding Israel of what they had heard God say. And surely as significant as *what* God said was *how* he said it:

> You came near and stood at the foot of the mountain, while the mountain burned with fire to the heart of heaven, wrapped in darkness, cloud, and gloom. Then the LORD spoke to you out of the midst of the fire. You heard the sound of words, but saw no form; there was only a voice. And he declared to you his covenant, which he commanded you to perform, that is, the Ten Commandments, and he wrote them on two tablets of stone. And the LORD commanded me at that time to teach you statutes and rules, that you might do them in the land that you are going over to possess. (Deut. 4:11–14)

One would think that it would be pretty hard to forget standing at the foot of a mountain that was on fire and hearing the voice of God thundering out of the fire. But, of course, none of the generation Moses was speaking to had actually stood at the foot of Sinai that day. It was their parents who had heard the thundering voice of the one who had brought them out of Egypt and was making his claim upon their lives in the form of the Ten Commandments. Moses is saying that when God spoke to their parents, he had the descendants in mind so that in a profound sense, as far as God is concerned, they were there "in" their parents. What was it that God said in his thundering voice from the fiery mountain?

> The LORD spoke with you face to face at the mountain, out of the midst of the fire, while I stood between the LORD and you at that time, to declare to you the word of the LORD. For you were afraid because of the fire, and you did not go up into the mountain. He said: "I am the LORD your God, who brought you out of the land of Egypt, out of the house of slavery. You shall have no other gods before me. You shall not make for yourself a carved image. . . . You shall not take the name of the LORD your God in vain. . . . Observe the Sabbath day, to keep it holy . . ." (Deut. 5:4–8, 11–12)

From there, Moses reiterated the Ten Commandments God had given to their parents, adding:

> These words the LORD spoke to all your assembly at the mountain out of the midst of the fire, the cloud, and the thick darkness, with a loud voice; and he added no more. And he wrote them on two tablets of stone and gave them to me. (Deut. 5:22)

There they were, the words of the God who made the heavens and the earth, engraved in stone. Moses remembered well how the people had responded that day forty years before. They had said to Moses:

> For who is there of all flesh, that has heard the voice of the living God speaking out of the midst of fire as we have, and has still lived? Go near and hear all that the LORD our God will say, and speak to us all that the LORD our God will speak to you, and *we will hear and do it*. (Deut. 5:26–27)

"We will hear and do it," they had said. If that had only been true. It seems God wishes it had been true too. Moses quotes God as saying:

> Oh that they had such a heart as this always, to fear me and to keep all my commandments, that it might go well with them and with their descendants forever! (Deut. 5:29)

God heard their determination to obey, but he knew that they did not yet have the heart for it. What was needed was for these words to be written not only on stone tablets but also on their hearts:

> And these words that I command you today shall be on your heart. You shall teach them diligently to your children, and shall talk of them when you sit in your house, and when you walk by the way, and when you lie down, and when you rise. You shall bind them as a sign on your hand, and they shall be as frontlets between your eyes. You shall write them on the doorposts of your house and on your gates. (Deut. 6:6–9)

What God has said cannot be taken lightly. It must be worked into the fabric of their lives becoming the fodder for their conversations and the very foundation of their homes.

Remember Who You Are

When our children leave the nest of home, we hope that they will carry and invest themselves and engage with others in a way that is consistent with the identity and values of our family. That is what Israel is to do when they enter into Canaan. They need to remember who they are, and specifically *whose* they are:

> For you are a people holy to the LORD your God. The LORD your God has chosen you to be a people for his treasured possession, out of all the peoples who are on the face of the earth. It was not because you were more in number than any other people that the LORD set his love on you and chose you, for you were the fewest of all peoples, but it is because the LORD loves you and is keeping the oath that he swore to your fathers, that the LORD has brought you out with a mighty hand and redeemed you from the house of slavery, from the hand of Pharaoh king of Egypt. (Deut. 7:6–8)

Israel was chosen by God to be a beacon of godlikeness that would radiate throughout the world. They were to be his royal priests, representing him, declaring him, so that all nations would be blessed through them. It was through them that God intended to accomplish his grand purpose in the world—to glorify himself by bringing salvation, a salvation that would come to the whole world through one special descendant of these chosen people.

Remember the Lessons You've Learned

But for them to be all that God intended was going to require some refinement, some rubbing off of the rough edges, which is exactly how God used the forty years spent wandering in the wilderness. We might think that those were wasted years spent going nowhere. But when God makes us wait, that time of waiting is never wasted. The forty years in the wilderness would be wasted only if Israel did not remember all that the Lord had taught them there:

> And you shall remember the whole way that the LORD your God has led you these forty years in the wilderness, that he might humble you, testing you to know what was in your heart, whether you would keep his commandments or not. And he humbled you and let you hunger and fed you with manna, which you did not know, nor did your fathers know, that he might make you know that man does not live by bread alone, but man lives by every word that comes from the mouth of the LORD. (Deut. 8:2–3)

God intended for Israel to develop genuine humility as they were forced to face up to their true selves in the desert—a place where no one could hide behind pretense and pride. Evidently it was not an accident that they went some time without food and felt the discomfort of hunger before God sent the manna. What they perceived as lack was actually a gift that would help them come to terms with their need for God and his provision. Over the years, they learned to rely on God's provision day by day. This dependence on God was never intended to be a temporary stop-gap measure until they could get back to taking care of themselves. Every day that they had to wait for God's provision, their dependence upon God should have become more a part of them. Hopefully, it will have become a habit that will not be broken once they are living in the land of milk and honey.

By depending upon God's promise to provide manna day by day, the Israelites were to learn that "man lives by every word that comes from the mouth of the LORD." What were the words that came by the mouth of the Lord that they were to live by? They were God's promise to give them the land; the promised blessings for obedience and curses for disobedience; the assurance that the law was for their good always; the instructions for sacrifice and sanctification, feasts and festivals; and the announcement of God's intention to bless the whole world through them. The same mouth that had promised to miraculously send manna every morning and had delivered on that promise also made these other promises, so every day as they ate the manna, it should have instilled confidence that all of God's promises are as good as done.

The question, as they stood on the boundary of Canaan was, would Israel believe and act on everything God had said? Would they trust his guidance, obey his commands, and cherish his promise? Moses knew that the goodness and abundance they were about to enter into might lull them into forgetting the source of those blessings. The reason he is telling them to remember all of these things is that he knows they are likely to forget.

> Take care lest you forget the LORD your God by not keeping his command-
> ments and his rules and his statutes, which I command you today, lest,
> when you have eaten and are full and have built good houses and live in
> them, and when your herds and flocks multiply and your silver and gold
> is multiplied and all that you have is multiplied, then your heart be lifted
> up, and you forget the LORD your God. . . . Beware lest you say in your
> heart, "My power and the might of my hand have gotten me this wealth."
> (Deut. 8:11–17)

If we don't nurture our remembering of God's provision, we slip into the delusion that we are the ones who provide for ourselves. We figure that we've earned it, we deserve it, and it is ours to do with as we please. But we must remember, along with the Israelites, that everything we have, everything we are, everything we enjoy, has been given to us by God, and we are simply stewards of his gifts. We must take care lest we forget.

Remember What Is Required

Moses spoke to Israel and told them to remember what they had done, what they had heard, who they are, and what they had learned. Then, in Deuteronomy 10, Moses tells them to remember what the LORD requires of them.

> And now, Israel, what does the LORD your God require of you, but to fear the LORD your God, to walk in all his ways, to love him, to serve the LORD your God with all your heart and with all your soul, and to keep the commandments and statutes of the LORD, which I am commanding you today for your good? . . . Circumcise therefore the foreskin of your heart, and be no longer stubborn. (Deut. 10:12–16)

Fear the Lord, walk in all his ways, love him, serve him, keep his commandments, and don't be stubborn. It sounds simple enough, but while it is simple, certainly it isn't easy. When we read ahead into the Old Testament, we read the glad story of the Israelites entering into and enjoying the land and life God had for them in Canaan, but we also read the sad story of how, over time, they didn't remember and obey all of the things Moses told them. In the years to come, they did not fear the Lord, they did not walk in his ways, they did not love him or serve him or keep his commandments. In fact, they experienced many of the curses Moses warned them about should they disobey God. Eventually they were enslaved, scattered, and exiled from the Land of Promise. It would seem to be a sad ending to a sad story.

Remember What God Has Promised

And it would be the end if it were up to them to turn things around. But it is not up to them. These are God's people, and he has no intention of allowing them to be alienated from him and his promises forever. Here at the end of Deuteronomy we discover that the Spirit of God gave Moses the prophetic eyes to see how God will bring about their restoration to the land. Moses actually told the people about God's promise to one day restore them to the land even before they had entered the land.

> When all these things come upon you, the blessing and the curse, which I have set before you, and you call them to mind among all the nations where the LORD your God has driven you, and return to the LORD your God, you and your children, and obey his voice in all that I command you today, with all your heart and with all your soul, then the LORD your God will

restore your fortunes and have mercy on you, and he will gather you again from all the peoples where the LORD your God has scattered you. If your outcasts are in the uttermost parts of heaven, from there the LORD your God will gather you, and from there he will take you. And the LORD your God will bring you into the land that your fathers possessed, that you may possess it. And he will make you more prosperous and numerous than your fathers. And the LORD your God will circumcise your heart and the heart of your offspring, so that you will love the LORD your God with all your heart and with all your soul, that you may live. (Deut. 30:1–6)

Here is the foundation for hope as they reckon with the reality of their future failure. Their hope is not based on something as flimsy as their ability to obey, but on something as solid as God's promise. God has promised not just to bring them back to the land but to

> *Their hope is not based on something as flimsy as their ability to obey, but on something as solid as God's promise.*

do something in their hearts. Earlier in Deuteronomy (10:16), the people were told to circumcise their hearts. But how were they going to do that? How could they, by their own power and will, cut away their sinful stubbornness toward God, their deliberate forgetfulness of his ways? They couldn't. While they had the natural ability, they didn't have the moral ability. God promised, through his prophet Moses, that he would one day do for them what they could not do for themselves. We know that God always provides to us what he requires of us, and this was no exception.

Years later, through the prophet Jeremiah, God sent Israel a reminder of this same promise:

> Behold, the days are coming, declares the LORD, when I will make a new covenant with the house of Israel and the house of Judah, not like the covenant that I made with their fathers on the day when I took them by the hand to bring them out of the land of Egypt, my covenant that they broke. . . . I will put my law within them, and I will write it on their hearts. (Jer. 31:31–33)

And through the prophet Ezekiel, he sent yet another reminder of this promise:

> I will take you from the nations and gather you from all the countries and
> bring you into your own land. I will sprinkle clean water on you, and you
> shall be clean from all your uncleannesses, and from all your idols I will
> cleanse you. And I will give you a new heart, and a new spirit I will put
> within you. And I will remove the heart of stone from your flesh and give
> you a heart of flesh. And I will put my Spirit within you, and cause you
> to walk in my statutes and be careful to obey my rules. (Ezek. 36:24–27)

God promised to do something in their hearts by his Spirit that
would enable his people to keep his law—not because they had to, but
because they would want to.

When Jesus, the greatest of all prophets, finally came, the Israelites
had turned the law delivered to them by Moses into an unbearable
burden and seemed to have completely and conveniently forgotten its
demands upon their affections. Matthew describes a scene in which a
diligent keeper of the law came to Jesus:

> "Teacher, which is the great commandment in the Law?" And he said to
> him, "You shall love the Lord your God with all your heart and with all
> your soul and with all your mind." (Matt. 22:36–37)

Of course, the Pharisee knew this command from Deuteronomy 6:5.
In fact, as a faithful Jew he would have repeated it twice a day. But, as
Jesus said, "this people honors me with their lips, but their heart is far
from me" (Matt. 15:8). Jesus knew that something had to happen in
their hearts. The clear evidence that they had no real love for God was
that they hated Jesus. "If God were your Father, you would love me,"
he said (John 8:42). Jesus also knew what it would cost for them to be
able to love the Lord with all of their hearts. It would come at the cost
of his life:

> The Lord Jesus on the night when he was betrayed took bread, and when
> he had given thanks, he broke it, and said, "This is my body which is for
> you. Do this in remembrance of me." In the same way also he took the
> cup, after supper, saying, "This cup is the new covenant in my blood. Do
> this, as often as you drink it, in remembrance of me." (1 Cor. 11:23–25)

Like Moses, he was charging his hearers to remember. But it was not all the demands of the old covenant God had made with the people in Moses's day that they must remember, but rather the benefits of the new covenant. They would need to remember the day that Moses had prophesied about, the day when God circumcised their hearts by cutting off his own Son from the land of the living. They would need to remember the darkness that came down in the middle of the day as the full force of the curses, warned about in Deuteronomy, came down on an innocent Christ. They must remember it, savor it, and embrace it. They must rely on his death on the cross as their own so that they will be able to say, "I have been crucified with Christ. It is no longer I who live, but Christ who lives in me" (Gal. 2:20). What is needed for our hearts to be circumcised is to be united to Christ by faith so that his circumcision becomes ours. This is how our sinful stubbornness and inability to love God is cut away from our hearts.

> *In him* also you were circumcised with a circumcision made without hands, by putting off the body of the flesh, by the circumcision of Christ, having been buried with him in baptism, in which you were also raised with him through faith in the powerful working of God, who raised him from the dead. And you, who were dead in your trespasses and the uncircumcision of your flesh, God made alive together with him, having forgiven us all our trespasses, by canceling the record of debt that stood against us with its legal demands. This he set aside, nailing it to the cross. (Col. 2:11–14)

We must be "in him," identified with him, tethered to him. The only way we will ever be able to love the Lord with all of our heart and with all of our soul and with all of our mind is as we abide in the only one who has ever loved God in this way. As *his* pure heart toward God begins to beat in *your* chest, you will experience a growing passion for God and an increasing desire to walk in his way. Joined to Christ, you need not fear that the curses of the covenant will come down on you for your lack of love and obedience to God, because the curse for disobedience that you deserve came down upon him so that you might enjoy the favor and blessing that he deserves. Jesus, the mediator of this better covenant, has loved and served and obeyed the Lord perfectly in your place and gladly transfers that merit to you as a gift, even as his Spirit works in you to make this love and obedience more of a reality in your daily life.

> *Jesus has loved and served and obeyed the Lord perfectly in your place and gladly transfers that merit to you as a gift, even as his Spirit works in you to make this love and obedience more of a reality in your daily life.*

Do you long for more than a living-by-the-rules relationship with God? Something more than dry duty? Of course you do. What we long for is for something real and transforming to happen in our hearts. We want our hardened hearts to become soft with new affections for God. We want to find ourselves obeying God from an intrinsic desire rather than an imposed demand. This is exactly what God has promised to give to us. And not just to us, but to our children.

If we go back to Deuteronomy, we find that the promise of God was to "circumcise your heart *and the heart of your offspring.*" This is why instead of merely pointing our children toward being good, we must continually point them toward the one who can circumcise their hearts so that they will learn to love obeying God's law, which is first and foremost about loving God with their whole being. Until this supernatural work is done by the Spirit of God, they have no heart to love the Lord, no power to obey him.

What can we do? Just as Moses instructed, we make the Word of God the center of our home, purposefully creating an atmosphere in which his Word is read and discussed and revered. We pray that God, by his Spirit, will do what only he can do, which is to call our children to spiritual life by uniting them to Christ. We challenge them to choose the God who chose them in Christ before the foundation of the world. And we live before them in such a way that they can see the beauty of having a circumcised heart. Can your children see that God continues to cut away what is hard and resistant toward him in *your* heart? Can they see developing in you an ever-deepening intimate love for Christ because you know him better today than you did last year? Have they ever heard you humbly confess a specific sin, or seen you depend on God's power to forsake sin? This is what it looks like when God circumcises and writes his law on our hearts. This is the way we kindle the fires of love until he comes. When he comes, his purifying work in us will be complete so that loving him with all of our heart, soul, mind, and strength will no longer be our aim but our experience.

Can you just imagine with me the day when we cross over into the heavenly land God has promised to give us, when the change that must happen in our hearts is finally complete? On that day, we will love the Lord our God with all of our heart, as nothing and no one will compete for our affections. On that day, we'll love the Lord with all of our mind, as all of our stubborn blindspots and willful ignorance will be gone for good. We will love the Lord with all of our soul, as his glory radiates into our very being. We will love him with all of our might, as nothing trivial or temporal will sap us of strength or focus on loving him.

The good news of the gospel is that although you and I have not remembered all that we are to remember, although we have not loved the Lord exclusively, obediently, and passionately, although we have lived as though his promises are not precious to us, there is one who has done so in our stead. He is at work in us by his Spirit, cutting away all of our stubborn resistance toward God. He is causing something to happen in our hearts.

Looking Forward
When the Lord Your God Brings You into the Land

As Moses spoke to the people on the edge of entering into Canaan, he gave them instructions on what they were to do to take possession of it.

> When the LORD your God brings you into the land that you are entering to take possession of it, and clears away many nations before you, the Hittites, the Girgashites, the Amorites, the Canaanites, the Perizzites, the Hivites, and the Jebusites, seven nations more numerous and mightier than you, and when the LORD your God gives them over to you, and you defeat them, then you must devote them to complete destruction. You shall make no covenant with them and show no mercy to them. (Deut. 7:1–2)

If we read these instructions to the Israelites with no understanding of God's greater purpose in the world, we can't help but be a bit offended by what appears to be the worst kind of nationalism, racism, and genocide. We must read Deuteronomy in context of what we know to be God's intention for Israel as declared long before to Abraham: all nations will be blessed through Israel. But we must also recognize that the promise that all the nations of the earth would ultimately be blessed through Israel did not mean that particular nations in history would not be judged through Israel.

The destruction of the people living in the Promised Land had nothing to do with petty earthly politics but everything to do with the judgment of God falling on those who hate him. Those living in Canaan were the descendants of Ham, who did a detestable thing to his father, Noah. And evidently Ham brought up all of his children in his wicked ways. They sacrificed children to their gods and practiced sexual immorality. Their problem was not that they did not know about the God of Israel. In fact, they knew all about Israel's God (Num. 14:14–15). They just didn't want him.

When we read about the fearful judgment that fell on the nations living in the Promised Land, we must realize that this was a war unlike any other war, a war beyond ordinary earthly politics. This war, and the

Bible's record of it, sets before all generations a picture or pattern for the great judgment day to come—the day when all of the human race who live in rebellion against God and his people will be eternally evicted from the holy land, the recreated earth, where God intends to dwell forever with his people.

No one can be in doubt of what the return of Christ will be like for those who do not love him and refuse his mercy while it may be found. In that day there will be no mercy. He will come to take possession of his land, and either we are of those who will be driven out and destroyed or of those who will inherit his land with him. The new creation can be the home of righteousness and peace only if it is purged of wickedness. If Jesus were to compromise with the evil dwelling in the world on that day, we would have no hope for a future of perfect goodness and justice. So the fact that he is coming in righteous anger to purge the universe of evil is actually the greatest, most comforting truth in the universe. He will not let any evil pollute his new creation.

> The one who conquers will have this heritage, and I will be his
> God and he will be my son. But as for the cowardly, the faith-
> less, the detestable, as for murderers, the sexually immoral,
> sorcerers, idolaters, and all liars, their portion will be in the
> lake that burns with fire and sulfur, which is the second death.
> (Rev. 21:7–8)

While those who hate God will have no future in his new creation, those who love him can anticipate an eternal inheritance in God's glorious land. And just as Deuteronomy 7 begins with a picture of the reality of the coming judgment, it ends with a glorious vision of the abundant life that awaits God's people in the new creation.

> Because you listen to these rules and keep and do them, the
> LORD your God will keep with you the covenant and the stead-
> fast love that he swore to your fathers. He will love you, bless
> you, and multiply you. He will also bless the fruit of your womb
> and the fruit of your ground, your grain and your wine and your
> oil, the increase of your herds and the young of your flock, in
> the land that he swore to your fathers to give you. You shall be
> blessed above all peoples. There shall not be male or female

barren among you or among your livestock. And the LORD will take away from you all sickness, and none of the evil diseases of Egypt, which you knew, will he inflict on you, but he will lay them on all who hate you. (Deut. 7:12–15)

What Moses promised those on the brink of the land of Canaan was a mini-experience of the resurrection life to come in the new creation for all who will embrace the covenant of God from the heart.[2]

Love and Obey

Getting the Discussion Going

1. From your experience as a parent, or as a child, what kinds of things do parents long for their children to remember when they leave home?

Getting to the Heart of It

2. When we come to Deuteronomy after reading Exodus, Numbers, and Leviticus, we might sense that it is repeating much of what we've read in the books that precede it, and, in actuality, it is. Why do you think Moses repeated and recorded the content of this book for those who were preparing to enter the land, and how does it benefit us, as the people of God, to hear this repetition?

3. It is clear throughout Deuteronomy that loving God and obeying God are intertwined. That truth is also punctuated throughout the New Testament. How would you say that loving God and obeying God relate to each other? (Read together John 14:15–21 for Jesus's words about this.)

4. When we read the Bible, many of us zero in on what we are supposed to do, and if that is all we see when we read it, we can become hopeless about our ability to do it all. But the more we study the Bible, the more we discover that the imperatives in the Bible (commands that tell

us what we should do) are always based on indicatives (declarations of what God has done). That is clearly evident here in Deuteronomy. While there are many steep commands given to God's people—love him, obey him, serve him, choose him, and circumcise your heart—these commands are all based on what God has done for them. What are some of the indicatives Moses declares in Deuteronomy that serve as a foundation for the imperatives? (For help see 4:20; 7:6; 10:20–22; 11:1–12; 26:16–19; 30:6.)

5. How would you explain to someone what it means to have a circumcised heart and how that happens?

6. What would you say to someone who read the book of Deuteronomy and said, "Forget it. I can't do this." What hope in the gospel would you have to offer them?

7. Obviously God wants more than our dry duty of obedience but wants us to love him. In the Personal Bible Study you were asked what you think it means to love the Lord with all of your heart, soul, mind, and strength, and how you think it happens. Would several of you share with us what you wrote?

Getting Personal

8. In the context of calling Israel to love the Lord, the Israelites were instructed to remember that they had been slaves, to remember their past disobedience, to remember the laws God had given and the promises he had made, and to remember how God chose them and set his love on them. How do you think it might help you to kindle love for Christ if you were to make time and space to nurture your remembrance of these same things?

Getting How It Fits into the Big Picture

9. Throughout this whole study we've been tracing the story of Israel's being rescued from slavery, delivered through the death of an innocent lamb, and guided and provided for in the wilderness, and now

preparing to cross over into the Promised Land, and we have seen in it a picture of our own salvation, justification, sanctification, and glorification. How has this study helped you to understand the need for Christ to come and the meaning of his life, death, and resurrection in a new way?

Bibliography

Books and Articles

Clowney, Edmund P. "The Final Temple." *Westminster Theological Journal* 35 (1973): 156–91.

———. *The Unfolding Mystery: Discovering Christ in the Old Testament*. Phillipsburg, NJ: P&R, 1988.

Dever, Mark. *The Message of the Old Testament: Promises Made*. Wheaton, IL: Crossway, 2006.

Duguid, Iain M. *Numbers: God's Presence in the Wilderness*. Wheaton, IL: Crossway, 2006.

Duncan, Ligon. "The Face of Moses." Sermon. First Presbyterian Church, Jackson, MS, undated. http://www.fpcjackson.org/resources/sermons.

ESV Study Bible, English Standard Version. Wheaton, IL: Crossway, 2008.

Evers, Stan K. *Christ in Exodus: Using New Testament Keys to Unlock Truth in Exodus*. London: Grace Publications Trust, 2010.

Gibson, John. "Finally an Obedient Son." http://beginningwithmoses.org/bt-brief ings/171/finally-.-.-.-an-obedient-son.

Guthrie, Nancy. *The One Year Book of Discovering Jesus in the Old Testament*. Carol Stream, IL: Tyndale, 2010.

Hamilton, James, Jr. *God's Glory in Salvation through Judgment: A Biblical Theology*. Wheaton, IL: Crossway, 2010.

Mathews, Kenneth A. *Leviticus: Holy God, Holy People*. Preaching the Word. Wheaton, IL: Crossway, 2009.

Pink, Arthur W. *Gleanings in Exodus*. Chicago, IL: Moody, 1928.

Robertson, O. Palmer. *The Israel of God: Yesterday, Today, and Tomorrow*. Phillipsburg, NJ: P&R, 2000.

Ryken, Philip Graham. *Exodus: Saved for God's Glory*. Preaching the Word. Wheaton, IL: Crossway, 2005.

Williams, Michael D. *Far as the Curse Is Found: The Covenant Story of Redemption*. Phillipsburg, NJ: P&R, 2005.

Wright, Christopher J. H. *Deuteronomy*. New International Bible Commentary. Peabody, MA: Hendrickson, 1996.

Audio

Beynon, Nigel. "The Real Thing." Sermon series on Hebrews. St. Helen's Bishopsgate Church, London, October 1998–February 1999.

Blackham, Paul. "Biblical Skin Care." Sermon. All Souls Church, Langham Place, London, October 10, 1999.

———. "The Blood that Divided." Sermon. All Souls Church, Langham Place, London, November 11, 2001.

Dennis, Jon. "Freedom: The Rise of an Unstoppable People." Sermon series on Exodus. Holy Trinity Church, Chicago, IL, April 11–August 21, 2010.

DeYoung, Kevin. "Revelation 22:1–5." Sermon. University Reformed Church, Lansing, MI, August 5, 2007.

Ferguson, Sinclair B. "Exodus II." Sermon. First Presbyterian Church, Columbia, SC, December 30, 2007.

———. "The Great High Priest." First Presbyterian Church, Columbia, SC, January 11, 2009.

———. "Jesus, Greater Than Moses." Sermon. Park Cities Presbyterian Church, Dallas, TX, October 13, 2004.

———. "Jesus, Our Great High Priest." Sermon. Park Cities Presbyterian Church, Dallas, TX, May 4, 2005.

———. "Moses: Portrait of God's Presence." Sermon. Westminster Theological Seminary, undated.

Fesko, John. "Circumcise Your Heart." Sermon. Geneva Orthodox Presbyterian Church, Woodstock, GA, undated.

Goligher, Liam. "The Final Word." Sermon series on Hebrews. Duke Street Church, London, September 5, 2004–August 28, 2005.

———. "Generation eXodus." Sermon. Duke Street Church, London, October 2, 2005.

———. "The Grace of Law." Sermon. Duke Street Church, London, October 24, 2010.

———. "Scripture: Ends or Means?" Sermon. Duke Street Church, London, September 30, 2007.

———. "The Temptation of Jesus." Sermon. Duke Street Church, London, England, May 9, 2010.

Hedges, Brian. "Renewal and Remembrance: The Message of Deuteronomy." Sermon. Fulkerson Park Baptist Church, Niles, MI, August 13, 2006.

———. "Wilderness and Wandering: The Message of Numbers." Sermon. Fulkerson Park Baptist Church, Niles, MI, August 6, 2006.

Horton, Michael. "Exodus, Exile, and Conquest." *White Horse Inn* podcast, January 22, 2011.

———. "God's Story vs. Our Stories." *White Horse Inn* podcast, June 14, 2009.

Keller, Timothy J. "Bible: Ends or Means?" Sermon. Redeemer Presbyterian Church, New York, November 30, 1997.

———. "Christ: Our Treasury (The Book of Hebrews)" Sermon series. Redeemer Presbyterian Church, New York, September 8 –November 10, 2002.

———. "The Gospel according to Moses: Discovering the Lost Language of Salvation." Sermon series. Redeemer Presbyterian Church, New York, February 6–May 5, 2005.

———. "Sin as Slavery." Sermon. Redeemer Presbyterian Church, New York, March 17, 1996.

Moffatt, Justin. "Living Outstanding Lives." Sermon series. Christ Church, St. Ives, Australia, October 3–17, 2004.

Murray, David. "Lessons from the Life of Moses." Unpublished lecture notes. Puritan Reformed Theological Seminary, Grand Rapids, MI, August, 2005.

Pakula, Martin. "Testing of the Son of God." Sermon. Christ Church, St. Ives, Australia, March 29, 1998.

Perkins, Gavin. "The Kingdom and the Law." Sermon. Christ Church, St. Ives, Australia, October 28, 2007.

Piper, John. "The Hardening of Pharaoh and the Hope of the World." Sermon. Bethlehem Baptist Church, Minneapolis, MN, February 9, 2003.

———. "The Lust of Ignorance and the Life of Holiness." Sermon. Bethlehem Baptist Church, Minneapolis, MN, December 5, 1993.

———. "Our High Priest Is the Son of God Perfect Forever." Sermon. Bethlehem Baptist Church, Minneapolis, MN, December 8, 1996.

———. "The Son of Man Must Be Lifted Up—Like the Serpent." Sermon. Bethlehem Baptist Church, Minneapolis, MN, April 5, 2009.

———. "You Have Come to Mount Zion." Sermon. Bethlehem Baptist Church, Minneapolis, MN, September 7, 1997.

Tice, Rico. "A Night to Remember." Sermon. All Souls Church, Langham Place, London, June 1, 1997.

———. "The Plagues." Sermon. All Souls Church, Langham Place, London October 19, 2008.

———. "The Spies Who Wobbled." Sermon. All Souls Church, Langham Place, London November 3, 2002.

Woodhouse, John. "Rescued by God." Sermon series on Exodus. Christ Church, St. Ives, Australia, April 14–June 30, 1996.

———. "Words Worth Hearing." Sermon series on Deuteronomy. Christ Church, St. Ives, Australia, April 23–June 25, 1995.

Notes

Week 1: A Prophet like Me

1 Iain M. Duguid, *Numbers: God's Presence in the Wilderness* (Wheaton, IL: Crossway, 2006), 251.

2 These observations on why God may have given instructions to take the staff and strike the rock come from David Murray, who shared with me his unpublished series of lecture notes, "Lessons from the Life of Moses," given at Puritan Reformed Theological Seminary, Grand Rapids, MI, August 2005.

3 See Gen. 49:24; Deut. 32:4; Ps. 78:35.

4 Duguid, *Numbers*, 253.

5 James Montgomery Boice, *Foundations of the Christian Faith: A Comprehensive and Readable Theology* (Downers Grove, IL: InterVarsity, 1986), 253–54.

6 Philip Graham Ryken, *Exodus: Saved for God's Glory*, Preaching the Word (Wheaton, IL: Crossway, 2005), 1034.

Week 2: Slavery and a Savior

1 Adapted from the chart "Covenant Call and Dialogue," *ESV Study Bible* (Wheaton, IL: Crossway, 2008), 148.

2 I was helped in understanding this progression of Pharaoh's plans by John Woodhouse's sermon "What on Earth Is God Doing?," given at Christ Church, St. Ives, Australia, April 14, 1996.

3 Josephus, *The Antiquities of the Jews*, 2.210–216.

4 This explanation of the linguistics of the name "Moses" comes from Philip Graham Ryken, *Exodus: Saved for God's Glory*, Preaching the Word (Wheaton, IL: Crossway, 2005), 48.

5 This list of subjects Moses would have studied as the son of Pharaoh comes from James K. Hoffmeier, *Israel in Egypt* (Oxford: Oxford University Press, 1999), 142–43.

6 Sinclair Ferguson, "Moses: Portrait of God's Presence," sermon, Westminster Theological Seminary, Philadephia, PA, n.d.

7 John Piper, "I Am Who I Am," sermon, Bethlehem Baptist Church, Minneapolis, September 16, 1984.

8 Michael Williams, *Far as the Curse Is Found: The Covenant Story of Redemption* (Phillipsburg, NJ: P&R, 2005), 32.

Week 3: Plagues and Passover

1 Philip Graham Ryken provides this insightful tracing of the story of the lamb throughout God's story in *Exodus: Saved for God's Glory*, Preaching the Word (Wheaton, IL: Crossway, 2005), 330.

2 Liam Goligher describes this likely drama in Israelite homes in his sermon "Generation eXodus," Duke Street Church, London, October 2, 2005.

3 Paul Blackham describes this likely drama in Egyptian homes in "The Blood That Divided," sermon, All Souls Church, Langham Place, London, November 1, 2001.

Week 4: Salvation and Provision

1 Timothy J. Keller describes these differing responses of faith in "The Great Escape," sermon, Redeemer Presbyterian Church, New York, January 6, 2002.

2 Jon Dennis gives this Hebrew linguistic interpretation in a sermon on Exodus 15, August 15, 2010, in the series "Freedom: Rise of an Unstoppable People," Holy Trinity Church, Chicago, IL.

3 John Piper, "Do Not Labor for the Food That Perishes," sermon, Bethlehem Baptist Church, Minneapolis, November 15, 2009.

4 Edmund P. Clowney's *The Unfolding Mystery* (Phillipsburg, NJ: P&R, 1988), 124–26, was very helpful to me in understanding this passage.

Week 5: The Giving of the Law

1 Michael D. Williams, *Far as the Curse Is Found: The Covenant Story of Redemption* (Phillipsburg, NJ: P&R, 2005), 151.

2 Martin Luther, *Lectures on Galatians, 1535*, trans. and ed. Jaroslav Pelikan, Luther's Works (St. Louis: Concordia, 1963), 26:327.

3 Ryken, *Exodus*, 530.

4 Ibid., 534.

5 Kevin DeYoung, "The Law of Love and the Love of Law," *DeYoung, Restless, and Reformed* blog, August 11, 2011, http://thegospelcoalition.org/blogs/kevindeyoung/2011/08/11/the-law-of-the-love-and-the-love-of-law.

6 Graeme Goldsworthy, *Gospel and Kingdom*, in *The Goldsworthy Trilogy: Gospel and Kingdom, Gospel and Wisdom, The Gospel in Revelation* (Exeter: Paternoster, 2000), 113.

7 Adapted from my book *The One Year Book of Discovering Jesus in the Old Testament* (Carol Stream, IL: Tyndale, 2005), April 9.

Week 6: The Tabernacle

1 Philip Graham Ryken, *Exodus: Saved for God's Glory*, Preaching the Word (Wheaton, IL: Crossway, 2005), 821.

2 This detail on the curtain comes from David M. Levy, *The Tabernacle: Shadows of the Messiah* (Bellmawr, NJ: Friends of Israel Gospel Ministry, 1993), 71.

Week 8: Sacrifice and Sanctification

1 Vern S. Poythress, *The Shadow of Christ in the Law of Moses* (Phillipsburg, NJ: P&R, 1991), 11.

2 Kevin DeYoung, "Burnt Offerings," sermon, University Reformed Church, East Lansing, MI, February 15, 2009.

3 This definition of *holiness* is adapted from R. C. Sproul, *The Holiness of God*, 2nd ed. (Carol Steam, IL: Tyndale, 1998), 37–38.

4 This definition of *holiness* is adapted from John Piper, "The Holiness of God, Our Sin, and the Love of Jesus," sermon, Bethlehem Baptist Church, Minneapolis, April 16, 1981.

5 Paul Blackham, *Book by Book Study Guide: Leviticus* (London: Biblical Frameworks, 2008), 52.

6 "Introduction to Leviticus," in the *ESV Study Bible* (Wheaton, IL: Crossway, 2008), 212.

7 John Woodhouse, "I the Lord Your God Am Holy," sermon, Katoomba Youth Convention, Sydney, Australia, 1986.

8 Justin Moffatt, "Why You Need to Be Clean," sermon, Christ Church, St. Ives, Australia, November 17, 2004.

Week 9: In the Wilderness

1 This idea of the Israelites' looking at life through the knothole of their craving comes from Tuck Bartholomew in his sermon "Leadership and Community," Redeemer Presbyterian Church, New York, November 17, 2002.

2 O. Palmer Robertson, *The Israel of God: Yesterday, Today and Tomorrow* (Phillipsburg, NJ: P&R, 2000), 95.

3 John Gibson, "Finally . . . an Obedient Son" (http://beginningwithmoses.org/bt-briefings/171/finally-.-.-.-an-obedient-son), n.d.

Week 10: Love and Obey

1 Mark Dever, *The Message of the Old Testament: Promises Made* (Wheaton, IL: Crossway, 2006), 155.

2 This "Looking Forward" reflects numerous insights gained from Paul Blackham, "No Compromise!," sermon, All Souls Church, Langham Place, London, June 30, 2002.

For additional content, downloads,
and resources for leaders, please visit:

www.SeeingJesusInTheOldTestament.com

Also Available in the
Seeing Jesus in the Old Testament Series

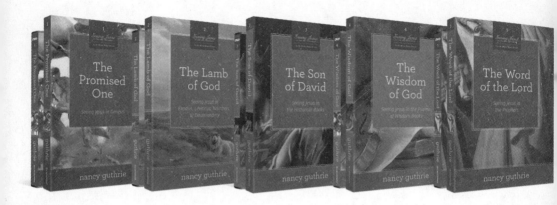

The Promised One: *Seeing Jesus in Genesis*

The Lamb of God: *Seeing Jesus in Exodus, Leviticus, Numbers, and Deuteronomy*

The Son of David: *Seeing Jesus in the Historical Books*

The Wisdom of God: *Seeing Jesus in the Psalms and Wisdom Books*

The Word of the Lord: *Seeing Jesus in the Prophets*

A companion DVD is also available for each study.

SeeingJesusInTheOldTestament.com